ROBBO

MY AUTOBIOGRAPHY

ROBBO
MY AUTOBIOGRAPHY

BRYAN ROBSON
with Derick Allsop

HODDER &
STOUGHTON

Copyright © 2006 by Bryan Robson

First published in Great Britain in 2006 by Hodder & Stoughton
A division of Hodder Headline

The right of Bryan Robson to be identified as the
Author of the Work has been asserted by him in accordance
with the Copyright, Designs and Patents Act 1988.

A Hodder & Stoughton Book

1

A CIP catalogue record for this title is available from the British Library

Trade Paperback ISBN 0 340 92264 8
Hardback ISBN 0 340 83956 2

Typeset in Sabon by Hewer Text UK Ltd, Edinburgh
Printed and bound by Mackays of Chatham Ltd, Chatham, Kent

Hodder Headline's policy is to use papers that are natural, renewable
and recyclable products and made from wood grown in sustainable forests.
The logging and manufacturing processes are expected to conform to
the environmental regulations of the country of origin.

Hodder & Stoughton Ltd
A division of Hodder Headline
338 Euston Road
London NW1 3BH

*For all my family, friends
and everyone who has supported me
through my career*

CONTENTS

Acknowledgements   ix

Introduction   1

1   Uphill task   3

2   Breaking new ground   17

3   United calling   33

4   Cup of joy   50

5   Foreign currency   69

6   Days of woe   83

7   Enter Sir Alex   102

8   Silver lining   116

9   Eurostars   136

10   Deliverance   153

11   England pride   175

12   Cruel fate   192

13   Bitter sweet   209

14   Buzzing Boro   222

15   Up to stay   239

16   New life with the Baggies   257

17   Talking a good game   277

Bryan Robson – career record   299

Index   305

ACKNOWLEDGEMENTS

Just like football, writing this book has been a team effort. It wouldn't have been possible without the assistance and encouragement of so many people, far too many to name, but we would like to thank in particular Keith Lamb, the FA press office, David Barber, the West Bromwich Albion press office, the Manchester United press office, Ray Matts, Graham Taylor, Jim Rosenthal, Bill Bradshaw and everyone at Hodder & Stoughton, especially Roddy Bloomfield and Natasha Laws, and copy editor Marion Paull. We greatly appreciate also the help, support and patience of Maureen, Denise, Claire, Charlotte and Ben Robson, and Sue, Natalie and Kate Allsop.

BR and DA

Photographic Acknowledgements

The author and publisher would like to thank the following for permission to reproduce photographs:

AFP/Getty Images, Colorsport/Andrew Cowie, Empics, Getty Images, Mirrorpix, Offside/Mark Leech, PA/Empics, Popperfoto.com, Sport & General/Empics, Brian Swain.

All other photographs are from private collections.

INTRODUCTION

My dad called me Robbo. He was Brian with an 'i'. He took me playing football for the first time when I was five. He also took me to my first proper match. He was there, with my mam, when I made my League debut and again when I first played for England. He was a long-distance lorry driver so he couldn't be there all the time, but whenever he could, he was there. Both my parents were. Thanks to them, I got into football and went on to have a fantastic career. Football was the only thing I ever wanted to do and it's given me an incredible life.

I probably didn't fully appreciate how fortunate I'd been in football and life until 10 May 2003. That was the day my dad died, aged seventy-two. He had cancer and it was awful to see him deteriorate the way he did. His death had a deep effect on me. It wasn't just the sadness and the grief. It gave me a different perspective on life. I realised what was really important. I would have given so much of that career back to have him with us a little longer.

Football had virtually taken over my life. As a player I made my name with West Bromwich Albion, then moved to Manchester United, the biggest club in the country, for a record transfer fee. I became captain of United and England. I won cups and championships with my club and played in three World Cups for my country. So much happened so quickly, but at least a player has time to switch off. As a player you just look after yourself. As a manager the job is always with you, in your mind even when you are not on the training ground or at your desk. The club, the players, the training, the matches, the results – they are all the manager's responsibility.

I had terrific times as manager of Middlesbrough, as well. We were promoted twice and reached three Cup finals. We brought in some great players and revived the place, but the price a manager has to pay is family life. I left for work before the kids were up and by the time I got home they were ready for bed. Then when things didn't go well I wondered what I was doing wrong and probably let things get on top of me. Sometimes it isn't the manager's fault. Sometimes the players aren't good enough. You're in charge, though, so you take the pressure and the flak, and eventually you can get the sack, as I did. It hurt because it was almost as if my achievements didn't count for anything. It hurt still more when I couldn't get another job.

When I got back into the game I was strengthened by experience and that new perspective. I was more relaxed, more decisive – didn't dally and let things fester. I was a better manager. I returned to my first club, West Brom, and we confounded everybody by pulling off our 'Great Escape' in 2005. My dad wouldn't have wanted me to throw in the towel. He would have wanted me to tough it out, just as I'd always done. I think I got that fighting spirit from him.

My dad had a right temper and so have I if I'm pushed too far. My mam has always been the placid one, so the aggressive, competitive side of my game must be from my dad. All the grandchildren called him Mr Grumpy. Perhaps it's a grandad or growing older trait. The family tell me I get more like him every day. I don't think I'm that bad – not yet, anyway. I just hope I can give as much to my kids as he gave to me.

1

UPHILL TASK

It is just another gentle climb on the rolling County Durham landscape, but to a boy of five it must have seemed an ascent of Himalayan proportions. More than forty years ago, a young Bryan Robson, along with his father, Brian, his sister, Susan, and their golden retriever, Shane, left their council house in the village of Witton Gilbert to walk up the hill to the football pitch at the top. Mrs Maureen Robson was at home, doubtless enjoying the respite. Up on the hill, Susan reluctantly went in goal, dad Brian teased little Bryan with his nifty footwork and Shane scurried around as dogs do. Little did any of them realise what that first Sunday morning kick-about for young Bryan would lead to.

Today the pitch is bordered on one side by modern houses. Beyond the other side, a new road runs in the direction of Durham city and its majestic cathedral. The pitch itself is probably little changed since the early sixties. A rough, undulating surface with tufts of grass would challenge the skills and commitment of a latter day Captain Marvel, let alone a youngster just discovering the wonders of this simple game one Sunday morning. Now, on a Thursday afternoon in late winter, rain is pounding the pitch on the hill. Junior goals, perhaps five yards wide and five feet high, are rusting and silent. The playground rides, too, are still and quiet, save for the beating sound of the rain. Yet, with a little imagination, it is not difficult to visualise the darting, tiny figure, trying to take the ball from his father and then running away with pure delight on his face, a lifelong love in his heart and the world at his feet.

Maureen Robson

I was the youngest of nine. My family were from Castle Eden, the other side of Durham. Bryan – we spelt it with a 'y' rather than an 'i' – was my second child. Susan was a couple of years older and Justin and Gary came later. Bryan was born at Brian's mother's home at Northlands, Chester-le-Street, on 11 January 1957. I had him at his gran's so that we had somebody to look after us. I had thrombosis after he was born. When I was well enough, we went back to our home a few miles away, in Witton Gilbert.

Bryan started kicking a ball when he was five. His dad used to take him to the local pitch up on the hill. Susan went with them, and Shane. It all began from there. Brian was a long-distance lorry driver and could be away for two, three or four weeks at a time. Our neighbours at Witton Gilbert, Jack and June Hardy, were very good with Bryan and Susan. When Brian was away, Jack used to take them down to the river. Brian was a good player, but he was in the army and went to Korea. He drove the armoured cars. I liked swimming and athletics.

Our Bryan is like his dad in a lot of ways. He's got a bit of his dad's temper! He's probably more like me off the pitch and his dad on it. He used to fight our Susan and chase her around the house. She would lock herself in the bathroom and he would knock hell out of the bathroom door to get to her. I've always told our Bryan to watch his temper. Now I tell him he's too old to be getting into trouble!

Bryan went to the infant school in Witton Gilbert, but he'd been there only about a year when we moved to our own house at South Pelaw, Chester-le-Street. Not long after, we moved again, to a nearby council estate. Bryan went to the junior and infant schools in Chester-le-Street, and then to the big school, Birtley Lord Lawson Comprehensive. He was very good at maths and could have done well at school if he'd concentrated on it, but he was always more interested in football. He played for three or four teams. The cubs had a good team and he only joined so that he could play for them.

All the boys were good footballers. I always thought our Justin was the best of the three but he got injured just when he was going into the first team at Newcastle and that ruined his career. They've all had their injuries. Gary's career was cut short, but for all Bryan's injuries he played on for a long time. He always had that determination, even as a youngster. Football was all he liked or cared about. He was only small but his PE master, Mr Chapman, was very good to him. He used to keep him back for training after school.

On Saturday mornings, all his pals used to come over here to meet and have a chat before school matches. I had an Austin Westminster, a big car, at the time and I used to take about twelve of them off to the match. I've always followed the boys playing football, with their dad being away so much. Nowadays you see lads hanging around on street corners, but ours never did. They used to come home from school and go down to the council playing fields where there were goalposts, and they played there. At about seven o'clock I'd go down and shout them in, or their grandma, who lived on the green, would shout them in. They used to go to her house for a drink when they were thirsty. Our Bryan used to say, 'Grandma, when I make it in football I'll buy you a leopardskin coat.' Unfortunately, he never got the chance. She died when she was sixty-seven.

A lot of clubs were after Bryan but West Brom were the best for a young boy to go to. They didn't put them in hostels, as a lot of clubs did. They put them into private houses and Bryan got nice lodgings. So did Gary, when he went there. One or two of the lads Bryan went down with from this area got homesick and had to come back. Bryan was a bit homesick at first, so at weekends we'd go down and get a family room at a hotel in Birmingham. He'd come over from his digs and stay with us.

Our other lads have had a lot to put up with because Bryan did so well. It was hard for them. They played for the county teams and people would say they only got there because of Bryan, but they were good enough. I knew that. Now they are playing for a local team, Whitehills, in the Northern Alliance League. Justin is the player-manager and turns out when he has to. Gary plays all the time. I used to get uptight when I watched any of them play. Now I watch Justin and Gary and tell myself not to get too excited – if they lose they lose – but sometimes I can't help it.

I worked as a school dinner lady for eighteen years. A lot of people used to say, 'Oh, you won't be speaking to us now that Bryan's captain of England,' that kind of thing. We thought it was marvellous and he made us really proud, but I don't think we ever changed. We watched our Bryan as often as we could, playing for his clubs and for England.

A LL I CAN EVER REMEMBER wanting to do was play football, which I suppose wasn't that unusual for a lad from the North East. In that part of the country there's a long tradition of producing players and the passion for the game is as obvious today as ever it was. The Charltons and Milburns are famous football folk from the North East, but there have been many, many more over the generations. Norman Hunter and Colin Todd, two of English football's finest defenders, were raised just a mile or two from where I was born, in Chester-le-Street. Football dominated sport in our region. All the schools played football. There was no rugby and very little cricket played in our area. Durham got into the County Championship only relatively recently.

I spent my first six years not far from Chester-le-Street, at a village called Witton Gilbert. Although the North East was known as a mining area, it wasn't all pits and slag heaps. I can remember plenty of green fields and open countryside. On Sunday mornings, when I was five and six, I used to go with my dad and our Sue up to a field at the top of a hill near our home. I think it was an old pit heap. There was a pitch up there and we'd kick a ball around. My dad was quite a good player but his time in the army had slowed him down a bit. He'd got on the beer and curries! Our dog, Shane, was a lot quicker than any of us.

I don't think I had any ideas about becoming a professional footballer at that stage. I just wanted to play for fun, and the older I got the more I played. In the summer we'd go to the beach at South Shields, a twenty-minute drive away, and play there. Even if my dad was away, working, my mam would take us across to the coast. Dad would often leave home on a Monday morning and we wouldn't see him again for a fortnight or more.

We moved to South Pelaw, in Chester-le-Street, to be nearer my gran. With my dad being away so much, he felt Mam might need the help. We had our own house but Mam and Dad decided to sell it and applied for a council house. Justin's arrival meant they had three kids to feed and I think my dad wanted to buy Mam a decent car. South Pelaw was fine by me because there was a field near Gran's where I played football with my mates after school.

Chester-le-Street is a market town. You can't miss the market place or the big railway viaduct, which looks down on the town centre. Pelaw Bank is a steep hill, leading up to where we lived. I liked going to the park with the family. We used to go for walks around the park and swim in the river. When I was older and came back home for weekends, I'd go with my dad to the pub or the working-men's club. Every other door is a pub in Chester-le-Street. I enjoyed going home.

My mam was the strict one at home. I suppose that was because my dad was away so much. He would tell her what to say to us. She'd give us a slap. A few of the drivers my dad worked with called him Robbo and I was quite young when he started calling me Robbo.

Some of my mates called me Roppa, which is what a Robson is commonly known as in the North East. The only time we went abroad on a family holiday was to Le Havre and Rouen, in France. My dad was used to that ferry route because he often went from Southampton to Le Havre. We went to Skegness with my aunt and uncle from Newark quite a lot, for long weekends in caravans. My mam and dad went abroad more often later.

I didn't get in too much bother as a kid because I was always playing football. I did go bird-nesting and had a great egg collection. I sold it to this lad for fifteen quid, which was a lot of dough at the time. The maddest thing I did was to play a game of chicken on bikes. Three of us had a bet on who could go the farthest down the hill with his eyes closed. There was a slight bend in the road and I hit the kerb, flew over the handlebars and went straight into a brick wall, knocking myself out. I was about eleven or twelve.

I wasn't very big but I wouldn't be pushed around and I did have a few fights. Two ginger nuts from school picked on me. One day they waited for me at the top of Pelaw Bank and jumped me. I had a right good scrap with them, but ended up with a shiner. When I got home my dad asked me what had happened. He said I should go down to the field and get them one at a time. I said I'd get them at school and I did, separately.

A lad at school used to tag on to our gang and offer me an apple. Just about every day he'd come up to me and say, 'Roppa, do you want my apple?' and I'd say, 'No, it's OK.' But on a couple of days the school bully, Dave Kay, nicked his apple and gave him a slap on the head. So the next day I said, 'Give us your apple,' and when Dave Kay, who was a big lad, came across to get the apple again, I grabbed hold of him. 'Do you want the apple?' I said, showing it to him. 'You're not getting it today.'

He started laughing and the next thing I knew we were scuffling and all the other kids were round us in a circle in the playground, egging us on. He battered me, really, but I got in one or two good ones. Thankfully, the teachers broke us up before he could do too much damage to me. Then the two of us got the cane for fighting. So that was a really good decision – get a battering and the cane, all for an apple!

That was at Birtley Lord Lawson, a big new comprehensive school I'd moved to from Birtley South Secondary Modern. I was never too keen on school. I would say I was very average when it came to school work. Mam was always telling me off for not doing better. She would be on at me to get my homework done when all I wanted to do was play football. My school reports all had comments like: 'If he tried as hard at his school work as he does at football he'd be a far better scholar.' My two favourite subjects were geography and history. I just couldn't get interested in any of the others. I didn't have the motivation or desire to concentrate on them. The maths teacher used to hammer me – literally. He threw chalk and anything else he could lay his hands on at me.

I got a bit of stick from my mates because I did cookery at school. We had a choice of metalwork, woodwork or cookery. I didn't fancy metalwork or woodwork and I thought cookery might be useful later in life. I was the only lad in the cookery class. The trouble was that we had to take our cookery stuff to school in a basket, so I used to get a girl from down the road to take mine in for me.

It was pretty obvious to me and everybody else that I was never going to be an academic. I was lucky to be among the last of the fifteen-year-old school-leavers. The next age group had to stay on until they were sixteen. That was definitely a result for me!

Mind you, I did realise that if I wasn't going to be a professional footballer, I would have to earn my living some other way, and I decided I'd like to be a PE teacher. I knew I would have to knuckle down at school and get my qualifications if that was going to be my target, and I had an excellent role model in Bill Chapman, our PE teacher. He was the one teacher I made a favourable impression upon and he became a big influence on my football development. Football was always number one for me but I loved most sports. Running has always been one of my strengths. I competed at school in cross-country and the 400 metres.

By then I was a big Newcastle United fan and often went to matches at St James' Park, but the first professional football match I ever saw was at Sunderland – an FA Cup replay against Manchester United in March 1964. Dad took me to see our local rivals because it was such a big match and United were a glamour team. They were the Cup holders and had some of the greatest players in the game. That night their side included Bobby Charlton, Denis Law and George Best. I was mesmerised by the whole occasion and atmosphere. The match ended in a 2–2 draw but United went on to win the second replay. Not long after that, my dad took me to St James' for the first time, to see Newcastle v. Northampton Town in the old Second Division, and I was hooked. The buzz about the place was incredible and this young lad couldn't wait for more. From that day on, I went to Newcastle's home matches whenever I could. I played for the school in the morning and cheered on Newcastle in the afternoon – Saturdays were just perfect.

Newcastle's League Championship successes were all back in the early part of the last century, but they won the FA Cup three times in the fifties and have always been one of the big clubs in the English game. They have found it more difficult to win trophies in recent times, but in 1969 they lifted the Inter-Cities Fairs Cup – now called the UEFA Cup – after an unbelievable campaign. My hero in those days was Wyn Davies, a big, no-nonsense centre-forward who battered everybody in his path. The continental teams just couldn't cope with him. He absolutely murdered them in the air and set up his team-mates for fun. It made me appreciate from an early age that aerial power could be so important in football. I also liked Bobby

Moncur, who was a really cool, commanding left-half. In the first leg of the final we beat Ujpest Dozsa, of Hungary, 3–0 at St James' in front of a 60,000 crowd. We won the return leg in Budapest 3–2 to complete a fantastic 6–2 aggregate win.

There was a great tradition of dominant centre-forwards at Newcastle. 'Wor' Jackie Milburn was a legend in the black and white stripes and you'll hear Geordie fans reminiscing about him to this day, even if they never saw him play. My dad did see him and he used to tell me about his amazing goal-scoring feats. The whole family were fans, my mam included, although her favourite was Bobby Mitchell, a terrific little winger. In later years, Newcastle found new centre-forwards to worship in Malcolm Macdonald and Alan Shearer. It's as if the team can never be complete without a marauding, Roy of the Rovers style leader of the line.

I was also a big England fan, especially after we won the World Cup in 1966. I watched that at home with my mam and dad. The player I liked most from that team was Bobby Moore. He played a similar role to Moncur's, the defensive half-back. I've always admired good central defenders. I never imagined back then that I would one day wear the England shirt and, just like Moore, captain my country.

Even though I idolised Wyn Davies and Bobby Moncur, I always preferred playing as an attacking midfielder and that was the role I enjoyed through most of my professional career. As a youngster I just wanted to be involved in the play as much as possible. I'd run all over the park, chasing the ball and, when I had it, surging forward to try to score. I scored a lot of goals from midfield for my school teams. I got eleven in one match but it cost me. That was the day my dad stopped giving me 50p a goal. He had been paying me by the goal instead of giving me pocket money, but after that match he said he couldn't afford it.

I heard the local cubs had a good football team and some of the lads there kept on at me to join them. So I became a cub just to be able to play for their team. They had a great run in the district knock-out cup competition and we won the final 11–0.

We always had a good school team, although we usually met our match in a school from Washington. They have produced quite a few professional players down the years, including Gary Rowell, Wilf Rostron and Joe Bolton. We were probably the two best teams in the area.

I was captain of the school team and then made skipper of the Washington and district team. One of my proudest moments was leading them out in the final of the Hartlepool Hospital Cup. We met Darlington at Sacriston, a village between Chester-le-Street and Witton Gilbert. It was a massive occasion for us – we even had proper nets and corner flags – and we ran out to a crowd of about 200. We thought it was the FA Cup final. We didn't let ourselves down, either, winning 2–0. The hardest part for me was making a little speech at the end. I muttered a few words of thanks and then, when the ordeal was over, enjoyed our victory with the rest of the lads and our families.

Everything wasn't always so rosy, though. My first sending off came in a school match, against Chester-le-Street Grammar. We were losing and my temper started to fray. I kicked one or two of their players – one or two too many for the liking of the teacher who was refereeing the match. He gave me my marching orders and I trudged off, still fuming.

I got into trouble another time for messing around during a practice match at school. Some other lads had been ordered to run around the pitch as punishment for breaking windows. I passed the ball to one of them as he ran by and he kicked it back but it went past me and ran out of play. The teacher wasn't amused and said, 'If you want to join them, you can.' So I got lumped in with them, had to lap the pitch and then got two whacks of the cane across the backside.

The first suggestion that I might make it as a player came from my cousin Maurice, who used to travel up from Birmingham to visit us. I called him Uncle Maurice because he seemed so much older than me – actually by about ten years. He loved football and enjoyed a kick-about, although I drove him daft by nagging him to keep on playing when he was ready to go down to the pub for a pint. He always said that he was convinced I had it in me to be a player. I wasn't so sure, just hopeful that I might get a chance. By the age of thirteen, I'd done well at school and district level. I was small, but that didn't bother me at all. I was never afraid to mix it with bigger lads.

If I had a vague dream about becoming a professional footballer, it became a real ambition one Saturday afternoon. I'd come home after playing for the school team and was settling down to watch 'Grand-stand' on television. Dad was down at the social club. A knock came on the door and a man introduced himself to my mam as a scout from Burnley Football Club. He gave her his card and asked if he could have a chat with me. Mam showed him into the lounge. He said he'd seen me playing for the school that morning and in a few other games. He told me Burnley would like me to go down for a week's trial. He said he didn't need an answer straightaway, but if I wanted to go down in the next school holiday to let him know. He said I should speak to my dad and have a think about it. As soon as he left I said to my mam, 'I don't need to speak to Dad, I'm going.'

My mam said I wasn't to go around bragging to everybody about the scout coming to our house, but I couldn't wait to tell my school mates on the Monday. I was so excited I couldn't keep it in. I had to tell a couple of my pals who were really keen on football that I'd been offered a trial by Burnley. I never sensed any jealousy or ill-feeling from the other lads at school or in the neighbourhood. They seemed genuinely pleased for me. Soon more scouts came knocking on our door. I had a week's trial at Burnley, where I stayed in a hostel, and another at Coventry, where I also stayed in a hostel. Sheffield

Wednesday showed an interest, as did West Bromwich Albion – and Newcastle.

You might think that once Newcastle came in there could be no doubt where I wanted to go. This was my local team, the team I supported. I couldn't possibly be interested in any other club, but my hopes at St James' soon faded. I went up to Newcastle on a few evenings to train and they gave my dad a couple of tickets for a match, but somehow it didn't feel right. I just didn't enjoy it there.

Going to West Brom was totally different. I went down initially for a week and they put me in a hotel rather than a hostel. They took their young triallists to games and the theatre, and generally gave us more time and attention than the other clubs did. I felt they were genuinely kind and thoughtful. The whole atmosphere was friendlier and more encouraging for a young lad away from home. West Brom did everything they could to look after us and get the best out of us. Right from the start I enjoyed the coaching there, and the chief scout, Reg 'Paddy' Ryan, was great. It didn't take me long to decide this was the club I wanted to join.

They were just as quick in reaching the conclusion that they would have to build me up physically if I was to have any realistic prospect of succeeding in the game. That was where Bill Chapman became such an important influence on my career. I told him West Brom said I needed to be bigger and stronger, but he was happy that I had plenty of time to develop. He went out of his way to devise a training programme for me, which I did two evenings a week. He set up a weights circuit, tailored specifically for my needs. He knew exactly what he was doing. He understood what was beneficial and what wasn't for the bone structure of a young lad. So I never did heavy weights. Instead, he had me lifting lighter weights repetitively. Over the weeks and months, those circuits did me the world of good. I grew fitter and stronger, which was a big help when I went back down to West Brom for training during the school holidays. I'll always be grateful to Bill Chapman for the help and support he gave me. We've kept in touch and I think he was pleased and proud to follow my progress in the game.

When you have scouts from League clubs knocking at the door you're bound to get ideas about a career in football, but then you go training with them and realise how competitive it is. They are casting the net for the best lads they can find and yet most of those will never make the grade. I knew I was still a long way from becoming a professional footballer. The moment I thought I had a chance at The Hawthorns came at the end of Easter holiday training with an invitation to join them for six weeks during the summer. I was fourteen and a year away from a decision on whether or not I would be taken on as an apprentice. By asking me down for a lengthy stint like that they were virtually treating me as an apprentice – and paying me accordingly. They gave me £5 a week and put me up in digs. It struck me as a significant move by Albion and all the vibes I got that summer indicated they wanted me to stay with the club. I really felt I could be on my way.

There's no doubt that the weight circuits I'd done with Bill Chapman made it easier for me to adapt to the training sessions of a professional football club. Don Howe, who took over from Alan Ashman as manager of West Brom in 1971, was a hard taskmaster. He has rightly earned a great reputation for his coaching ability, but he also put his players through rigorous fitness routines. He ran his players and he made sure they worked on demanding weight routines. The sessions I'd put in back at my school gym went a long way towards preparing me for an apprenticeship at The Hawthorns.

My full-time job at the club was confirmed in the summer of 1972. I'd just left school and, although everybody had been saying I would be OK, I walked nervously into Don's little office to hear his verdict. To my relief, he told me I had the job. I was an apprentice professional. My pay was £5 a week for the first year, £8 for the second. The club paid my board and lodging but no other expenses, so I was hardly going to be rolling in money. That didn't bother me. All I wanted was to be on the books. I can remember Paddy Ryan was there to offer his congratulations and encouragement. Some lads were told they wouldn't be staying, and they left distraught. Some were in tears. I didn't need anyone to tell me how lucky I was.

Don made it clear, though, that this was only the start of the steep climb. I would have to work hard and play well over the next two years to justify a full professional contract. I would also have to start growing – and quickly.

2

BREAKING NEW GROUND

W EST BROMWICH ALBION were determined to do all they could to make me grow. I was little more than five foot tall and six and a half stone wet through at the age of fifteen. They insisted I went on a special diet, designed to put on the inches and the pounds. In the morning I had what looked to me like a lethal concoction of raw eggs, sherry, sugar and a pint of milk. For my evening meal the plate would be piled high with loads of boiled potatoes. I'm sure there was other stuff in there, but in my mind's eye all I can see is that mountain of potatoes.

As if that wasn't enough to tackle, I had to drink a bottle of Guinness. They told me it would be good for me, but it tasted horrible and I hated having to force it down. I had to keep telling myself it would be worth it and I did grow pretty quickly through my middle and late teens.

My digs were at Hamstead, a few minutes' bus ride from The Hawthorns. The landlady, Mrs Curtis, happened to be the gran of a good mate. Everything was fine to start with. She made sure I kept to my diet and watched over me as I gulped down the raw eggs and the Guinness. I would often go to the snooker hall with some of the other apprentices for a couple of hours after training, and then back to the digs early in the evening. Mrs Curtis was happy with that. She was quite strict rather than motherly and liked me in early so that she could lock up for the night.

After a while I started going out on the odd night with my cousin Maurice, who lived just up the road. He'd take me somewhere for a bite to eat or I'd just go round to his place. I'd get back at around eleven o'clock and I could tell she wasn't too pleased. One night I went out with the other players and didn't get back until midnight. I tried the door and realised she'd locked me out. I ended up having to sleep at the house across the road. Fortunately, I'd got to know the guy who lived there because I played snooker with him every now and then. He let me have a bed at his place.

After that, I decided it was probably time to get new digs. I wasn't one for going out on the town every night, and even if I wanted to I couldn't afford it, but I was a normal lad who liked to have a bit of fun from time to time and I didn't fancy having to keep begging a bed from the neighbours. So after about eighteen months I moved in with Ron and Irene Hinton at nearby Great Barr. They had a son, Pete, and made me feel really welcome. Ron was an Albion fan and loved to talk football. It was like being back at home.

Although I was able to settle at West Brom from the first day I went to the club on trial, I did find it difficult to cope with that first full year away from home. I was still a young lad and I could understand why so many talented players of my age couldn't stick it out. I had bouts of homesickness and, again, Albion were very good about it. They allowed me to go home for weekends and that helped me get through those nervous early stages of my career. The familiar surroundings gave me that bit of comfort when I needed it. It was good to be back in my own room, surrounded by all the foreign football club pennants my dad brought from his trips. He went to Italy fairly often so I had pennants from Juventus and many of the other major *Serie A* clubs. I brought one back from a trial I had at Coventry!

In the summer, before joining West Brom for my first pre-season as an apprentice, I had eight to ten weeks at home and sometimes went with my dad on his trips abroad. He transported all sorts of stuff, even huge caterpillar trucks. He'd maybe deliver a load to France and then go on to Italy, pick up something there and bring it back. I went to Naples a couple of times with him, helping him load and unload the wagon. We'd be away for a fortnight. We slept on bunks in the back of the cab. Sometimes the long days on the road got a bit boring, but then you'd meet up with the other drivers in the evening, have something to eat and Dad would have a drink. The camaraderie on the road was great. It was a terrific experience for a young lad and introduced me to Italian food. I have loved pasta ever since. It was good to be out with my dad, in a man's world. I also got some holiday work at the depot of Cavewood, the company he worked for. I'd do odd jobs, such as filling in holes in the yard, or driving the forklift truck. It earned me a few extra quid, which was always useful.

I've always liked to go back up to Chester-le-Street whenever possible, to see the family and go for a pint with some of my old mates. I found it funny going back later in my career, when I was playing for Manchester United and England, and later still when I became a manager. I'd be sitting in a pub with a few of my pals from schooldays, and they'd be telling me, 'Ah, but you know, Jimmy was a better player than you were . . .' or 'Johnny had more skill than you . . .' I'd just laugh because I've heard it so often over the years. To be honest, I still think I was the best player at school, but talent alone isn't enough. It's what you do with that talent and how you develop it that matters.

A few of the lads back then were good players and might have had a chance, but you have to apply yourself and work at it. The players who get the best out of themselves are those who dedicate themselves to the job. People go on about the fact that I liked to have a pint and enjoy life, which I did. I make no apologies for that. But I had that pint at the right time and I made sure it never interfered with my preparations for a match. I was 100 per cent ready to be the best I could be whenever I was picked.

I was probably just fortunate I had that determination even as a youngster at school. Cross-country runs would sometimes be agony. I'd be tired and have a massive stitch in my side, but I would never stop. I would run through it. When I became a footballer, I could run hard for ninety minutes and I know the effort I put in as a lad at school gave me that strength and stamina. I tell the young players I have now to give it their best shot and make the most of the gift they have. Too many young players with great natural talent are just play-acting. That's why they become average rather than outstanding players. If you work hard and dedicate yourself and still don't make it, at least you know you've given it everything. To have that talent and not get the best out of it is unforgivable.

Don Howe had left me in no doubt about what I had to do, although I didn't have a lot of direct contact with him in those first couple of years. His main concern was obviously the first team. The person I worked under was Albert McPherson, the youth-team coach. He was good with the kids and Paddy Ryan was never far away, so the atmosphere was always friendly. Paddy nearly always joined us after training for a bite to eat and a chat. He had a great knack of putting the younger players at their ease.

I didn't really mix with the senior players in my early days at the club and I soon learned that it paid to keep a respectful distance from them. As an apprentice I had to take my turn making cups of tea for them, collecting their kit, cleaning their boots, sweeping the dressing-room floor and doing all the other chores that were part of the job in those days. Clubs aren't allowed to make the YTS lads do jobs like that now and I sometimes think we pamper them. A few menial tasks do a youngster no harm and perhaps somewhere between past and present practices would be ideal.

One day when I had to go to collect the first-team players' kit I walked into the dressing room without knocking – big mistake. They were sitting on the benches, taking off their kit and chatting. John Kaye, one of the senior players, turned towards me and barked, 'You, out. Knock next time you want to come in.' So I went back out, knocked on the door and waited till they told me to come in. When I did, they said I had to serve a punishment. They told me to dance with a mop in the middle of the dressing room. Did I do as I was told? You bet I did. I was absolutely crapping myself!

I learned my lesson and didn't intend to upset the old boys again. I saw some of the other lads having to do outrageous things as punishment for getting on the wrong side of the first-team players. They were ordered to run around the training pitch stark naked because of some little thing they might have done wrong. Another 'sentence' was to have boot polish or dubbing smeared all over you. It was just part of normal life at a football club. It happened everywhere. We accepted that was the way it was and just tried our best to keep out of the first team's way.

For the most part I succeeded in keeping my nose clean, but I got picked on again – or to be more precise picked up – one day at the training ground. I was playing pool in the dining room when the first-team players strolled in. Jim Cumbes, a goalkeeper who must have been six feet four inches tall, came up to me, picked me up by my legs, held me upside down and started shaking me. 'You can't be an apprentice, you're a midget,' he said. The other players were having a good laugh, but I was more bothered about my money, which fell out of my pockets and rolled all over the floor. Jim, who also played cricket and is now chief executive of Lancashire Cricket Club, eventually put me down and left me to scamper around, trying to find all my coins.

There weren't so many laughs among the first-team players at the end of the 1972–73 season because they were relegated from the First Division, which was then the top tier in English football, to the

Second. That didn't really affect the apprentices because we were still a long way from making the first team. I was trying to establish myself in the youth team. I had been in and out of the side all through that first season. The good thing was that relegation didn't seem to make any difference to the way the club operated. There were no cost-cutting measures, we had the same training ground, the same travel arrangements and our kit was still laundered for us.

That summer the youth team had a pre-season tournament in Augsburg, Germany. It was a great experience for young players, playing foreign opposition and being abroad as a team for the first time. My game definitely took a leap forward on that tour. I had always been full of confidence in school matches, but that hadn't been the case in my first season as an apprentice. In Germany, I suddenly started getting involved much more and making an impact. I felt the whole pre-season preparations went well for me. It's a major step for a schoolboy coming into his first pre-season training sessions. Full-time training, mornings and afternoons, every day, is gruelling. It's draining for a young lad. You want all the rest you can get. I never had any problems or doubts about my fitness during that first year, because I could tell I was getting bigger and stronger, but I knew my game could improve. Coming back for that second year, after a summer's rest, I did feel the difference. I was so much more confident.

We had a good youth team and competition for places was stiff, but I kept up my form through that season and won a regular place. I even played alongside a couple of West Brom legends, both now dead, sadly – goalkeeper John Osborne and Jeff Astle, who scored the winning goal in the 1968 FA Cup final against Everton. You couldn't help but learn from those two overage players. Ossie, by then a part-time player, brought invaluable experience to the team and it rubbed off on all of us. Another of the legends from that era was Graham Williams, who goes down in history as the first player to try to stop George Best. He marked Bestie on his debut for Manchester United in 1963 – or at least he tried to. The joke at the club was that Graham couldn't get close enough to George to kick him.

I thought I had a decent season in the youth side but, more importantly, I appeared to be impressing the club because towards the end of the term I was called up for my reserve-team debut. It proved a bruising experience. The match was against Everton reserves at Goodison Park, and I was picked at left-back. I played in a number of positions in my early years at The Hawthorns and didn't really mind so long as I was playing. I also played central defence and wide on the left. I was naturally left footed, although I worked on my right foot and over the years it became reasonably effective. I even managed to score quite regularly with my right foot, mainly because I wasn't afraid to have a go with it. Too many players are unwilling to use their 'swinger'. My favourite position was undoubtedly central midfield and I believe I was always at my best in that role, covering the ground from box to box. I was quite useful in the air and the more I grew the more important my heading became – in both goal areas.

Anyway, I was excited at the prospect of playing at such a famous ground as Goodison Park, which had been one of the 1966 World Cup grounds. Nerves didn't usually get the better of me, but I must admit my stomach was churning as kick-off approached – not that there was anything like a World Cup atmosphere once we ran out on to the pitch. It was, after all, a Central League fixture and the crowd amounted to a scattering of spectators. As soon as the match got under way, I felt fine. The pace was quicker than I'd been used to, but I thought that what little I had to do in the first half I did OK.

Then in the second half I had a timely reminder that I was mixing it with the big boys. Everton knocked the ball forward and I decided I would let it run out of play for a throw-in. I got the call of 'man on' but felt sure I would be able to shield the ball over the line. The man I had been warned about wasn't prepared to let me have my way. He barged into me and sent me sprawling on the cinder track. I was badly grazed down one side and had to be bandaged up. We won the game 2–1, but the real plus for me was the insight into this higher level of the game. Reserve-team football is another huge jump for a young lad, literally the difference between men and boys. The name of that player who sent me away from Goodison with a sore souvenir? Joe Royle. The big centre-forward was making his come-back from injury and had no intention of making life easy for some kid called Robson.

During the summer of 1974 I faced another D-day. Don had to decide whether or not I'd done enough to graduate from the ranks of the apprentices to join the fully fledged professional staff. I was hopeful because I thought I'd made good progress over the previous season. I'd even made the breakthrough into the reserves. I couldn't be sure, though, just as none of the other lads could be sure, and in those days there was no question of anyone marking your cards for you. It was felt that wouldn't be fair. These days clubs give their players a lot more notice, drop little hints and generally handle the situation far more delicately. It's something we took great care over when I returned to West Brom as manager. Back then it was black or white, in or out. So we all had to sit in the dressing room at The Hawthorns and wait to be called, one at a time, to the manager's office. Some of the other lads came out with tears in their eyes, devastated. I didn't have to ask how they'd got on.

Then it was my turn. I was so nervous because I knew that I could be on the next train back to the North East with my dreams in ruins. Moments later I was relieved, elated and feeling quite rich. The manager put in front of me a pro contract worth £28 a week, plus a signing-on fee of £250. I signed the contract as quickly as I could and then went to find a phone box to tell my mam the news. My next stop was the building society to open a savings account. I was seventeen and on top of the world. This was real money for a lad from Chester-le-Street, but the main feeling was that I'd got my foot in the door of professional football.

All the signs that following season continued to look promising. I played regularly for the reserves and, when the first team began to stutter, I wondered whether I might even come into the reckoning for a senior call-up. The talk around the club, though, was not about the prospects of a youngster in the reserves, but the future of the manager. The local press were speculating that Don Howe's job could be on the line. The board eventually announced that they would not be renewing Don's contract at the end of the season, and since only a few fixtures remained, he decided he didn't want to hang around any longer. He said his goodbyes and that was it.

Although I hadn't had a lot of dealings with Don – I'd worked with Albert McPherson, Brian Whitehouse and Bill Asprey – he had always been very supportive and I was grateful to him for giving me my job. I was pleased our paths crossed some years later, when he was the England coach. In fact, our paths have crossed throughout my career. He and I also worked together as coaches alongside Terry Venables with the national team, and when I went on a Pro-licence course at Warwick University, Don was the lecturer.

The more contact I had with him, the more I appreciated what an outstanding coach he was, certainly one of the best I've ever worked with. It's probably true to say he was more cut out to be a coach than a manager. There is a difference and Don just wanted to be out on the training pitch, working with the players, rather than having to contend with all the other parts of managing. If anything, he liked coaching too much. He was so intense and enthusiastic that I sometimes wondered whether he didn't over-train his players. But as lads at West Brom we loved to be out there on the pitch, and the good habits you pick up at that age should be ingrained for the rest of your career.

Don's sudden departure from The Hawthorns meant the club had to put someone in temporary charge for the remaining three matches, and the caretaker role was handed to our reserve-team trainer, Brian Whitehouse. The club made it clear they were looking outside for Don's full-time replacement, but Brian obviously wanted to make his mark. He definitely caught my attention when he pinned up the team-sheet for his first match as boss, away to York City. He had made changes – and I was one of the players he brought in. I made my first-team debut on Saturday, 12 April 1975. I was eighteen and to be playing League football at that age was way beyond anything I could have dreamed of when I joined Albion.

My mam and dad came down to watch me play at Bootham Crescent. Brian told me I had earned my chance and the senior players did their best to make me feel at ease. Brian played me in midfield but said he wanted to make my job simpler by giving me a man-marking job on their captain. I remember doing a lot of chasing and coming off the pitch at the end tired but pretty happy. We won 3–1. Brian's shake-up of the side had brought West Brom their first success away from home since Christmas.

Brian must have been reasonably satisfied with my contribution because he kept me in the team for the following match, against Cardiff City, at The Hawthorns. The crowd were brilliant with me on my home debut, especially when I scored. Brian told me to play my natural game this time, so I was able to get forward and be much more involved. We had been playing for about ten minutes when I ran into the box and put us in front from close range. It was just the most fantastic feeling, yet weird also, to hear my name being chanted by the fans. We went on to win 2–0, but the most nerve-racking part of the day was still to come. I had to face the press.

Until then I'd never spoken to national newspaper reporters, although I'd been interviewed occasionally by the local lads. When I came out of the dressing room, all the national boys were waiting to interview me. This was far more intimidating than playing because it was totally new to me. At that time clubs weren't geared up to advise their young players on how to deal with the press. They didn't put them through media training courses, as they do now. The reports were very complimentary, though, and my mam and dad started collecting the cuttings for their scrapbooks.

I was flying and couldn't wait for the next match, away to Nottingham Forest. I managed to score again and, although we lost 2–1, I felt pretty good. I had scored two goals in my first three League matches and was sick that the season had come to an end. I wanted to keep playing. Fortunately, I had the chance to do so – for my country. I was picked for the England youth team's trip to Switzerland for the mini World Cup. Other players in the squad included Glenn Hoddle, Ray Wilkins, Peter Barnes, Alan Curbishley and Steve Wicks. With so much midfield talent to choose from, the manager, Ken Burton, played me at centre-half. By then I was over five feet ten inches tall and felt comfortable in that role. We went through the tournament undefeated and beat Finland 1–0 in the final with a 'golden goal' scored by Ray. Winning the Cup rounded off an unbelievable season for me.

I suppose that trip and our eventual win made me start thinking about the possibility of becoming a full England international. I also wondered what my position would be. The mini World Cup had gone well for me, but when I reflected on those goals for Albion I realised I could never be totally content playing anywhere except central midfield. As for the senior England team, that was another world. I still had to hold down a regular first-team place with West Brom and to do that I needed to convince a new manager that I was worth it.

The new boss was Johnny Giles, the former Manchester United, Leeds United and Republic of Ireland midfield player. He arrived as player-manager and left us in no doubt that he was still tremendously skilful and effective as a player. His passing, with either foot, was exceptional. We had a chat and I told him I preferred to play in central midfield, but of course I realised there would be plenty of competition in that department, not least from the gaffer. He brought in a few new faces, including England's World Cup hat-trick hero Geoff Hurst, and I played in a variety of positions that season. One match I would be centre-half, another left-back, another midfield, another on the bench. That didn't concern me too much. I knew I still had a lot to learn and was happy just to be involved with the first-team squad.

I found John Giles great to work with. As far as I was aware, so did the other players. We played five-a-side every day in training, but with the intensity of a real game. We had a lot of sit-up routines and finished with sprints. All the hard work had been done pre-season. We enjoyed our training and the spirit in the camp was good. John liked to take us on trips every now and then. He allowed us to down a few pints and encouraged us to have a sing-song. He brought in fellow Irishmen Mick Martin and Paddy Mulligan and they always made sure we were in good voice. They were real characters, always cracking jokes and getting up to pranks.

The laughs were on Mick one day, though, when he turned up for training wearing a pair of white shoes. He got merciless ribbing and there was more to come. After training he tried to slip into his shoes but they wouldn't move. Willie Johnston, the Scottish winger, had nailed them to the floor. That incident must have stuck in my mind because I did the same thing to Ray Wilkins when we were team-mates at Manchester United. He left me stranded in Leeds after we'd gone together in his car and I had to get a taxi all the way back home. So I took my revenge by nailing his shoes to the floor at the United training ground.

John Trewick, one of the other younger players, and I became good pals and roomed together on trips. Some of the other players at

Albion when I was breaking into the first team were Len Cantello, Asa Hartford, Alistair Robertson, Tony Brown and Ally Brown. They were all good to this quiet lad from the North East. Len was especially helpful. He more or less took me under his wing. He'd invite me to join him for a pint, and ask me round to his house for a meal with him and his wife. He 'kidnapped' me one weekend and took me back to his home in Manchester. I remember going to his dad's club, but not much else. It was Len who first told me I'd play for my country. During a match for West Brom he said to me, 'Keep playing like this and one day you'll play for England.' I thought he was just getting carried away with the friendly bit.

My attitude was always positive despite not having a regular first-team place that season. I got the impression that John Giles was still trying to judge me and assess where I could best serve the team, and I realised that playing in different positions would benefit my education in the game. The time for specialising would come.

Optimism was growing at the club as we went through that season. After a shaky start under the new boss, we picked up, got on a roll to join the promotion chase and arrived at Oldham for our last match, knowing that a win would take us back to the First Division. We had a fantastic following at Boundary Park that day and, although I wasn't in the starting line-up, I felt very much part of the Albion effort.

One goal was enough to give us the result we needed and it came, appropriately, from Tony Brown. 'Bomber' was a goal machine. From distance or close range, he was a natural. He was a marvellous striker of the ball and hit some breathtaking volleys in his time. He could bend the ball, chip it, do almost anything with it. The timing of his runs into the area was uncanny and he was ice cool under pressure. That day he was again the right man in the right place for us. All the tension of the occasion was blown away at the final whistle. Thousands of our fans swarmed on to the pitch. John Giles and his team had delivered and I was confident we had the quality to hold our own in the First Division.

My personal battle for regular first-team football continued at the start of the following season, 1976–77. I came in for the injured player-manager in a League Cup match against Liverpool at The Hawthorns only to be told I would have to make way for him in the League meeting away to neighbours Birmingham. For the first time I plucked up the courage to voice my disappointment and the following day Giles said he had changed his mind – he would be substitute. Just when I thought I was making a significant breakthrough I was struck down by a break of a very different kind.

I was playing at left-back in the match against Tottenham in October when I went in to challenge Chris Jones as he lined up a shot. I nicked the ball away from him, but his boot caught me and I went down with a strange ache in my left leg. I tried to carry on but couldn't and had to be carried off. We thought it was just bruised and I didn't worry too much about it. Besides, we beat Spurs 4–2 to go third in the League. Over the weekend, though, the pain got worse and on the Monday I was taken to hospital for an X-ray that revealed my left leg was broken. The good news, they said, was that I should be playing again within weeks.

Five weeks and many hours of muscle-building exercises later I was ready for my comeback, a reserve game against Stoke City at The Hawthorns. I was in midfield and had no worries about going in for a fifty-fifty tackle with Denis Smith, Stoke's long-serving centre-half. The sudden pain left me in no doubt this time. I knew it was broken again and I also knew I had come back too soon.

I decided to relieve the boredom and frustration of another lay-off by joining my dad on one of his trips, this time to Grenoble. My friend Pete Hill – Mrs Curtis' grandson – came for the ride as well. I was on crutches but didn't think that would be a problem, and the change of scenery definitely bucked me up. I was in even better spirits after we dropped off the load and popped into a bar in Grenoble. Later, the three of us made our way back to the cab somewhat worse for wear, and next morning we remembered little of our night out – in particular, where my crutches were. I'd lost them. Every time we stopped on the way back, poor old Pete had to give me a piggyback. Dad dropped us off at West Bromwich but before he left he said he'd have a last look around for my crutches – and found them in the back of the trailer. Pete wasn't best pleased.

Everybody at the club, and the manager especially, went to great lengths to reassure me that I could make a full recovery. I was told to be patient and not rush my return. By Christmas, I felt I was ready and was recalled, at left-back, for the home match against Bristol City. Whatever worries I had, nagging away at the back of my mind, quickly disappeared. I came through that game, the leg felt as good as new and all I thought about was staying in the team. Things were really looking up when I scored my first hat-trick, against Ipswich Town at The Hawthorns. We hammered them 4–0 and it seemed I couldn't do anything wrong. One of my goals was a particularly satisfying strike, the others were down to anticipation.

Selection for the England Under-21 squad followed but I was withdrawn by West Brom because they had a match. As consolations go, it wasn't so bad. We drew 2–2 with Manchester United and I scored on my first appearance at Old Trafford. I felt I was really on my way in the game. Instead, I was soon on my familiar way to the hospital.

During a game against the other Manchester club, City, at The Hawthorns in April 1977, I went into a tackle with Dennis Tueart and my right ankle cracked. I was becoming an expert on fractures and had no illusions about the extent of the injury. The expressions on the faces of my team-mates told me I was right. I saw the same looks in the ambulance. My mam and girlfriend, Denise, went with me on that dreaded journey and they couldn't hide their concern. The hospital verdict was a formality. I had suffered a third broken leg in seven months.

I got plenty of sympathy from the club and the fans, but I was aware that people were beginning to ask whether I was too injury prone to make it as a professional footballer. The doctors insisted it was a clean break and that there was no reason why I shouldn't be back, good as new. John Giles and all the medical and coaching staff were equally encouraging. The season was coming to an end, so I had all summer to heal and regain my fitness. Then it was up to me to prove myself.

3

UNITED CALLING

THE SUMMER of 1977 was like serving a sentence of hard labour. I pushed myself to the limit to be in the best possible condition for the new season. All the effort paid off and as the first game approached the ankle was fine, just as the doctors said it would be, and my self-belief was as strong as ever. West Bromwich Albion were re-established as a First Division club and I felt I was ready to make a more regular contribution. That personal ambition became a more realistic aim when I learned that one of my midfield rivals had left the club. Johnny Giles, our player-manager, decided to go back to his homeland to take up a post with Shamrock Rovers.

Our new boss was an Albion old boy, Ronnie Allen, a goal-scoring hero of the team that won the FA Cup in 1954. He had been Giles's chief scout and he quickly settled into his new role. We made a good start and I had the regular place I wanted, but in mid-season it was all change again. Ronnie accepted a big offer to go to Saudi Arabia and the club captain, John Wile, was put in temporary charge. By then, results had taken a dip and I was one of the casualties of the subsequent team shake-up. That was how things stood early in 1978 when we were introduced to our fourth manager in a matter of months.

Ron Atkinson had made people sit up and take note by leading Cambridge United from the Fourth Division to the brink of the

Second in consecutive seasons. He also attracted plenty of attention with his formidable physical presence – not for nothing was he known as Big Ron – and with the sheer power of his personality. You would never describe Ron as shy and retiring. He became known in football and the media as 'Flash', 'Mr Bojangles' and other such names, and he did little to discourage that flamboyant public image. Much of it came from his tongue-in-cheek, fun-loving attitude to life, but basically he was a down-to-earth, fair-minded, regular bloke.

As soon as he walked into The Hawthorns the place lit up. He was lively and jovial, totally different from the previous managers I'd known at the club. He was more like one of the lads than the boss. What mattered to the club, players and fans, of course, was whether he could produce results and he set about proving that he could. He was very much a football man and when it came to the job, he was serious all right. He brought in Colin Addison, another outgoing character, as his assistant. I went on to develop an excellent working relationship with Ron and eventually rejoined him at Manchester United, but I can't say I had an instant rapport with him. He left me out of the FA Cup semi-final team and I was far from impressed. We lost that tie, 3–1, to Ipswich Town, who went on to lift the trophy.

My mood improved in the later stages of the season, when Ron recalled me and I began to show him what I could do, but I still needed to feel I had a future with Albion. I was twenty-one and desperate to progress. Ron told me that if I got my head down and kept on working at my game, I would have an important role to play at Albion. We had qualified for Europe and had plenty to look forward to. He insisted I was going nowhere – except China!

Our tour of the world's most populous country, in the summer of 1978, has become the stuff of legend. The eighteen-day trip included five matches. This, though, was far more than a football assignment. We were effectively ambassadors for the English game and the English nation. Apparently, the Chinese authorities were keen for a western team to visit their country and our FA were anxious to oblige. Albion's chairman, Bert Millichip, who became a distinguished figure in international football as chairman of the FA, pulled all the right diplomatic strings to entrust his club with the unprecedented mission.

It was an amazing experience for all of us and certainly, for me, an insight into a society and culture I could never have imagined. We visited communes where we had to bend our heads to walk into the tiny, very basic homes. Everything was small and simple – the chairs, tables and beds. The outlet from the stove went through a hole in the roof. The people were unbelievably hospitable and polite. Our every move was recorded by a 'World in Action' TV crew and inevitably we were taken to the Great Wall of China. John Trewick's remark that day is now almost as famous as the massive construction itself. 'Once you've seen one wall, you've seen them all,' he said. People still ask whether he really did say that and I assure them he did. It's right there, on camera.

We were guests of honour at a succession of marathon banquets, which was just as well since there was certainly nowhere to go for a night out. Some of the food was good, some . . . well, not quite what we were used to at our local Chinese restaurant. I like to try different food but I drew the line at sea slugs. Alistair Robertson, sitting next to me, went for it and he was served a big black creature with long antennae. I winced as he somehow got it down his neck. I think he was thankful for the beer that finally washed it down. We booked tables at a highly recommended restaurant one night and were enjoying our meal until we were urged to hurry and leave. It closed at nine and that was that, no arguments.

The best night out we had was at the Shanghai Circus. The acts were fantastic, but for some reason they wouldn't allow the cameras in. Other than that, we spent most of our spare time occupied with footballers' usual pastime – playing cards.

We were originally due to play four matches, but the possibility of another came up and Ron asked us if we were willing to take it on. The lads voted unanimously to play the extra game, which shows how much time we had on our hands. Overall it was an adventure that I think most of us now cherish. I have been on loads of trips and visited most parts of the world since then, but Albion in China stands out in my mind. People still talk about it, which shows what a special trip it was.

Spending all that time together, in unfamiliar surroundings and sometimes sensitive circumstances, might have strained relations in the camp, but it served as a valuable bonding exercise long before that term became common. Team spirit was sky high. Ron and Colin created an excellent working atmosphere. We went about our training and matches in a thoroughly professional and committed manner, yet there were always smiles and chirpy banter about the place. We enjoyed our football and with every reason. Ron moulded a side that had the courage – and ability – to take on the best.

Tony Godden made the goalkeeping position his own, Derek Statham emerged as an outstanding left-back, John Wile and Alistair Robertson were as commanding as ever in the middle of the defence, Len Cantello was a class act in midfield and Tony Brown just couldn't stop scoring goals – but what made us one of the most exciting and talked-about teams in the land was that we had the Three Degrees. Brendan Batson, a tremendous right-back, Laurie Cunningham, a winger with pace and flair, and Cyrille Regis, an awesome centre-forward, were given that nickname after we went along to the opening of Andy Gray's nightclub in Birmingham. The real Three Degrees, the American girl group, were there and it was too good a photo opportunity to miss. Albion's three black players and the three black singers happily posed for pictures, Andy got his publicity and, from that moment, we had our very own Three Degrees.

That stunt, I'm convinced, helped break down the prejudice against black and coloured players in this country, as did Viv Anderson's selection as the first black England international. Barring the occasional, isolated incident, it is simply not an issue in this country now, yet less than thirty years ago racism still shamed our game. I used to get letters from people asking me how I could play for a club that had so many black players in their team. It wasn't uncommon for players to have bananas thrown at them from the crowd. I remember a match at The Hawthorns when the away fans left hundreds of banana skins at the Smethwick End. We have come a long way since then but, unfortunately, the same can't be said for some countries in Europe.

Brendan, Laurie and Cyrille all had a major impact on that season and helped us on brilliant runs at home and abroad. We topped the First Division at one stage and finished the term in third place. One of the highlights was a spectacular 5–3 win against Manchester United at Old Trafford. We came back from 3–2 down to stun the big Christmas holiday crowd. Cunningham was at his mesmerising best and United just couldn't live with the sheer power of Regis. We reached the fifth round of the FA Cup and the quarter-finals of the UEFA Cup after some fantastic performances. The most memorable night of that campaign was our triumph over Valencia. We held the Spanish team, which included Argentina's World Cup hero Mario Kempes, 1–1 away and two goals by Tony Brown gave us an aggregate victory at a bouncing Hawthorns.

Injuries and club commitments had prevented me from totting up a few England Under-21 appearances before I got my chance that season, at the age of twenty-two. Two overage players were allowed and I took my place in the team against Wales at a wintry Swansea. We won 1–0, thanks to a goal by Glenn Hoddle. I was on national duty again at the end of the season, rejoining the Under-21s for a European tour and then making my England B debut against Austria

B in Klagenfurt. I put the B side in front with one of my better long-range efforts, only for the match to be abandoned because of a spectacular storm.

I still had the most important trip that summer ahead of me – my delayed honeymoon. I had met Denise Brindley at a local pub, where she was celebrating her twenty-first birthday with friends. We chatted and I asked for her phone number. A couple of nights later we went to the pictures and soon I was smitten. She was no starry-eyed football groupie. In fact, she wasn't a football fan at all, which I was quite pleased about. Denise loved horses and was happier show-jumping than watching football at weekends. On Sundays, I went along to watch her.

Denise was born in Wednesbury, just outside West Bromwich, and was secretary to an accountant. She had a few secretarial jobs. Her dad, George, wasn't really into football, either. When we started getting serious about each other, Denise's mum, Doreen, turned to George and said, 'Don't worry about him, he might get a proper job one of these days.' George and Doreen were great and made me feel very welcome. We hit it off straightaway.

George and Doreen helped me out with furniture when I bought a flat in Great Barr. They were buying new wardrobes so they gave me their old ones, which looked pretty new to me. They also gave me a bed for the spare room. All I had when I moved in was one bed, a settee and a telly. I bought a fridge from my old sparring partner, Joe Royle. Our mutual friend, Asa Hartford, organised that little deal. A much bigger deal for me was buying the flat, which had two bedrooms, a lounge and kitchen. It cost £18,000, which meant sacrificing having a car to raise enough money for the deposit. The older players advised me to invest in property as soon as I could. I figured that if I could keep my place in the first team and pick up some bonus money, I would be able to afford another car before too long. In the meantime, I didn't mind catching the bus to the training ground, about twenty minutes away.

I'd not had much luck with cars, anyway. Like most young lads, I was excited about getting my first set of wheels and I've always liked cars. My first was an old Chrysler, or to be more accurate, an old banger. Smoke billowed from the back every time I started it up. I bought it from my aunt. She and her husband were car dealers and did repairs as well, so they sorted me out. It didn't last long, though, so my mam and dad let me have the Austin Westminster. That had reached the age when it was just about to drop to pieces, but it was still a really comfortable car and great for me, driving from the Midlands back up to Chester-le-Street. One day it got nicked and when I went to the Birmingham police compound a day or two later, the wheels, battery and all sorts of stuff had gone. I got it fixed, though, and it kept me going until I decided I ought to get something a bit flashier.

I bought a yellow Ford Capri and then changed that for a blue Capri 3000. That was some motor – or it was before I wrote it off. I went to pick up Willie Johnston, who didn't drive, and I was doing, I swear, no more than 30mph when I hit a patch of black ice and skidded into a lamp post. The impact buckled a wheel and broke the chassis. Willie and I didn't have a mark, but my beloved Capri was history. I was still without a car when I met Denise. I hadn't got around to sorting out the insurance money and in the meantime decided to check the property market.

I borrowed Denise's Mini one day to go to the ground but as I was leaving, a wagon reversed into me. A couple of the other players saw the accident and were killing themselves laughing. I didn't think it was so funny, especially as I had to go and pick up Denise from horse riding. I said to her, 'You'll not believe what's happened.' She went round to the side of her nice new Mini and saw for herself – the side was smashed in.

Denise and I fixed our wedding for 2 June 1979, thinking there wouldn't be too many complications through football commitments. In fact, our big day came in the middle of a hectic period that left me barely enough time for the chapel service in West Bromwich. Ron took us to an end-of-season tournament in Denmark and we returned on the Thursday, two days before the wedding. I had my stag night, with a few of the lads at a local pub, on the Friday and flew out with the England Under-21 squad on the Sunday. We finally got round to a honeymoon after the England B game in Austria and settled down to married life in our three-bed semi in Great Barr.

At least the honeymoon was worth the wait. We went to Ibiza with Pete Hill and his girlfriend, Jane Wypler, and had a fantastic time. The four of us came out of a bar one day, having had a few drinks, and Denise jumped on my back. I carried her down the street to the beach and still she wouldn't let me put her down. So I ran on to the pier, carried on running to the end – and jumped off into the sea. She lost her shoes but it was worth it for the laugh.

Almost before I had time to dry out we were into another season. My form was generally good and, having played for my country at Under-21 and B level, I had ambitions of making the full England team. It seemed I wasn't the only one thinking along those lines. The local press started to clamour for my call-up and the *Birmingham Evening Mail* launched a campaign to put pressure on the England manager, Ron Greenwood. The sports editor decided his paper would organise a petition to support my case and Ray Matts, the senior football writer, wrote glowing articles in which he set out my credentials. Ray had followed every step of my career, initially for another local paper, the *Express and Star* in Wolverhampton, and then for the *Birmingham Evening Mail*. He reckoned that I had been overlooked, not only by the manager but also by the London-based national press, because I played for an 'unfashionable' Midlands club. He felt that Glenn Hoddle, for instance, had an advantage because he played for Tottenham.

The campaign gathered amazing momentum and, with Mattsy beating the drum, the response was staggering. The paper canvassed support outside the ground on match days and printed petition forms. More than a thousand readers sent in their completed and signed forms, which were then sent on to the FA offices in Lancaster Gate, with a carefully worded suggestion to Ron Greenwood that he might consider my claims. It was tremendously flattering to have that kind of backing from the media and the public.

Whether or not it influenced the England boss I don't know, but I didn't have to wait much longer to become a full international. Ron Atkinson called me in one day to tell me he had received a phone call from Ron Greenwood. I had been picked for a European Championship qualifying match against the Republic of Ireland, at Wembley, on 6 February 1980. It wasn't until I joined Manchester United that I fully appreciated the poignancy. My debut came on the twenty-second anniversary of the Munich air crash, which killed eight of the Busby Babes.

Whatever Ron Greenwood made of the press campaign, he didn't appear to hold it against me. As soon as I turned up at the England camp he came over to me and welcomed me on board. He couldn't have been more pleasant and considerate. He made sure I was put at my ease and two of the established players, Terry McDermott and Phil Thompson, went out of their way to make me feel I was one of the lads. I'll never forget that. I'll never forget pulling on the England shirt for the first time, either. I was in the starting line-up, as I was to be throughout my international career. Over the years I realised how lucky I was when I saw so many lads called up to the squad only to find themselves repeatedly sitting on the bench or even in the stand on match day.

The England team that night, in front of a 90,000 crowd, was: Clemence; Cherry, Thompson, Watson, Sansom; Keegan, McDermott, Robson, Cunningham; Johnson (Coppell), Woodcock.

It was good to have a club-mate, Laurie Cunningham, alongside me, but then it was no problem settling in with the rest of those players. Ray Clemence took his turn in goal as the manager persisted with his policy of alternating his two brilliant keepers. The other was Peter Shilton and neither man let down his country. I think that had I been in charge I would have made my choice and stuck with it, but Ron Greenwood maintained he could not split them. Shilts eventually made the position his own and I felt he just about had the edge over Clem, but we were so lucky to have two keepers of that calibre. Shilts went on to win an England record 125 caps. When you think how many more he might have had, it's an incredible tally.

I had a few pre-match nerves, which is normal, but I didn't feel overawed. The main sensation was one of pride, the realisation that I was stepping out to represent my country. It was my first appearance at Wembley and that in itself was the dream of most young players. The match was hardly a classic and I played more significant roles for England in later internationals, but I think I did OK and the result was all-important. We won 2–0, both goals coming from Keegan, so it was a case of job done. England were heading for the European Championship finals in Italy.

Although Ron Greenwood showed no hard feelings towards me over all the fuss created by the *Birmingham Evening Mail*'s 'Robson for England' campaign, he obviously hadn't forgotten Mattsy's involvement and couldn't resist the chance to have a little stab back at the man who probably became a pain in the bum for him. Ray was in Italy, reporting on England's progress at the European Championship, and introduced himself, as required, before asking Ron a question at a press conference. Apparently, Ron responded, 'Ah, so you're Roy Mopps.' That no doubt made Ron feel better and Mattsy, who has a good sense of humour, took it in good part. Besides, he's no doubt been called a lot worse in his long career – by me, for one, a few years later.

At West Brom, we still had work to do if we were to finish the season in a respectable position. Our exploits in 1978–79 were always going to be a hard act to follow and we had struggled to rediscover that devastating form in the early part of the following term. In fact, we had struggled to find any sort of form, scrambling around at the bottom rather than being lauded at the top of the table. We had been knocked out of the UEFA Cup in the first round and the FA Cup in the third. We improved after the turn of the year and ended the season tenth in the League, yet it was difficult to hide the general disappointment.

My emotions swung from anxiety to elation early the following season, although that had nothing to do with football. Denise gave birth to our first child. In the early hours of 17 September 1980, Denise woke up and said her waters had broken. She said the pains weren't too bad so I told her to relax and when they came on more we'd go to hospital. I made her a cup of tea, which was normal enough, but then I went off to start painting one of our rooms, which was far from normal for me – especially in the middle of the night. The room needed decorating so I decided to find the paint and a brush. I suppose that was my nerves getting the better of me. I just had to find something to occupy me rather than sit around waiting. It wasn't too long, though, before I had the job of taking Denise to hospital. I was with her as she gave birth to our little Claire and, as any father will tell you, it is the most magical experience.

Mother and baby were fine, and dad wasn't too bad either. Pride and joy replaced all that nervous tension. Suddenly we were a family and that meant extra responsibilities, which I think is no bad thing for a footballer. Having kids to care for helps a player mature more quickly. Family life gives him stability. In the modern game, when so many young players are on huge wages, they are less likely to go off the rails and do daft things if they have commitments at home. Single players have a lot of time on their hands and money in their pockets.

When they get bored they have the means to do whatever they want. When you have a family to bring up, you don't have time to be bored.

Ron Atkinson's teams are rarely boring and we recovered a touch of the familiar swagger during the 1980–81 season. Mick Brown was installed as Ron's new assistant and a fresh zest came into our football. We finished fourth in the First Division to book a return to European football and I managed ten goals in forty League appearances. That was a scoring standard I set myself for the rest of my career – I wasn't content unless I reached double figures. I had always liked to get forward from midfield and one manager after another had encouraged me to develop that instinct. Now it was paying off for me at the highest level of the English game.

Ron had been rebuilding the side as one or two players came towards the end of their careers and I readily accepted greater responsibility. I looked forward to playing an increasingly important role under Ron and Mick, but by the time I returned from an end-of-season tour with England, Ron Atkinson was no longer the manager of West Brom. He had been lured to Manchester United as successor to the sacked Dave Sexton. The Albion players didn't want Ron to leave, but I could understand why he was attracted to the job. United were an enormous club, with the kind of support and resources Albion simply couldn't match. Ron was ambitious and he had been offered one of the greatest challenges in football. It was a once-in-a-lifetime opportunity and he took it. With him went Mick Brown and the man who gave me my chance in senior football, Brian White-house, the club's reserve-team coach. Ronnie Allen, who had gone on from Saudi Arabia to Greece and Portugal, returned to his old job at The Hawthorns.

Ron Atkinson and I were getting on well but he had said nothing to me about the possibility of a move and made no suggestion that he would like me to join him. There were, though, doubts in my mind about Albion's future and their prospects of becoming a genuine force in the game. I had been convinced by one of the directors, Tom Silk, that the board had the ambition to take the club to the next level and I was more than happy to commit myself to that cause. Mr Silk was the money man at Albion and he talked to me about his determination to bring in the extra couple of quality players who would make that crucial difference. Tragically, Mr Silk was killed in a plane crash and it seemed to me that the club wasn't the same without him. Some of the hunger and desire were missing. We were standing still and if you stand still in any competitive business, you run the risk of going backwards. Ronnie Allen promised he would bring in players to build on the team we had, but instead people were walking out of the door.

Ron Atkinson and his coaching staff weren't the only significant departures. Len Cantello, like Steve Bruce one of the best English players never to have been capped, left for Bolton. Len was such a good player and, of course, he had taken me under his wing, so I was particularly sad to see him go. When they sold Laurie Cunningham to Real Madrid I thought to myself, 'Hold on a minute. Aren't we supposed to be building the team? How are we going to replace Laurie Cunningham?'

I spent that summer of 1981 wondering what lay ahead for West Bromwich Albion and for me. I was uneasy about the direction the club were taking. I wanted to progress, achieve success and win trophies and I came to the conclusion that I would not be able to do that at The Hawthorns. I would have to move.

Denise and I talked it over again and again. She was a Birmingham girl, all her family lived in the area and she had never been away from home, but she assured me she was willing to uproot if that was what I wanted. She could see I wasn't happy and understood my concerns. The unrest in the Albion camp was obvious to the media and soon speculation arose that I would be next to leave. I was linked with a number of clubs, notably United and Liverpool. Ronnie Allen told me he wanted me to stay and I was offered a new long-term contract worth a basic £1,000 a week. It was a fabulous offer for those days, but much as I wanted the best for my family in terms of living standards and security, money wasn't my main motivation. I simply wanted to be a winner. I decided I would turn down the new contract offer and ask for a transfer, but before I could deliver my reply I read all about it in the papers. I was livid. I told Ronnie Allen that details of the offer were supposed to be confidential. He said he didn't know how the story had got out, but I found out that it had been leaked by the club. That made me even more determined to leave and he asked me to put my request in writing. The board rejected it, but my mind was made up and the transfer rumour mill churned out daily updates on 'developments'.

I was told that the club would match anything Manchester United offered me. I pointed out that it was nothing to do with what United were offering because at that stage they hadn't made me an offer. There was a general assumption that I would be following Ron Atkinson to Old Trafford, but it was Remi Moses, another of our midfield players, heading for United that September in a £500,000 deal. United had discussed with Albion a possible package for Remi and me, yet I was still unable to get my release. I had to be patient – and so had United.

Some reports linked me with Arsenal, but that was never a possibility. I couldn't have lived in London. Liverpool was a different matter. If they had matched United's offer to Albion, I would probably have gone to Anfield. I know that United supporters won't like to hear me admit that, but at the time I didn't have the affection for United that I have now, and Liverpool were a fantastic team. Their consistent success not only in this country but also in Europe set them apart. Liverpool have achieved more League Championship and European Cup wins than any club in England. It would have been great to play with Kenny Dalglish, Ian Rush and Alan Hansen.

That would have been an excellent career move for me. It might also have convinced my critics that I was genuine in my desire for success and not merely gold-digging. If money had been my prime concern, I would have had no reason to quit Albion because they were willing to match United's pay.

In the event, Liverpool weren't prepared to compete with United. I was told they would go no higher than £1 million. Albion had held out for £2 million, but eventually accepted United's bid of £1.5 million, a British record transfer fee. I learned that the deal was done on 1 October. I had been training that morning and was back at home when I received a telephone call from Ronnie Allen, who said he wanted to see me. When I walked into his office, he said, 'The club have agreed a fee with Manchester United. You can go and speak to them.'

'Thanks very much, Gaffer,' I said.

'Before you go, leave your car keys on the desk.'

I had a club car by then, so I was suddenly left without my own transport. My accountant had to drive Denise and me up to Old Trafford that Thursday afternoon.

I left The Hawthorns with mixed feelings. West Brom had been great to me from the day I first went to the club. I made lifelong friends there. All the managers and coaches had helped me to develop and improve my game and become an England international. If I hadn't had ambitions to win trophies, it would have been a fantastic place to spend the rest of my career. I could have done a Tony Brown and spent twenty-odd years there, but I did have personal ambitions, and the local press, who had championed my cause to play for England, were now hammering me. I was dubbed a 'Judas', a 'money grabber' and much, much worse. That hurt because I felt I had played my part for the club, never given less than 100 per cent, and still didn't even know what my salary at United would be.

Accusations of greed come with the territory when a player looks for a move and I accept that. Harder to take was the criticism of my family. One article made out that every member of the Robson family bar the cat had had their say on my transfer. Denise has agreed to no more than a couple of interviews throughout my career. She's turned down the rest because she doesn't like to project herself or get involved. My parents were occasionally caught out by reporters knocking on the door. They would give a polite, innocent answer to a question and find their names splashed across the papers. No member of the family has ever looked for publicity or an ego trip through the media.

Ray Matts, once my supporter-in-chief, turned on me just as the other local men did. I thought it was ironic when, a couple of months later, he quit the *Birmingham Evening Mail* to join the *Daily Mail*. Whether his motivation was money or ambition I don't know, but I presume he felt it was the right career move for him. He now concedes I have a point.

I knew that once the clubs had reached agreement on the transfer, United would not have much of a problem persuading me to sign. They were prepared to pay a record fee, so I was sure the personal terms would be satisfactory. When we arrived at Old Trafford, to be met by Ron and the chairman, Martin Edwards, I wasn't disappointed. Mr Edwards actually offered me more than I had hoped for – £2,000 a week. The financial details were soon tied up and, despite those earlier injuries, there were no hitches with the medical. It was a pity we missed the five o'clock deadline for me to be eligible to play that Saturday, but the transfer saga had dragged on for three months so I could wait a few more days for my debut. I was just relieved all the wrangling had finished and Denise and I had a whole new life to look forward to.

The following day I was officially introduced as a United player at a press conference and on the Saturday formally signed on the dotted line, out on the Old Trafford pitch before United's home match against Wolverhampton Wanderers. A crowd of nearly 47,000 gave me a fantastic reception. The fans have been great to me ever since, even when I've returned with a visiting team. I was beginning to understand the scale of the move, and the challenge ahead. I wasn't so much nervous as excited. This was an opportunity any player would relish – huge club, huge stage, huge fan base, huge in every respect. I sat at a table, flanked by Ron and the chairman, pen poised, smiling for the cameras.

I'll never forget that day and I'll never be allowed to forget the pictures. I've had so much ribbing over the years because at the time I was one of the many footballers sporting the perm look. Kevin Keegan, Graeme Souness and Terry McDermott were among those who famously became curly mops. The reason I had my hair permed was for convenience, not for the fashion. It used to be a nightmare when I had a shower after training. It was all over the place. After I had it permed I could have a shower, run my fingers through my hair and that was it. I don't really regret it, even though some of my players have had a laugh at my expense since I became a manager. I've turned up in the dressing rooms at Middlesbrough and Albion to find an old picture of me and my locks stuck on the wall.

My hair was almost standing on end as I watched my new team in action from the stand that day at Old Trafford. They absolutely murdered Wolves. United won 5–0 but could have had twice as many goals. Sammy McIlroy, supposedly one of the players whose place was under threat because of my arrival, scored a hat-trick. Other people were no doubt thinking, as I was, sitting there watching United's stunning performance, 'How am I going to get into this team?'

4
CUP OF JOY

Denise Robson

I'd never heard of Bryan when I met him. I wasn't much of a football fan, although if I followed any team it was West Brom because I came from the area. My dad wasn't really a football fan, either, and the funny thing was that he had a bus company called Albion Coaches. None of the family were that bothered about football, but Bryan wasn't famous, anyway. He was eighteen. I was out with a load of girls on my twenty-first birthday and he just started chatting me up. Then, about a week later, he asked me out. We saw each other about once a week to start with and it went on from there. He got on well with my mum and dad. They liked him.

I'd no idea how good he was or how good he might be. He hadn't played for the team very often, but after about a year, people started talking about him. We just got on and started getting serious. I wouldn't say he was shy, but he was quiet. I'm two years, two months older than Bryan, but that has never been a problem. He was good with the kids and changed nappies in the day and things like that, but he never got up in the night with them. He said he had to get up to go to work in the morning, which was fair enough.

I thought Bryan had a strong accent, but when he took me to a working-men's club in Chester-le-Street I couldn't understand a word anybody was saying. When the comedian, Bobby Thompson, came on, Bryan had to translate for me – every word. Apparently, he was famous in the North East, but he was lost on me.

We were at a club on another night and a band was on, singing songs and telling jokes. They were a bit like the Grumbleweeds. I was sitting there with my Babycham and this guy in the band spat out a false tooth and it landed in my drink. So he said, 'Ah! What are you drinking?' and I said, in my Brummie accent, 'B-i-i-i-bycham.' He said, 'What?'

It was a big move when we went to Manchester. I'd never lived away from Birmingham but it was what Bryan wanted to do and you have to be prepared to move. It was the same when there was all that talk about Bryan going to Italy. I would have gone there, no problem. We were living away from our parents anyway, and it's only a two-hour flight to Italy. It would have been interesting to experience a different way of life, but we've had a home in Manchester ever since he first went to United and we've loved it. Even when we went to the North East, we kept the house in Hale.

I F I HAD CONCERNS about getting straight into the Manchester United team, there were no worries about settling into the squad. I wondered whether the mood at a club of their stature would be more serious than I'd been used to at West Bromwich Albion. I thought the players, so many more of them internationals and big names in football, might be a little reserved and distant compared with the easygoing, wisecracking pals I had down at The Haw-thorns, but I soon discovered those fears were totally unfounded. The lads were welcoming and the atmosphere in the camp was great. Footballers are footballers, no matter where you find them, and Old Trafford had the usual mix of characters and wind-up merchants.

It probably helped that I knew Ron Atkinson, Mick Brown and Brian Whitehouse, and was familiar with the kind of regime they liked to impose. Ron called me 'Pop' after the game's other Bryan

Robson, the Newcastle, West Ham, Sunderland and Carlisle player. Ron and I were on the same wavelength. He revelled in the charisma and glamour of United. He knew how big the job was and it never intimidated him. He saw no reason why he should change his style of managing, which meant the work would be hard yet fun. Ron demanded 100 per cent commitment but he also enjoyed a laugh with the players. His banter and enthusiasm were infectious. His man-management was excellent and the players respected him for the way he treated and trusted them.

When the serious training was done he would join in the five-a-sides and demonstrate the skills he reckoned never had the showcase they deserved. If Ray Wilkins was shaping to pass the ball to me and Ron was standing next to me, he would say, 'Run him off and use your legs.' That was just a con so that I would get out of the way and he could receive the ball. He loved to get involved at the end of the sessions, pretending he was Manny Kaltz, the West German World Cup right-back, crossing the ball to his own running commentary – 'It's Manny Kaltz, going down the wing, and he puts a great ball into the middle.' When we were shooting, he'd be Bobby Charlton, bombing them in from twenty-five yards. It was quality comedy for the lads, but you couldn't help wondering whether Ron actually believed it. He did have decent skill. Mobility? Well . . .

There were plenty of smiles and a strong camaraderie about the United camp. I knew Ray Wilkins and Steve Coppell through playing with England, and Remi Moses had joined from Albion just before me. It wasn't too long before I hit it off with the other lads, as well. We tended to stick around after training, have a bite to eat, a cup of tea and a chat in the canteen at the Cliff, United's training ground. That togetherness undoubtedly benefited performances on the pitch. Gary Bailey, John Gidman, Arthur Albiston, Martin Buchan, Gordon McQueen, Kevin Moran, Garry Birtles, Lou Macari, Frank Stapleton and Sammy McIlroy all welcomed me into the fold.

Lou and Gordon, the Little and Large of our Scottish fraternity, became particularly good mates. I soon found out about Lou's pranks and practical jokes. Anyone was fair game, as far as he was concerned. The other lads became wise to his sense of mischief but he would always prey on the unsuspecting. A press match at the Cliff was too good an opportunity to miss. The journalists came into the dressing room for their half-time cuppa and couldn't help noticing that it tasted . . . different. When one of them dug to the bottom of the urn, he discovered not only tea bags but the toe ends of socks. Lou had crept into the dressing room during the first half with a pair of scissors and snipped the reporters' socks.

On another infamous occasion, when the English press played their Italian counterparts before our European Cup-Winners' Cup tie against Juventus, the reports returned to the dressing room to find their ties had been cut in half. Apparently, the Italians didn't take it as well as the English lads, who knew full well who the culprit was. Lou had some diplomatic ground to make up on the return trip and handed out club ties. We hit it off straightaway, possibly because we both liked to go horse racing. He was teetotal, which was great for me. I had a chauffeur as well as a good pal.

Gordon is another of those guys you can't help liking. We went on to work together at Middlesbrough and have remained close friends.

Our captain was another Scot, Martin Buchan, but a totally different character. He was very much his own man and not everybody's cup of tea. An intelligent, thoughtful guy, he specialised in put-downs. I thought his sarcastic sense of humour could be funny and he was OK with me but not everyone found it so easy to get on with him. Some felt he was too cold and aloof. I think it's fair to say he and Ron were always heading for a clash of personalities. Martin took his position as captain really seriously. At the end of a match he would rush off the pitch, put on his tracksuit and stand at the door of the players' lounge, collecting guest tickets. As captain, he was responsible for handing out the tickets to the players and if anyone turned up without one, he would turn them away. If there was anyone in the lounge he felt shouldn't be there, he would throw them out. When I took over the captaincy, the lads said, 'This is a bit different!'

It takes all sorts to make a football club tick, as it does any other organisation, and it would be boring if we were all the same. Most importantly, this mix of characters added up to a potentially outstanding football team and it seemed to me that their performance against Wolves in October 1981 was just an indication of their capabilities. Martin, Gordon and Lou were Scottish internationals and we had excellent England, Northern Ireland and Republic of Ireland internationals, as well – and, coming through the ranks, a promising young Welsh player and an even younger boy from Northern Ireland had the talent to make their marks. Their names were Mark Hughes and Norman Whiteside.

Ron had wasted no time adding to the squad following his move from West Brom. Before I arrived he paid £1 million for Frank Stapleton, the Arsenal and Republic of Ireland centre-forward, and then picked up a relatively unknown Irish defender called Paul McGrath. We had quality and variety right through the squad. We had ability on the ball, vision, pace and strength. We had a gifted, powerful team and every reason to believe we could do well that season and beyond.

More immediate was the little matter of my Manchester United debut. To my relief, I was named in the team to play Tottenham Hotspur in the first leg of a Milk Cup tie – the League Cup was known as the Milk Cup at the time – at White Hart Lane on 7 October 1981. I had butterflies in my stomach, but that was normal before any big game, and generally I felt much the same as I did when I played for West Brom. We lost 1–0 and there was no suggestion that I should beat myself up about that. No one was expecting

Right: On South
Shields beach – aged
one and already
making a forward
run.

Below: My first
'team-mates' were
my dad, Brian, and
my sister, Susan.

Wyn Davies' power in the air made him my childhood hero.

Bobby Moncur was a class act for Newcastle United.

Don Howe was my first manager and our paths would cross again.

Len Cantello – a terrific player and a real pal.

Finding my feet with Albion in the old First Division.

Back from our legendary trip to China, I line up with team-mates Mick Martin (*left*), Ally Brown (*right*) and manager Ron Atkinson.

The 1978–79 West Bromwich Albion squad – I'm in the middle row, second from right. To the right of Big Ron is Colin Addison.

Nothing beats that goalscoring sensation – here against Fulham in the 1979–80 season.

Head first – beating Arsenal's John Hollins to the ball in 1980.

Taking on a master, Liverpool's Kenny Dalglish, in 1979.

Our wedding day line-up, 2 June 1979 (*left to right*): my dad Brian, my mam Maureen, Sue Egan, Denise's niece Natalie Brindley, my best man Steve Shaw, me, Denise, Denise's dad George Brindley, my aunt Lesley Eagleton, and Denise's mum Doreen.

So proud to wear the England shirt.

I find myself in a high-kicking duel with Tony Grealish on my England debut against the Republic of Ireland, 6 February 1980.

Hunting down my first international goal in the infamous defeat by Norway.

miracles on my first appearance for the club. We were beaten by the same score in the return leg and made an early exit from the competition. We were also bundled out of the FA Cup in our first tie, by Watford, who had a decent team during that period and reached the final in 1984.

In the League, the true measure of a team's capabilities, we were generally more convincing and effective. My First Division debut for United was in the highly charged showdown of a Manchester derby. We made the short journey over to Maine Road and drew 0–0 with City in a typically passionate, full-blooded encounter. I received a lot of complimentary reviews for my contribution that day, but to be honest I walked off the pitch feeling frustrated with myself. I had a couple of half chances and felt I might have put away at least one of them. I probably should have won us the match.

Something I did take from that match was possession of the United No. 7 shirt. At West Brom, especially during Johnny Giles' management, I played in several positions and had a variety of numbers on my back. That didn't particularly bother me because I just wanted to play as often as possible. Then it occurred to me that my better performances came when I wore the No. 7 shirt and I came to regard it as my lucky number. So when I joined United, I asked if anybody minded my having the number. Steve Coppell, who usually took that number, wasn't in the starting line-up against City and said he didn't have a problem with my wish, anyway. None of the other lads objected, either, so the No. 7 shirt was mine.

We had an excellent spell that autumn, beating, among others, Liverpool 2–1 at Anfield and Sunderland 5–1 at Roker Park. That match up in the North East, a re-run of the first fixture I saw as a young boy, brought another landmark in my career with United when I scored my first goal for the club. We were top of the League and buzzing. We had a tremendous spirit in the camp and I was hearing all the right noises about how I was settling in and getting used to the Manchester United way of life. It was nice to hear public and private words of encouragement and I tried to make out that the tag of 'Britain's most expensive footballer' didn't worry me when, in fact, it did. The truth was that it was far harder to cope with the burden than I had anticipated when I left The Hawthorns.

As a young lad, working my way up through the ranks at West Brom, there were no real expectations of me. I was allowed to learn and improve my game virtually unnoticed by the football world and public at large. Even after I made the breakthrough to the first team, I was always treated sympathetically by the Albion fans because they regarded me as one of their own. Once I had become a £1.5 million player, lining up with the biggest club in the country, it was an entirely different scenario. Suddenly, expectations soared and everything I did – every tackle, pass, run, shot or header – came under scrutiny. When we lost some of our momentum and results went against us, I definitely suffered. My self-belief never wavered. I was convinced I had the ability that Ron and United expected of me, but I also knew I wasn't myself. After starting quite well for my new club, I was under-performing. The pressure of the fee and all the attention undoubtedly took its toll.

Some players are adamant a big fee doesn't affect them, but that's not what I found. I don't mind admitting it affected my game. The more I thought about it, the worse the situation became. After games I was worrying myself sick because I knew I could play better than I had. I would think to myself, 'I cost all that money. I should be doing a lot more than that, I should be changing the game.' As a result, I probably tried too hard to justify the fee and started doing things I wouldn't normally have done. It took over my football brain and scrambled my thinking. I strayed away from my tried and trusted way of playing and started trying to do other people's jobs. I got myself into the wrong areas and did the wrong things. I couldn't get it out of my mind that Ron had spent a hell of a lot of money on me and other players, so surely we should have been up there at the top.

The weight of expectation was so much heavier at United because of the club's illustrious past. There was simply no escaping that heritage. Their success in the fifties and sixties cast a shadow over the teams of the seventies and eighties. United had last won the League Championship in 1967 and followed that up by lifting the European Cup, the premier club prize, twelve months later. They had managed to win the FA Cup in 1977, but that hardly satisfied demands in the boardroom or on the terraces at Old Trafford. Every passing year without the League title intensified the pressure on the manager and the players.

I was born the year before the Munich air crash so I have no memories of that wonderful fifties team, created by Matt Busby and his assistant, Jimmy Murphy, but like anyone with a love of football and an interest in its history, I was aware of the impact the Busby Babes made on the game. My generation grew up hearing about Roger Byrne, Eddie Colman, Billy Whelan, Tommy Taylor and, above all, Duncan Edwards. I was always particularly fascinated to listen to some of the stories about Duncan Edwards, who played more or less in my position. He was only twenty-one when he died and yet Ron and others talked about him as though he had completed a full career. The way everybody raved about him he really must have been some player.

Sir Matt had to rebuild his team and, a decade on from Munich, United were European champions. The sixties team is remembered in the main for the great trio of Bobby Charlton, Denis Law and George Best, but alongside them were Paddy Crerand, Nobby Stiles and Brian Kidd. They won the Championship twice and the FA Cup once before achieving their crowning glory. Every United fan who saw them – and even many who didn't – will tell you they played with a style and flamboyance that was as breathtaking as it was effective.

So this was the magnificent legacy Sir Matt left and the scale of the challenge that faced the United managers and players who dared to follow. As if you needed reminding, the trophies and mementos were on display in the lounges and guest rooms at Old Trafford. So were many of the players themselves. Bobby Charlton, who returned to the club as a director, Paddy Crerand, Bill Foulkes and David Sadler, all members of the side that beat Benfica in the 1968 European Cup final at Wembley, were still familiar figures at the ground.

Of course, Sir Matt himself, long retired from management, was the club's president and an immense and respected presence. He had an aura about him and an amazing way with people, a gift for making anyone he came into contact with feel special. He seemed to remember everybody's name and addressed them personally. I got to know him probably better than any of my contemporaries did. Denise and I became friends with a builder, Pete Molloy, and his wife, Lynn, who had known Sir Matt for many years. Pete and Lynn regularly had friends around at their house on Sundays and invited us to join them. Sir Matt was often one of the other guests and we sat chatting for hours, developing a friendship away from the football club.

When I bumped into Paddy Crerand, Denis Law or any of Sir Matt's former players and told them how I'd been chatting to their boss and what a lovely man he was, they would smile knowingly and tell me about the many times they were taken in by the Old Man's charms. Whenever they knocked on his door to ask for a rise or a new contract he would massage their egos and send them away apparently happy — but with not a penny more. They all told the same story. He also had a subtle way of dropping a player. He would call in his 'victim' and ask him how he thought he was playing. The player would modestly reply, 'Not bad.' Sir Matt would then say, 'That's what I thought, son. You're not really playing your best. I think you need a rest.'

That strikes a chord with me because when I was into the later stages of my career with United, Alex Ferguson would call me over and say he felt I needed a rest. By then, he had Paul Ince and Roy Keane in his midfield and I knew he was thinking my legs were beginning to go. Sir Matt and Sir Alex were very different men but each, in his own way, was prepared to make tough decisions, just as any manager has to. You can't achieve what Sir Matt did by being a charming gentleman all the time. It is quite clear that he was cunning and, when necessary, hard.

Sir Matt and his players earned the status they had at the club, but all the reminders of former glories merely piled the pressure on Ron and his team to deliver. What made the task still more difficult for me was living in a hotel. It took Denise and me a few months to sort out a house in the area, and until then I didn't really feel settled. I travelled back down to the Midlands when I could and appreciated the return to home comforts. We eventually moved to a four-bedroomed house with a nice garden in Hale, near Altrincham, early in 1982, and have had a home in the area ever since.

If the demands were greater at United, so were the potential rewards. The move to Old Trafford instantly raised my profile and expanded my scope for endorsements. Offers came in from all directions but fortunately I had just the man to handle my commercial affairs. I had met Harry Swales, a no-nonsense, straight-down-the-line Yorkshireman, when he was agent for the England team. He had been involved in showbusiness but became a hugely respected figure in football circles – and that can't be said of every agent. Kevin Keegan was his client for about eight years and Kevin effectively passed Harry on to me. When I left United, Alex Ferguson asked me if I could get Harry to look after Ryan Giggs. I was beginning to cut down on the commercial stuff by then, so Harry took on the young Welshman.

When I first broke into the England team, adidas gave me a

contract to endorse their products, but after I signed for United I was offered a boot deal by New Balance. They had a huge business in America, making running shoes, and were keen to get into the boots market. What attracted me to them was the chance to have my say on the design of the boot. They listened to my ideas, so I felt personally involved in the project, and we worked together for many years. Harry carefully examined the various other offers and made sure I didn't over-commit myself. He was a stickler for schedules and wouldn't stand for any messing around, which was OK by me. He'd insist I work no longer than the agreed time, when I would have been happy to stay on – so he was always regarded as the bad guy rather than me.

I went into partnership with Ronnie Wood – not the Rolling Stone – and took a stake in a chain of greetings cards shops, Birthdays. Ronnie is a top guy and probably my best mate. But any commercial work or personal appearances always came a distant second to football. I would never take on anything that required too much time or travel. I wouldn't allow anything to interfere with my training and rest periods. Besides, I knew I was in demand only because of my football and it would have been counter-productive to risk undermining my performances on the pitch.

Through that first season at United I was conscious that my performances fell short of the consistent standards I knew I was capable of and the fans were entitled to expect, but it wasn't exactly a flop for me or for the team. We finished third in the League, behind Liverpool and Ipswich Town, and I sensed that most people accepted we had made reasonable progress. Our home defeat by Liverpool ended any lingering title hopes we may have had and virtually confirmed the Anfield club as champions. We ran out of steam and goals during the crucial run-in. I ended the campaign with five goals from thirty-two appearances. One of those goals came on my return to The Hawthorns. I was given the hostile reception I fully expected, but we won 3–0. That was probably the best way to answer the fans' boos and jeers.

Ron continued to bring in new players. He was creating his own side, a process that needed time. One of his significant changes was confirming Ray Wilkins as captain. My England colleague took over the responsibility after Martin Buchan was injured, and retained it when the Scot came back into the team. Ron also introduced a young man who would be seen on a much bigger stage before the summer was over. Norman Whiteside, a powerful lad from Northern Ireland, made his League debut in our 1–0 win at Brighton at the age of sixteen. Weeks later he was playing for his country in the World Cup finals in Spain. United – and Ireland – had a real player on their hands.

World Cup duty kept me occupied that summer, too. We beat France in our opening match and I scored twice, the first after twenty-seven seconds, but we were eliminated at the second stage, even though we were undefeated. The tournament did my form and confidence a power of good, though, and I returned from Spain a different player. Much as I would have liked to stay involved in the World Cup, it was good to get home to see our new baby. Denise had given birth to Charlotte on 17 June, hours after the match against France, and I was at last able to hold our second daughter.

My whole life took an upturn in the summer of '82. I'd made a real breakthrough as an international player. I got an excellent press for my part in England's World Cup run, I received bumper bags of fan mail and the interest from would-be personal sponsors went up another notch. Harry was a busy man. I was eager to throw myself into a new season because I knew I had shaken off the shackles of my first term with United. I felt that nothing could hold me back. We had the makings of a Championship-challenging team and Ron gave us an extra dimension by signing Arnold Muhren, the Dutchman with a magic wand of a left foot. He had been a revelation with

Ipswich and although he was thirty-one, he played with a languid style that wasn't dependent on pace or high energy levels.

Arnold was particularly good for my game. He wasn't an orthodox winger who went past defenders. He was such a terrific passer and crosser of the ball that he could operate more as a 'sit-in' player and still be devastating. With Ray also sitting deep, it meant I was free to make more forward runs. Stevie Coppell, on the right, did take people on and cross from the line in the manner of a conventional winger, so we had the perfect balance in midfield.

Players come, players go and early that season Garry Birtles left United. He was one of the many – strikers especially – who struggled to make it at Old Trafford. Peter Davenport, Alan Brazil and Terry Gibson were other names on that list during my early years at the club. I knew from personal experience how difficult it was to handle the pressures at United, and for some it probably proved too much. Playing for the top clubs at the time, such as United, Liverpool and Arsenal, you had to have mental strength and resolve, as well as ability. Perhaps that was the difference between good players and great players. Those clubs had to have great strikers. Garry and Peter had made their names with Nottingham Forest, Alan with Ipswich, provincial teams where the expectations weren't as high as at United. When you come to United with a big price tag around your neck, people think you can influence every game and win every game. It just doesn't work like that.

Contrast their fortunes with Frank Stapleton's. He had made his name with Arsenal and was accustomed to the big-club syndrome, so he didn't suffer the trauma that appeared to stifle others. Frank was terrific in the air and scored his share of goals, but he was also expert at holding up the ball and bringing others into the game. He had the temperament to demonstrate that ability in the full glare of public attention.

You have to persevere and tell yourself you'll get through the difficult times. As a West Brom player I had done reasonably well against the Manchester Uniteds and Liverpools. You move to the big clubs for the challenge of being part of that all the time and you get nowhere if you shrink away from it. You've got to stand up and be counted. I scored twice as many goals in my second season, reaching my target of double figures, but then that was largely down to Arnie's role in the team.

I gave us the aggregate lead in the second leg of our UEFA Cup tie away to Valencia, but a dodgy refereeing decision gave them a penalty and we lost 2–1. It was a bitter disappointment to fall at the first hurdle of that competition, especially after the wonderful experience I'd had against the Spaniards with West Brom. We had been so close to achieving a great result at the Mestalla. Fortunately, there was consolation in store for us.

At one stage we were in contention for a domestic treble of League Championship, FA Cup and Milk Cup. Our opening tie in the Milk Cup had an important bearing on the rest of my career, at both club and international level. Ray Wilkins had been named by the new England manager, Bobby Robson, as his captain and I was appointed vice-captain, in succession to Kevin Keegan and Mick Mills respectively. Ray suffered a depressed fracture of the cheekbone in our match at Bournemouth, which put him out of the game for several weeks, and in his absence, I took over as skipper for United and England. When Ray returned, I retained the two jobs and he became my vice-captain.

I couldn't possibly have anticipated something like that. I had been at Old Trafford barely a year and became an England regular only a few months before that move. I hadn't been captain at West Brom and didn't even think about taking on the role. My only concern was to be in the team. It wasn't easy for Ray when he came back and I knew how disappointed he was, but he has tremendous character and he handled it with his customary dignity. He had become captain as a result of Martin Buchan's injury and now fate was taking it away from him in similar circumstances. Ray and I remained pals as well as team-mates and I believe we made a pretty effective partnership. I always welcomed and valued his opinions.

There was, in any case, an ironic twist to this tale. After beating Bournemouth, we knocked out Bradford City, Southampton and Nottingham Forest to reach the semi-finals of the Milk Cup. We virtually booked our place at Wembley by going four up in the away leg of our tie against Arsenal. Norman Whiteside underlined his potential with the first goal and a fearless performance. Arsenal pulled back two late goals, to give themselves hope, but we won 2–1 in the return at Old Trafford to go through to the final 6–3 on aggregate.

I knew, though, that I wouldn't be able to make that Wembley date with the champions-elect, Liverpool. I went down in a rut and tore my ankle ligaments in the second leg against Arsenal. I was wheeled away on a stretcher and taken to hospital. Ray went on as substitute and led us through to the final. When the job was done he came to see me in hospital, clutching a celebratory bottle of champagne. I appreciated the gesture, although I had mixed feelings that night. It was great that we had reached a final. I had joined United for such moments. Yet, with the big day little more than a month away, I had to accept I would not be fit to play my part in it. Ray would be leading the team out at Wembley.

My worry was that I might not be back in action before the end of the season – and a possible FA Cup final. We had, by then, reached the sixth round of that competition and fancied our chances of going all the way. Liverpool were again stretching clear at the top of the League, so our realistic aim had become a Cup double.

I was a frustrated spectator at the Milk Cup final, where Liverpool reminded us that they were still the team to beat. Even so, we didn't have the breaks that day. Our centre-halves, Gordon McQueen and

Kevin Moran, got injuries and many critics reckoned Liverpool's goalkeeper, Bruce Grobbelaar, was lucky not to be sent off for wiping out poor old Gordon. Norman scored a smashing early goal, but Liverpool took the match into extra time and Ronnie Whelan clinched their 2–1 win. The lads were disappointed, yet it wasn't the devastating blow some might have thought. They picked themselves up and tackled the later stages of the FA Cup with a show of real character and defiance.

We had beaten Everton 1–0 to set up another semi-final meeting with Arsenal and, despite my earlier fears, I recovered to reclaim my place for the tie at neutral Villa Park. It was a cracking game, worthy of the occasion, and our belief was hardly dented by Tony Woodcock's first-half goal for Arsenal. I equalised early in the second half and Norman, not for the first time, came up with a corker to send us through to our second final. We were heading back to Wembley and this time I intended to be out in the middle rather than on the sidelines.

The celebrations after the semi-final were typically rowdy and excited – a bit too much so for Kevin Moran. Our likeable Republic of Ireland centre-half had more than his fair share of cuts and bruises over the years so it was perhaps no surprise to see him carried off, near the end of the match at Villa Park, for another appointment with needle and thread. He was stitched up and ready to join in the fun when we got back to the dressing room. We were all larking about and flung Mick Brown into the bath, but as Mick flew through the air his flailing arm caught Kevin on the forehead and opened up the wound. So off he went for another five or six stitches, with the rest of the lads trying not too hard to hide their laughter.

That could have happened only to old Kev. He was always in the wars. He was such a brave, whole-hearted player that he never flinched. If a tackle or an aerial challenge had to be made, he would make it. I think one of the reasons he had so many cuts was his

65

background in Gaelic football. He jumped with his arms down by his side, rather than the way apprentices in association football are taught. Young players in our game learn to jump with their arms raised, so that they have some protection and also as a means of getting higher than their opponent. Kevin was exposed to a clash of heads and opponents' elbows and often came off worse when he went up for the ball.

Reaching two Cup finals in one season wasn't bad going, but Ron understandably wanted more. If he was to take the Championship from Liverpool, he would have to wait at least another year. They were on course for the title again and we had to accept third place again. Ron's search for a sharper cutting edge took him to Spain and Scotland. He signed my old West Brom team-mate Laurie Cunningham, the player he sold to Real Madrid, on loan with a view to a possible permanent transfer. Ron also followed up an approach by Charlie Nicholas' agent to check on the Celtic striker and liked what he saw. Nicholas eventually went to Arsenal but there was no mistaking Ron's intent. He was determined to take United back to the pinnacle of the game.

We still had to complete our 1982–83 League programme and a little more drama was in store. Remi Moses was sent off for butting Arsenal's Peter Nicolas in our 3–0 defeat at Highbury. Ron was furious because he had heard that they were going to provoke Remi, and was also given his marching orders for his angry protest. We were gutted for Remi, because the sending off meant he was suspended and out of the FA Cup final, against Brighton. We all felt angry as we left Highbury, but a few days in Majorca – Ron's idea of a break before the final – had the desired effect. We combined training with relaxation and recharged the batteries.

Ron's preparations for the final didn't go entirely to plan, though. Laurie failed a fitness test on a troublesome hamstring pull, so Alan Davies, a twenty-one-year-old with just three full first-team appearances behind him, was named in our team for Wembley. It was an unlucky break for Laurie, who was desperate to re-establish himself in the game after an unsettling spell in Spain, but a great opportunity for Alan and he didn't waste it.

Manchester-born Alan, who went on to win thirteen full caps with Wales, was a live wire that day and a constant threat. We started the final with the confidence of overwhelming favourites and saw nothing to worry us in the early stages, but Brighton, just relegated from the First Division, were up for it and took the lead through Gordon Smith. The jolt made us raise our game and Frank Stapleton equalised. When Ray put us ahead with a terrific twenty-five-yard bender, we seemed to have one hand on the trophy. Brighton didn't think so, though, and Gary Stevens' late goal sent us into extra time.

We had reached the 119th minute of the final when we were spared by the famous 'And Smith must score' incident that has passed into football folklore. The Scot was clean through, with Gary Bailey at his mercy. The now familiar commentary predicted a winner for Brighton, yet he buried the ball into our keeper's body. Smith has taken stick for that miss ever since, but everyone seems to overlook Gary's save, from near point-blank range. He not only stopped the shot but also clung on to the ball and kept us in the final. We were relieved yet knew we hadn't done ourselves justice that day. We intended to put the record straight in the replay, the following Thursday evening.

Ron backed the same eleven players to silence our critics and predicted his captain would score two goals. Alan Davies set me up for my first and, after Norman had extended our lead, I forced in another before half-time. We were three up and cruising. I was bundled over in the penalty area in the second half, but although some of the lads urged me to take the kick and complete my hat-trick, I wasn't even tempted. Arnie was our penalty taker and this was his moment. He put it away with his usual calmness. We won

4–0, the biggest win in a Wembley final. That was usually the way of it – the underdogs have one chance of an upset and if they don't take it, they are made to pay.

We had our trophy and I had my winner's medal after less than two years at the club. Wearing a United cap and scarf, tossed to me by supporters, I climbed those steps to the royal box and lifted the FA Cup. This was what I had dreamed about when I was a kid and yearned for since I became a professional footballer. The celebrations began down on the pitch, as we danced and sang, showing off our silverware to the equally delirious United fans. Ron and his staff were ecstatic. I was pleased for him and everybody connected with the club. It was Sir Matt's seventy-fourth birthday, so I was glad we'd made it a happy one for him. The songs continued to ring out and the champagne flowed on our private train that had pulled up for us at Wembley station. We partied all the way back to Manchester.

This, though, was by no means the end of the line.

5
FOREIGN CURRENCY

M ANCHESTER UNITED'S management and players were convinced the 1983 FA Cup triumph was just the start of something big. Ron Atkinson, who was born in Liverpool, knew he had to topple the consistently dominant Merseysiders if we were to become the new force in English football. Crucially, he had the backing of Martin Edwards, the chairman and chief executive, in his search for the added ingredients. Just like the fans, the players scour the papers for transfer gossip and in the dressing room they compare notes on the latest rumours. Players know their place could be threatened by a signing, yet generally new arrivals are welcomed because everybody wants the team to improve and win trophies.

For all the ambition of the boss and the chairman, they couldn't come up with the package to prevent Charlie Nicholas from joining Arsenal and decided against taking up an option to buy Laurie Cunningham, who was injured just before the final. Laurie didn't have much luck in his search for a permanent football home. He went back to Spain, then to France, had a loan spell at Leicester, two more clubs in Spain, one in Belgium, a non-contract stint with Wimbledon, and finally a move back to Spain, to join Rayo Vallecano. Tragically, he was killed in a car crash in Madrid in 1989.

One player who did come to United in that summer of 1983 was Arthur Graham, the Leeds United and Scotland winger. The downside of the deal was the realisation that Steve Coppell might have to concede defeat in his two-year struggle against injury. Arthur was effectively earmarked to fill that massive void. Stevie had been on the wrong end of an awful tackle, playing for England against Hungary, and hoped a cartilage operation would solve the recurring problems and save his career.

By October 1983, though, he reluctantly had to accept that he would never be able to play football at the highest level again and announced his retirement. It was a terrible blow, not only for Steve, who was an unselfish team player as well as an exciting, lethal winger, but also for United and the game as a whole. He was twenty-eight and should have been approaching his peak, and he was such a terrific bloke – modest, preferring to keep a low profile. Stevie's misfortune was another reminder that a footballer's career, no matter how lucrative and privileged, can be cut short at any time.

Another departure was our former captain, Martin Buchan, who joined Oldham Athletic, and midfield player Ashley Grimes went to Coventry City, as Ron made way for new faces. Some may have wondered whether we needed reinforcements after we beat Liverpool 2–0 in the Charity Shield, the season's traditional curtain-raiser, and went on to win eight of our first eleven League matches. Our performance against the champions was hugely encouraging psychologically, and we carried that momentum into the League campaign. Our early run included another victory over Liverpool and an away win against Arsenal.

Again we reached the top of the First Division and again we felt we were capable of staying there. Ray Wilkins started the season brilliantly. As a young player he scored a lot of goals but he had settled into a deeper role, spraying those long passes with radar precision. Ray had to take a bit of stick for supposedly playing sideways, but he understood the importance of keeping possession and knew when to pick the telling through ball. What's more, he had the skill to execute it, and he could still produce that lovely clean strike, as he proved with that bender against Brighton in the FA Cup final.

For all Ray's quality and the outstanding ability in every department of our team, we again failed to keep up our Championship challenge. Injuries and lapses in concentration through the winter cost us dear. We had a good record head-to-head against Liverpool, but they kept winning the title because of their greater consistency. We dropped too many points against teams in the middle and lower parts of the First Division, sides we should have put away with goals and effort to spare. When we had to cover for injuries and perhaps needed to freshen up the team, our lack of genuine strength in depth let us down.

Ron responded by signing striker Garth Crooks from Tottenham, another player who was with us for only a short spell, and lining up Jesper Olsen, a young Danish winger. Jesper was making a name for himself on the international scene and England had been the victims on one of his unplayable days, the previous year. He couldn't join us until the following summer, and in the meantime our domestic season went from bad to worse.

Our problem against smaller clubs was embarrassingly exposed in the Milk Cup and the FA Cup. We had reached the finals of both competitions in the previous season, but this time around we were eliminated by two Third Division sides. Oxford United, a club Ron had once played for, took us to a second replay, at their ground, in the fourth round of the Milk Cup and won the tie in extra time. In our defence, they did have some good players and we undoubtedly suffered through injuries. Gordon McQueen missed the match and I had to go off after kicking the underneath of Wayne Biggins' foot. My boot split and my foot was swollen like a balloon. As if to add insult to injury, it was Biggins, Oxford's substitute, who scored the winner for Jim Smith's team.

71

No excuses were good enough for us or the boss. Ron was livid. If anyone thought Ron wasn't serious enough about the job and perhaps too soft with his players, they should have seen him in action that night. He gave us a hell of a tongue lashing. He reckoned it was the worst he'd ever felt after a match – but that lasted for just another couple of weeks or so. He was even more furious when we were beaten 2–0 away by Bournemouth in the third round of the FA Cup and lost our prized trophy.

This time he didn't just give us a verbal bashing, he made us really suffer for our flop. He ordered us to report to our training ground at the Cliff the following morning, Sunday, to take our punishment. He marched us into the gym, which at the time had a cinder pitch, and told us, 'If you're not going to run on a Saturday, you can run on a Sunday instead.' He ran us . . . and ran us . . . and ran us until we were sweating buckets and some of the lads were almost on their knees. So much for 'Mr Softie'.

Ron challenged us to make up for it in Europe and we hardly needed the psychological gee-up to follow the physical pain. We were as desperate as he was to put the humiliation of our Milk Cup and FA Cup defeats behind us.

Our Cup-Winners' Cup campaign had got off to an unpromising start. We were drawn against the technically gifted Czech team Dukla Prague, who put us in serious danger of another first-round knock-out by continental competition. They took the lead an hour into the first leg at Old Trafford and no one could argue they didn't look the part. I suffered a recurrence of an ankle injury and went off ten minutes from the end, leaving the lads with a difficult task. To their credit, they kept plugging away and in the last minute the Dukla keeper brought down Frank Stapleton to give us a penalty and a desperately needed lifeline. Arnold Muhren had been substituted, so Ray Wilkins accepted the responsibility from the spot and equalised. The Czech players obviously still felt they had done enough because they celebrated at the final whistle, but we believed that we were very much in business.

We needed belief when we went behind again in the second leg, but I equalised and, twelve minutes from time, Frank Stapleton headed us in front. Frank struggled with an ankle injury for much of the match, yet was determined to carry on. He had a small splint put on the ankle to support it. Norman Whiteside willingly did the donkeywork up front and Frank was in the right place at the right time to tilt the tie our way. Gary Bailey's timing was vital, too. He pulled off some terrific saves after the Czechs made it 2–2 on the night. We still had the advantage on the away goals rule, although one of our players didn't realise it. Arnold thought we needed a winner so, with only a couple of minutes to go, he crossed the ball from the wing rather than try to keep it in the corner and run down the clock. He wasn't too popular with the lads for that, but fortunately we held on. The tie finished 3–3 on aggregate and our second away goal had proved decisive.

The Bulgarian side, Spartak Varna, gave us far fewer problems in the next round. Arthur Graham and I scored the goals in a 2–1 first-leg away win that didn't really reflect our superiority. We missed loads of chances that could have made the return meeting a formality. As it was, we never looked like slipping up at Old Trafford. Two first-half goals by Frank Stapleton killed off the tie and completed a 4–1 aggregate victory. It meant United had reached a European quarter-final for the first time in fifteen years.

We knew we were into the business end of the Cup-Winners' Cup when the draw paired us with Barcelona and set up a first-leg date at the magnificent Camp Nou. Barcelona, managed by Luis Cesar Menotti, who had led Argentina to World Cup victory in 1978, had a star-studded team, but the most dazzling was undoubtedly a certain Diego Armando Maradona. The little Argentine magician, who joined the Spaniards after the 1982 World Cup finals for a fee of

£4.2 million, was already being linked with another move, this time to Italy, where a two-year ban on the signing of foreign players was about to come into force. Speculation suggested the top Italian teams were scouring Europe for reinforcements while they could and early that year I was one of the players reported to be on the hit list of clubs such as Sampdoria, Torino and Fiorentina.

The World Cup finals in Spain had been a showcase for many players and the exposure appeared to raise my currency in the game. United's progress to the last eight of the Cup-Winners' Cup probably attracted more attention, and agents started contacting me, confirming the interest from Italian clubs. I was told that Juventus and Milan also wanted me and sure enough, I had their agents on the phone. Tapping players, which became such a contentious issue at the time of the Ashley Cole affair, is nothing new. It has been part of football since the year dot. The agents told me I could earn far more money in Italy than in England and painted the tempting picture of a luxurious lifestyle. At that time, wages had reached nowhere near the levels that are familiar to us in the English game today. The highest earners were on about £100,000 a year, which was regarded as good money. Now, of course, top players demand that kind of figure per week.

The approaches undeniably interested me, although I made it clear I was in no hurry to leave United. Besides, the club had more pressing business on their hands. Tycoon Robert Maxwell, chairman of Oxford United, was not content with knocking us out of the Milk Cup. He wanted to own United as well. He tried to buy control of the club from Martin Edwards, who, along with his brother, Roger, owned 70 per cent of the shares. Martin had a meeting with Maxwell but rejected his offer, which was said to be worth £10 million. When Malcolm Glazer moved in to take over the club twenty-one years later, the deal cost almost £800 million. Players don't take too much notice of the politics at a club and at United there is always so much happening that they get used to it. They just want to get on with their training and prepare for the next match.

It wasn't too difficult for us to keep our eye on the ball with a trip to Barcelona coming up. We needed no warning about Maradona's ability, but we were told to beware, also, his knack of conning the referee into giving him free-kicks just outside the penalty area. On the night, though, he didn't cause us too many problems. He apparently wasn't fully fit and Barcelona eventually substituted him. We contained most of their players for most of the match, yet lost 2–0, and I left the pitch feeling particularly frustrated.

An own goal by Graeme Hogg, a young defender making his European debut, put Barcelona in front, but I had an excellent chance to equalise. For perhaps the only time in my career, I switched off. I was clean through, one on one with the keeper, and thought I was offside, so I casually flicked the ball and watched it bounce off the top of the crossbar. To my horror, the flag stayed down – I'd blown it. I had another decent chance and squandered that, too. Then, in the last minute, Francisco Rojo scored a cracker to give them a two-goal cushion. I was sick and remember doing a piece in the *Sun* newspaper saying I owed the club and the fans big-style in the second leg.

I knew I had to make up for my mistakes in the Camp Nou and thankfully I did. A lot of fans and pundits reckon I produced my best-ever performance for United in the return leg against Barcelona. I am not so sure about that, but there is no disputing the importance of the two goals I scored on a spectacular Old Trafford night. They brought us level on aggregate by the fifty-first minute and sixty seconds later we led, through Frank Stapleton. Barcelona rallied, as they had to, but we showed our resilience and even a fully recovered Maradona couldn't save them. We had won 3–2 over the two legs. Every man in our team played an heroic part that night, and so did every one of our fans.

All night the atmosphere had been fantastic, the best I ever experienced in my time at Old Trafford. The packed ground was shaking with the noise. The passion of the crowd, the drama and the excitement were unbelievable, and at the end, the explosion of joy just about took the roof off the place. The players hardly had time to congratulate each other before they were mobbed by thousands of fans, spilling on to the pitch. I was lifted off my feet and carried shoulder high. My name was being sung and my back slapped till it hurt – or at least it would have done if I hadn't been so elated. It was one of those nights you dream about and treasure for the rest of your life.

We felt we were capable of taking on and beating anybody after that comeback, and the semi-final gave us another opportunity to test ourselves against a European super-power. Next up were Juventus, one of the Italian clubs being linked with a bid for me. The transfer rumour mill cranked up a gear following our victory over Barcelona. I heard all sorts of stories that Juventus, often referred to as the Manchester United of Italy because of their widespread national and international appeal, were under pressure from some of their most important players to sign me. Their French star, Michel Platini, my favourite player at the time, seemingly told the club he would commit himself to a long-term contract if they bought me. Paolo Rossi, hero of Italy's 1982 World Cup success, was reported to have made similar pleas. Juve had several members of the Italian national team and a fabulous heritage.

Like every United player, I relished the prospect of facing the Italian champions elect, but fate had other ideas. I pulled my hamstring in training just before the home leg and knew I had no chance of playing in Turin, let alone at Old Trafford. I just couldn't believe it – nor, it seems, could the Juve management. They thought it was a bit of kidology on United's part when news of my mishap was released. It was true, all right, and with Ray Wilkins and Arnold

Muhren also out of the side that night we had to field a makeshift team. The task became still more difficult when Rossi gave Juve an early lead, but the lads never allowed their heads to drop and Alan Davies, making his first appearance since the FA Cup final, eleven months earlier, levelled the first leg at 1–1. Alan didn't play many first-team matches for us in an injury-affected career, but those two were massive and he didn't let us down. Sadly, he committed suicide in 1992, at the age of thirty.

I was again a helpless spectator in Turin as the Poland international, Zbigniew Boniek, put Juventus ahead. Just as at Old Trafford, though, our team refused to buckle and big Norman, who came on for Frank, equalised. My hopes of playing in a European final were still alive as Gary Bailey, a generally underrated goalkeeper, produced another outstanding performance. Gary had his critics – he was never allowed to forget the cross that eluded him and presented Arsenal with their winner in the 1979 FA Cup final – but he produced some brilliant, match-saving displays for us and it looked as though he had done it again. The tie appeared to be heading for extra time when Rossi showed what a lethal predator he was to knock us out.

The lads who played were cut up and I felt no better. Juventus did have the edge on the night, but when you find yourself in a situation like that you can't help wondering whether you might have made a little difference and perhaps influenced the outcome. That was all academic, though, and I saw no point in tormenting myself over it.

My enforced absence from playing duties in Turin did, at least, give me an opportunity to find out from Juventus the strength of their interest in signing me. I had spoken to Ron about the situation and asked him where I stood. His ambition was to build United into a European force and he said that he wanted me to stay to help him complete the job. He told me he would speak to Martin Edwards and came back to repeat that they didn't want me to go. Significantly, though, he added that if they received an offer of £3 million for me, they would have to accept it. Every player has his price and I was no different. United gave me permission to speak to Juventus in Turin because they thought they were going to get their £3 million. I met the general manager of the club on the day before the match. He assured me they did want me and I was given the impression they were aiming to replace, ironically, Boniek. Word had it that he was a little too fond of the nightlife for Juventus' liking.

I went back home with plenty to think about. I had still more to chew over following another Italian trip, this time to Genoa. While I was still recovering from the hamstring injury, Trevor Francis, the England international striker who played for Sampdoria, invited Denise and me over for a week. I went along with Trevor to watch the team train. The coaching staff were very friendly and asked me to join the other players for lunch.

Denise was as impressed with Italy as I was. We discussed the possibility of moving, in case something did develop from all the interest shown in me, and we agreed it would be an opportunity too good to miss. We were sure we could settle in Italy. I could have earned about four times as much as I was being paid at United and the footballing challenge was immense. Some of the greatest players in the game were already playing in Italy's *Serie A* and more followed. I liked everything I saw at Sampdoria. They spoke to me a number of times and I was told they were eager to sign me. There was speculation that Liam Brady, the Republic of Ireland's former Arsenal playmaker, was going to be offered to United in an exchange deal.

I must admit, though, that I was more attracted by the prospect of playing with Juventus – and Platini. I'd spoken to him at England-France matches and seemed to strike up a bit of a rapport with him. The thought of linking up with him appealed to me and I like to think we would have combined well. I probably would have gone to Juventus if United had agreed a fee with them.

In the end, all the talking led to nothing. United priced me out of the market. None of the Italian clubs would go to £3 million, so I stayed at Old Trafford. That certainly wasn't a problem for me. I shared Ron's desire to take United back to the top and was happy at the club. I never asked for a transfer and never instigated the discussions for a move.

A couple of weeks after our second leg against Juventus, United did sell an England midfield player to an Italian club. I think most of us were surprised to learn that Ray Wilkins, my partner and good pal with club and country, had agreed to join Milan in a £1.4 million transfer that was completed at the end of the season. On the one hand I was sorry to see Ray leave because he was such an outstanding player and we were bound to miss him. He and I operated really effectively together on the pitch and got on brilliantly off it. On the other, I could appreciate why he felt he couldn't turn down the chance, because I had gone down this very road. I knew exactly how he had weighed up the pros and cons. It was a fantastic new challenge, both professionally and personally, and the rewards on offer meant security for the future. Sure, there was a degree of risk in uprooting and going to a foreign country. Such a move doesn't suit everybody, but Ray was a mature, intelligent, sensible type of guy. He knew that if the move didn't work out for him, he would be able to find another club and just put it down to experience.

Ray had an excellent season for us in 1983–84, missing just a couple of matches in the whole campaign. He came back from all the disappointments of the previous season, when he fractured his cheekbone, lost the United and England captaincy and secured a place in the FA Cup final team only after Remi Moses was suspended, to show his true class. That was a measure of the guy's character, as well as his ability. Milan were clearly impressed by what they had seen of him on their scouting missions and he left United with the best wishes of his team-mates.

We didn't have to wait long to discover how Ron intended using the cash from Ray's transfer. He earmarked £600,000 to nick Gordon Strachan, Aberdeen's Scotland international winger, from under the nose of Cologne. The German club weren't best pleased to be gazumped, but despite their protests, Ron got his man. He had already set up the signing of Denmark's Jesper Olsen, from Ajax, and that deal, too, eventually went through. Gordon was a key figure in the success story of Alex Ferguson's Aberdeen. He won Championship and Cup medals in Scotland and played in the 1983 European Cup-Winners' Cup-winning side.

Gordon was a smashing player with a great attitude to the job and always a bundle of mischief – a wicked wind-up merchant. He enjoyed a long, successful career and a lot was made of his strict diet, especially his intake of bananas. He certainly trained hard and was a committed non-drinker, but it was funny to hear Fergie reveal some years later that the wee ginger one loved his fish suppers.

Another newcomer that summer of 1984 was Alan Brazil, Tottenham's Scottish international striker, who made his reputation playing for Ipswich Town. Ron was still striving to give us the extra firepower he believed we needed to bridge the gap from nearly men to champions. We had our high points during the season just completed, notably against Barcelona in the Cup-Winners' Cup, but also in the League. A run of four wins on the trot, ending with a 4–0 hammering of Arsenal at Old Trafford, took us back to the top of the First Division at Liverpool's expense, but we couldn't stay there and erratic form again proved our undoing. We won just two of our remaining ten League fixtures and none of our last five, which wasn't anywhere near good enough for a team with title hopes.

In truth, you tend to take your foot off the gas a bit when you think the Championship has gone and you have a Cup to chase. It's a mental thing. When you are still in with a chance you have no problem pushing and staying closer to the leaders, but once they start disappearing out of view you are more likely to slip up in games you should win. So Liverpool became champions yet again, while we dropped down to fourth. We had the consolation of a place in the following season's UEFA Cup, but no one at Old Trafford could claim they were satisfied.

From a personal standpoint, I had to be pleased with my general form and twelve goals in the League, plus four in Europe, was a useful haul. My overall game had progressed over the two-year period following the 1982 World Cup and the interest from Italian clubs served, if nothing else, to reinforce my self-confidence. At the age of twenty-seven, I felt I was approaching my peak. The years between twenty-seven and thirty-two should be your best in the game because you have the perfect balance of experience and physical condition. You have come through the learning years and should be as fit as you are ever going to be. So I was looking forward to the next five years for the fulfilment of my ambitions at both club and international level.

I think being given the captaincy was probably another factor that helped me. Some players will tell you their form suffered after becoming skipper because they found the added responsibility a burden and a distraction from their own game. Others shy away from it because they feel it's simply not for them. But I never found the job a burden or a handicap. In fact, I relished the responsibility and believe I thrived on it. Ever since I was a young lad I wanted to be involved in a match as much as possible, which is why I loved playing in midfield. As captain, you have the opportunity, and duty, to be even more involved.

When things aren't going particularly well for the team you are conscious that the manager, players and fans are looking to you to do something about it. There's nothing like a challenge to make you dig deeper. I believe a captain can make a difference and influence the course of a match. He should be able to lift players when things aren't going well and give them self-belief. I like to think I led by example, whether it was going forward to score, heading away from my own area or tackling in midfield. I think football people generally, and managers in particular, like to see that aggression and commitment in their captains.

You have to know when it's right to have a go at your team-mates and when they need words of encouragement. They know it's nothing personal if they get a volley. As captain, you have to recognise that all players are different and you may have to deal with them differently to get the best out of them. The hardest part is sticking to your job when your own form is below par. You still have to lead and try to do and say the right things regardless. You can't afford to hide or shirk your responsibility in any way.

My responsibility through that summer of 1984 was to rest and then prepare as well as I could to skipper United to a more successful season next time around.

6
DAYS OF WOE

N EW SEASON, new players, new strip, new contract. For one reason or another, fresh optimism filled the Old Trafford air. On the eve of the 1984–85 League opener, I posed with our summer international recruits, Gordon Strachan, Jesper Olsen and Alan Brazil, all wearing our latest kit and confident smiles. All the conjecture about a move to Italian football had died down and I was eager to remove any lingering uncertainties about my future. United, in turn, were just as keen for me to sign an extended contract with them. We eventually agreed a seven-year deal, worth around £1 million, which tied me to the club through my peak years and guaranteed my family financial security.

It was a huge commitment on both sides, but showed the faith we had in one another. After the talks with Italian clubs came to nothing, I asked the chairman about the prospects of a new contract at United. He readily agreed we should sort out a long-term deal and I was glad to get the business settled. For professional and personal reasons, there couldn't have been a better outcome. I was satisfied that everyone at Old Trafford had the ambition to take the club forward, and Denise and I were happy to be staying in the Manchester area. A few months later we bought the house in Hale that has been our home ever since.

Ron Atkinson suggested that by the time I reached my early

thirties I could drop back from midfield to centre-back and prolong my career. Other players, such as the Scotland international Dave Mackay, had benefited from such a switch. Playing at the back demands less stamina and I wasn't a stranger to the role, anyway. I felt very comfortable playing there. What it does demand, apart from the willingness to tackle and head, is an ability to read the game and 100 per cent discipline. I think I qualified on most counts, but to be honest I found it a little boring playing back there. The discipline of holding my position, week in, week out, would probably have done my head in. You have to keep your defensive mind tuned in all the time and resist the temptation to join in the play. That wasn't for me. I had to be involved, I had to make those forward runs, although I did sit in a little more in the later stages of my career.

Back in 1984, I could run for fun. Any thoughts that we would be quickly out of the blocks, though, soon disappeared. We began our First Division programme with four successive draws and were wondering what we had to do to get it right. Then we thumped Newcastle 5–0, everyone was raving about our football and the bookies were making us favourites for the title. That win was satisfying for Ron because a couple of his new boys, Gordon and Jesper, scored three of the goals. Mark Hughes, promoted from the ranks, claimed another and perhaps the pick of the five went to the much underrated Remi Moses. Remi answered a lot of his doubters in that match. He was a far better player than many gave him credit for.

That result set us off and we began to look like the team we all wanted to be. Strach soon justified Ron's perseverance in signing him, Jesper took over the regular left-side role from Arnold Muhren and, although Alan didn't settle so quickly, we found the firepower we were looking for. It came from Hughes. Ron allowed Peter Beardsley to go because Brian Whitehouse told him that a young Welsh lad in the reserves would make it in the first team. Sparky, as

Mark was known, got his chance that season and was a revelation, scoring some of the spectacular goals that were to become his trademark and bagging two hat-tricks. He was a great striker of the ball, as strong as a bull, and became an excellent leader of the line, holding up the ball as well as anyone.

Our revived team enjoyed a terrific autumn, and again we were tipped to bring down the Liverpool fortress. We put five past West Ham, but suffered an ominous setback when Everton hammered us 5–0 at Goodison Park. As if to prove that was no fluke, they knocked us out of the Milk Cup with a 2–1 win at Old Trafford.

We were made to work hard to progress in the UEFA Cup. After a relatively straightforward 5–2 aggregate victory against Raba Gyor, a little-known Hungarian club, we needed an extra-time penalty, converted by Strach, to break the deadlock and the nervous tension against the Dutch side, PSV Eindhoven. Over the years we were lucky to have some excellent penalty takers and Gordon was definitely one of them. That narrow victory was followed by two more close encounters, this time with Dundee United. They had a good team at the time and Paul Sturrock, who later came down to England as a manager, was a lethal marksman for them. They held us 2–2 at Old Trafford and thought they had done the hard part. There was little between us again in Scotland, but Arnie's late, deflected shot, gave us a 5–4 aggregate win and a passage to the quarter-finals.

Our form hit an all-too-familiar topsy-turvy patch and even Strachan seemed to lose his sense of direction. He missed three penalties out of four as we wasted the chance to strengthen our Championship bid. Ron gave us another rocket after we lost at bottom club Stoke City and then we were beaten at home by Sheffield Wednesday. We managed to avoid another banana skin at Bournemouth, beating them 3–0 in the third round of the FA Cup, but in a League match at home to Coventry City on 12 January 1985, I took a tumble that was to have repercussions for me and, some seventeen months later, for England.

A costly defeat by Coventry was made worse by the freak accident, which left me in agony. It was a freezing cold day and the surface difficult. I had raced towards the far post, anticipating Mike Duxbury's deep centre, and was almost over the goal-line as I met the ball with my head. My momentum was such that I couldn't stop myself somersaulting over an advertising board. That wouldn't have been a problem, except that I landed, shoulder-first, on the transformer box of our newly installed underground heating system. I knew straightaway that it was a bad injury because the pain was so severe. I had dislocated my shoulder.

I was carried off, clutching my right shoulder, and Jim McGregor, our physiotherapist, quickly realised I would have to go to hospital. I had to wait, though, because a woman at the match had gone into labour and she was given priority over me for use of the ambulance. When I eventually got to the hospital we had to decide, after consultation with the doctors, whether I should have surgery. The shoulder was put back in place and the medical advice was that, because it was the first dislocation, we should allow it to heal naturally. An operation would have put me out for at least ten weeks, virtually the rest of the season, whereas rest and treatment might enable me to return in less than six weeks.

Hindsight is a wonderful thing, of course, and at the time I was prepared to accept the guidance of experts. If I had known that there was such a good chance of the shoulder coming out again, I would have told the surgeons to sew it up then and there. It would have been far better to get the problem sorted for good. The shoulder did come out again, more than once, and everyone involved was a loser. I missed many more matches for United than I would have done after an immediate operation, and the recurring injury ruined my 1986 World Cup hopes with England. It also took me longer to recover from the original dislocation than was expected and I didn't return to the United team until more than two months later.

At the time, I was just glad to be back and we still had plenty to play for. We were clinging to the leading pack in the Championship race, we had reached the semi-finals of the FA Cup and were in the middle of a finely balanced UEFA Cup quarter-final. Our progress in the domestic knock-out competition had been fairly smooth. We avenged that painful League defeat against Coventry by knocking them out of the Cup, then swept past Blackburn Rovers and West Ham United. In Europe, our opponents were the Hungarian side, Videoton. Their spoiling tactics made it difficult for the lads but Frank's goal gave us a 1–0 lead to take into the away leg.

My comeback was in a League fixture at West Ham. I was named as substitute and got the call to action on the hour. We had looked the better team yet somehow trailed 2–1. I had been on for about six minutes when I met Jesper's corner kick with a flicked header. The last time I had gone up to head a cross I landed in hospital. This time I saw the ball clip a post on its way into the net and we were celebrating an equaliser. Just as importantly, I came through that half-hour test unscathed. The shoulder gave me no problems and, although I may have been a little tentative in that match, I was ready to make up for lost time by throwing myself into what was left of the season.

Next up was the return leg of our UEFA Cup quarter-final against Videoton. They drew level on aggregate with a wickedly deflected free-kick that gave Gary Bailey no chance, but for most of the match we murdered them on a glue-pot of a pitch. They managed to take us into extra time and then survived our valid penalty appeals when Jesper was tripped. There was more penalty anguish for us in the shoot-out. It went to sudden death and Sparky's effort was saved. Our European campaign was over and 'gutted' doesn't begin to explain our feelings that night.

The great thing about football is that you soon have something else to aim for and we had vital matches to play back home. A classic header by Frank kept us on the title trail with a 1–0 win at Liverpool, who were also our opponents in the FA Cup semi-final at Goodison Park. We took the lead twice in a tie we dominated for long spells, but we couldn't kill them off and Paul Walsh scored their second equaliser just before the end of extra time. That meant we would have to do it all again in a replay at Maine Road.

In another of those great battles with Liverpool, we showed once more that we were capable of rising to the big occasion. We needed to after going in at half-time a goal down, but we turned the tie around with two goals that were as satisfying as they were imp-ortant. I equalised early in the second half, carrying the ball from deep and then cracking it before their defenders could close in. Bruce Grobbelaar got a fingertip to the ball, but couldn't keep it out. The momentum was with us and Sparky scored a brilliant winner.

We were through to another final and our fans went crazy. Beating Liverpool, who were still such a strong team, made it an even more memorable night. I went towards our fans after the final whistle, but before I knew it I was surrounded by hundreds of them. They swarmed on to the pitch and lifted me on to their shoulders. I didn't stay up there for long, though. In the chaos of the celebrations, I fell off. Mounted police moved in to rescue me, but I was fine. Our fans made sure of that. They were just happy and a bit exuberant. We all were.

So we were on our way to Wembley, but off course as far as the Championship was concerned, finishing fourth in the First Division table. That made us even more determined to complete the 1984–85 term on a high note, although the team waiting for us in the final were the new champions, Everton. They had an excellent, well-balanced side and fancied their chances of making it a double. We had other ideas.

It was a tight match and, for the most part, fairly uneventful. Everton might have felt they had the edge and must have thought they were going to get their hands on the Cup as well as the Championship trophy when we were reduced to ten men with twelve minutes of normal time left. Kevin Moran became the first player to be sent off in an FA Cup final after bringing down Peter Reid, who had broken towards goal after a rare lapse by Paul McGrath. I'm sure Paul would have got round and covered the run because Reidy wasn't the quickest of players. He certainly didn't have Paul's pace and would never have got away from him. Kevin's foul wasn't a bad one and he was just as livid as the rest of us with the referee, Peter Willis. Pete also pleaded on Kevin's behalf – that's the sort of bloke he was – but the referee wouldn't budge. Kevin was off.

If Everton figured the match was theirs for the taking, they were mistaken. The sense of injustice fired us up and you wouldn't have known we were outnumbered. Every one of our players found a little extra – we had to when the match went into extra time. We would have done well to force a replay but we did better than that, thanks to young Norman. With ten minutes left, he took the ball out on the right and faced up to their left-back, Pat van den Hauwe. Norman shifted it to his favoured left foot, cut inside and, using van den Hauwe as a shield, bent a fantastic shot into the far corner. Neville Southall was one of the best goalkeepers in the business and had played his part in Everton's success that season, but he couldn't do anything about that effort. The ball rippled the net and we were in dreamland. We saw off those last, long minutes and had our second FA Cup victory in three seasons.

I lifted the Cup again and held on to another medal as we took our lap of honour around the Wembley pitch. Norman was the centre of attention as far as the photographers were concerned and rightly so. He was just a few days past his twentieth birthday but had already made a big impact on football, both at club and international level. The plaudits were still being handed to Norman when we paraded the Cup in an open-topped bus the following day. There were a few sore heads on that top deck, but that didn't subdue the lads as we were cheered all the way from Altrincham to Manchester Town Hall, in Albert Square. The turnout of fans was fabulous and the lads were on a high all day. The only blot on the celebrations was the ban on Kevin receiving a medal. The FA had never been faced with a situation like this before but later, at a meeting of the Cup committee, they relented and agreed Kevin should have his medal.

It was great to end a mixed season with some silverware and I would never want to diminish the significance of that old pot, but our club should have been winning the League again by then and once more we'd not been good enough. Everton had stopped Liverpool's run and deserved their crack at the European Cup the following season. For tragic reasons, they didn't get the chance to play in the premier club tournament, just as we missed out on the European Cup-Winners' Cup. English clubs were outlawed from continental competition following the disaster at the Juventus-Liverpool 1985 European Cup final at the Heysel Stadium, Brussels, where thirty-nine fans, most of them Italian, died.

Our form in the early phase of the 1985–86 season suggested we were capable of taking on all-comers. Arnold Muhren and Arthur Graham had moved on, so Ron bought Peter Barnes, the former Manchester City and England player, from Coventry for £50,000. Ron was always a big fan of Peter's and he liked wingers. For Peter it was a chance to resurrect his career, which had dipped after some brilliant performances when he was young. Everton got a little revenge by beating us in the Charity Shield match but we were all flying when we began our League campaign with a 4–0 thrashing of Aston Villa, and that set the tone and tempo of our assault on the Championship.

We won our first ten League matches. Our football was devastating and the goals flowed. Just about everybody in the game agreed we looked unstoppable. That incredible sequence of wins continued like this: Ipswich (away) 1–0; Arsenal (away) 2–1; West Ham (home) 2–0; Forest (away) 3–1; Newcastle (home) 3–0; Oxford (home) 3–0; Manchester City (away) 3–0; West Brom (away) 5–1; Southampton (home) 1–0. It was the club's best-ever start to a season and many pundits were telling us we were already certainties for the Championship. We weren't prepared to say that publicly at the time, but we believed we were at last on our way to claiming that title.

The winning run couldn't last forever, of course, and it ended at Luton, where we were held to a 1–1 draw. That wasn't a major setback and we beat Queen's Park Rangers 2–0 at Old Trafford. The team was strong in every department and also well balanced. Our self-belief wasn't shaken at all at that stage. We dropped our first home points in a 1–1 draw against Liverpool, then won 2–1 at Chelsea and 2–0 at home to Coventry, matches I missed because of a hamstring strain. I returned for the trip to Sheffield Wednesday, on 10 November, only to be forced out of the match with a recurrence of the injury after fourteen minutes. Seven minutes from time, Wednesday scored the only goal and our fifteen-match unbeaten run was over.

We still led the Championship, but we could see our season unravelling. Injuries and our rivals began to catch up with us. We just didn't have a big enough squad to cope. John Gidman had broken his leg, Gordon Strachan missed matches with a couple of injuries and Remi Moses twisted his ankle crossing the ball. It seemed so innocuous at the time, yet that injury eventually ended Remi's career. The muscle down the side of his leg never fully redeveloped. I hoped to be back in December, but broke down in training with a pulled calf muscle. On top of the casualty list, some players were struggling for form and confidence. Ron left out Gary Bailey and brought in Chris Turner for a few matches, while Alan Brazil was having a hard time trying to please our more critical fans.

Liverpool knocked us out of the Milk Cup, but our priority was the League and Ron tried to shore up the team with reinforcements. He brought in Colin Gibson, who could play left-back or left-side midfield, from Aston Villa, John Sivebaek, a Danish defender, and Terry Gibson, a striker, as part of an exchange deal that took Alan Brazil to Coventry. Alan hadn't been able to hold down a regular place because, even though Norman Whiteside had dropped back to midfield, Frank Stapleton and Mark Hughes were established as our front pair. When Alan did come into the team, he got terrible abuse from some sections of the crowd. Eventually, he decided he couldn't take any more of it and wanted away. We all felt for him.

Alan was a terrific guy and got on with all of the lads. I went racing with him and we had a lot of fun together. He had an exceptional record at Ipswich and everybody thought he would have slotted nicely into our team. We saw what he was capable of in training. He had the touch, movement, build-up play and finishing ability of a top performer and was a great striker of the ball, but he was another of those players who couldn't quite handle the Old Trafford stage. He seemed a little overawed by the scale of United and everything that came with the club. Unfortunately, Terry didn't really come off for us, either, and Peter Davenport was about to experience the ordeal. Peter, a quick and devastating striker with Nottingham Forest, never really looked at his best after joining us in March 1986.

The wins virtually dried up for us in the second half of the season and we dropped out of contention for the Championship. We couldn't even console ourselves with the FA Cup this time. West Ham made sure of that in a fifth-round replay at Old Trafford. It became a nightmare period for the club as a whole and for me personally. I played just a few minutes' football in three months because of the hamstring and calf injuries, and trouble hounded me for the rest of the campaign.

It didn't help my morale to keep hearing and reading that I was injury prone. Some reports made out that I had some inherent weakness. The fact is that injuries are part of the game and the way I played always left me open to the possibility of getting hurt. People kept telling me I was too brave for my own good, but I wouldn't have changed my style or reined in my commitment for anything. For a start, you are asking for trouble when you hold something back in tackles, and I wouldn't have been half the player I was if I had played any other way. I played something like 850-plus games and finally retired just before my fortieth birthday. That's hardly the record of an injury-prone player.

When you are a high-profile player, your injuries are going to be noticed. As captain of Manchester United and England, every minor niggle becomes a major issue. I might have played more matches if it hadn't been for the injuries but I'm not complaining about that. I take the view that I was very fortunate to have had such a long and satisfying career.

The hamstring problem I had that season was typical of an injury any player can get when he puts so much energy and enthusiasm into his game. My hamstring literally ripped. Players will tear muscles from time to time. I was perhaps more susceptible to that type of injury because I had a bit of an imbalance as a result of breaking my ankle back at West Brom. Physiotherapists advised me to wear a boot inner lining and strap my ankle to improve my balance, but there is only so much protection you can give yourself. I broke my nose three times and had my share of routine sprains, strains, dead legs, cuts and bruises. You expect that. Many players were far worse off than I was. A lot of promising careers were ended prematurely by injuries. Some of my closest friends and team-mates were among the unlucky ones.

Both my brothers had their careers cut short. Our Gary, who, like me, played for West Brom, then went to Bradford and Gateshead, finally had to pack in because of ankle problems. Our Justin never really had the chance to get his professional career off the ground. He was with Newcastle and had loads of promise. He got into the first-team squad when he was eighteen or nineteen and was picked as a substitute. The Newcastle manager, Willie McFaul, told him he would get his chance in the next game. During the week, Justin played in a reserve match and damaged his cruciate knee ligaments. That was the end for him.

Nowadays, with the fitness regimes and technology we have in devising training schedules, we are able to reduce the rate of injuries that were commonplace twenty or more years ago. That is by no means a criticism of Ron Atkinson or Manchester United. It was the same at every club in the country. Football, like everything else, has changed over the course of a generation. Pre-season training used to involve hard cross-country runs, pounding up hills, and then more running. We would run six miles at a time. We ran for lap after lap around the pitch. Now the training is far more scientifically con-trolled. We still have long runs pre-season, but we break them up with stretching exercises. My players now run no more than a mile in any one go.

In the eighties it wasn't unusual to have a high-tempo five-a-side game the morning after a big night match. You might have started out wanting a bit of light-hearted exercise and a touch of the ball, but players are naturally competitive and were still on a high. They couldn't resist throwing themselves into the game and often ended up overdoing it. The result was sometimes a needless hamstring strain or calf-muscle pull. I know, because it happened to me. Today's players will have a gentle warm-down and stretches the day after a match. The whole philosophy is very different and much better for the players.

In January 1986, the club decided a different type of treatment and environment might be the tonic I needed. I went to a clinic in

Amsterdam, run by a Dutchman with the very un-Dutch sounding name of Richard Smith. He worked with the Denmark international team and was recommended by Jesper Olsen. He put me through the hardest week's training and treatment I ever had. It was agony. Richard believed in a deep friction and ice method of treatment. His staff rubbed scar tissue away from the tear in the muscle until it bled, then dispersed the blood with ice. I sat with ice on my leg for twenty minutes after each massage. I was also given lots of skipping and exercise routines, more like the kind of training boxers would be familiar with.

They were long and hard days. I had to be at the clinic by seven o'clock in the morning and one night I didn't get back to my hotel until just before midnight to find a message from Ron, which read: 'I hope you're having a good time.' He thought I must have been out on the town, having a drink. So I phoned him and explained I had only just finished my last session of treatment. Far from going out on the town, I just wanted to sleep. I assured him the treatment and training had been worthwhile. It certainly worked for me and I returned home feeling fit and raring to go again.

The target for my return was an FA Cup fourth-round tie against Sunderland at Roker Park, which of course brought back memories of the first match I saw as a young lad, twenty-two years before. This match, though, left me with a very different impression. I was sent off for the first and last time in my senior football career. Barry Venison, the Sunderland defender, and I slid into a tackle and he held me down. I swung out to knock his arm away and as I did my foot caught him on the head. It was totally accidental. The referee hadn't seen the incident because he was following the play, but the linesman called him over and interpreted it as a deliberate kick. It wasn't. I was angry that I had been held and just tried to free myself. I wanted to get on with the match. The referee didn't want to hear my side of the story and decided I had to go.

Ron was furious and had a right go at Jimmy Hill for criticising me on the BBC's 'Match of the Day' programme that night. There was a feeling I might have been too revved up and eager after being out for so long but that wasn't the case. It was frustrating to be sent off when I had put so much effort into getting fit again, but the lads came through the tie with a 0–0 draw and we beat Sunderland 3–0 in the replay. The dismissal cost me a suspension and I even had the threat of an extended ban for allegedly bringing the game into disrepute hanging over me. That was typical of the jumped-up charges you can be hit with when you are the captain of Manchester United and England. Some people weren't content with a straightforward suspension. The FA eventually dropped the case and I think there were one or two red faces down at Lancaster Gate.

Despite that welcome reprieve, I soon had to face up to another spell out of the game. I dislocated my shoulder again in the fifth round of the FA Cup at West Ham, on 5 March. I slid into a tackle, hit the ground with my elbow and felt the shoulder pop out. Jim McGregor led me off the pitch to the dressing room, laid me down on the treatment table, with my arm hanging over the side, and pushed the shoulder back in. I felt OK after that. I played cards with the lads on the journey home.

That was the second time the shoulder had dislocated and we again had to decide on the course of action to take. An operation was the obvious answer, but the surgeon told me I would need ten weeks to recover. That would have put me out for the rest of the season as far as United were concerned and leave me with only one week to train for the World Cup finals. I realised I would have had no chance of justifying my place in Mexico with so little preparation. I got helpful advice from all sorts of people, including the jump jockeys, John Francome and Peter Scudamore. They were no strangers to dislocations and recommended exercises to strengthen my shoulder. I decided to go with the exercises and did up to a thousand press-ups a day as part of my regular programme.

I played again three and a half weeks later, armed with not only the benefit of those exercises but also a protective harness that I had been told was widely used in Australian rugby league. I scored a late equaliser in the match at Birmingham, but didn't carry on using the harness. I found it too restrictive. I couldn't raise my arm sufficiently to get my balance and kick the ball properly. The shoulder came through the test and gave me no problem for the rest of the season. A hamstring strain put me out of our last three League fixtures, as well as the England-Scotland match, but I had no doubts I would be playing for my country in the World Cup finals.

Our form at United was less certain. West Ham knocked us out of the FA Cup in the fifth-round replay and successive home defeats, against Chelsea and our jinx team, Sheffield Wednesday, effectively put us out of the Championship chase. We were five points behind Liverpool and Everton, and some fans vented their frustration by calling for Ron's head. The gloom clouded the final weeks of the season. We finished fourth, which was a massive disappointment for all of us after the brilliant start we'd had. Our bid nose-dived and I still say the main reason was the catalogue of injuries with which we had to contend. Our supporters probably weren't too pleased, either, to learn that Sparky had been sold to Barcelona. United obviously figured the £2 million fee was too good to refuse and I could understand Sparky wanting to take on the challenge.

We needed to start afresh in the 1986–87 season, but Ron had more problems on his hands before a ball was kicked in anger. I had to have an operation after dislocating my shoulder again at the World Cup in Mexico, and I missed our first four matches. Ron had gone berserk because I'd stayed with England until they were knocked out of the tournament rather than return straightaway for surgery.

I was still able to join the team on a pre-season trip to Amsterdam, when seven of our players were fined for staying out drinking – and I wasn't one of them! We assembled for our evening meal and Ron realised a number of the lads were missing. He looked over to our table and, no doubt to his surprise, saw the usual suspects – Whiteside, McGrath, Moran and me – all present and correct. The missing players were his non-drinkers, so he was worried something serious might have happened to them. Unusually, they had been drinking and eventually came back to the hotel wrecked. Jesper Olsen, Chris Turner, Gary Walsh, Mike Duxbury, Terry Gibson, Clayton Blackmore and Peter Barnes were all fined for their little escapade.

Three defeats from the first three League matches intensified the pressure on the team and the manager. The lads picked up our first point at Leicester and we thrashed Southampton 5–1 to raise hopes that we could get back on track. Instead, we lost another three on the trot and slumped to joint bottom of the First Division. The writing was on the wall – the League was already out of the question. We hadn't been able to pull it off with stronger teams than the one we had that season, so what chance was there? The truth is that we had one or two players who were not good enough for Manchester United.

There was no question of Ron 'losing the dressing room'. The players liked him as a bloke and respected him as a manager. He showed no particular signs of strain or stress, remaining bubbly around the training ground. Talk about his lack of discipline was a load of rubbish, yet it seemed that everything was going against him. The last thing he needed was headlines about a punch-up involving two of his players, but that's what he got.

The players in question were Remi Moses and Jesper Olsen, and it was the biggest mismatch imaginable. Remi wasn't a big lad, but he absolutely battered Jesper. The fight took place on the training pitch.

Jesper went over the top on Remi, who wasn't happy about the tackle and gave Jesper a menacing stare. Jesper came back at him with a defiant, 'Yeah, what are you going to do about it?' kind of response. Remi showed him. He went bang, bang, bang, and that was the end of it. There was blood all over the place.

United tried to cover up the incident, saying Olsen had to have eleven stitches put in a wound after a clash of heads in a five-a-side, but it happened all right. It was bloodier than most skirmishes you are likely to get at a club, but rows and fights are going to blow up every now and then. Newcastle's Lee Bowyer and Kieron Dyer and one or two others have exchanged blows during a match. You can't expect around two dozen blokes in any workplace, and especially in a highly competitive, contact-sport environment, to get on all the time. Even in training, you can identify the winners and, if they are caught by a nasty tackle, they will react. Aggression can spill over. It was unfortunate for Ron that this bust-up got into the press. He could have done without it – and so could Jesper!

Another lengthening injury list limited Ron's options, but he was fast losing sympathy among the supporters and our 4–1 defeat in a Littlewoods League Cup replay at Southampton proved the last straw. Less than forty-eight hours later, on 6 November 1986, Ron Atkinson was sacked.

Ron reacted as only Ron could. He invited friends around to his house in Rochdale for a few drinks. Some of the injured players, who weren't going to be in the team that weekend, went along to join him. Denise and I went across. So did Norman and Gordon. It wasn't long before Strach had taken over as the DJ. 'Big Spender' and 'Gold-finger' boomed out and Ron was suitably amused. It was typical of Ron to take his sacking in that way. He wasn't one to hide away. I'm sure it hurt him, though. He said at the time that he ought to have quit that summer, but his pride wouldn't let him.

He knew the score, as all of us in the game do. When Manchester United are in the position we were in, you accept they are going to do something about it. There were suggestions that matters in Ron's private life affected the board's decision, but I don't think that was the case. I believed the club when they said the decision was made for purely football reasons. Our results weren't good enough, so you could argue the club were justified in wanting a change of manager.

The poor run and Ron's dismissal hurt our pride and reputation as well as his. As players, we felt we had let him down. When any manager is sacked his players should accept a share of the blame. We had to recognise it was partly our fault. By that stage, though, I felt we didn't have enough players capable of fulfilling the ambitions and expectations of Manchester United and as a manager you are judged to a large extent on your signings. If you bring in top players and deliver results, that is good management. If your signings don't work out, you are open to criticism. Ron made a lot of very good signings and was unlucky with some, who had looked very good, such as Brazil and Davenport. A few, it has to be said, just weren't up to the job at United.

Ron's balance in the transfer market showed a deficit of £1.3 million, which isn't bad over five years – hardly extravagant for a club of United's stature. He won the FA Cup twice and his team were consistently among the League leaders. His sides played with flair and adventure, very much in the United tradition, and the fans enjoyed some fantastic, exciting performances. And yet he perhaps never quite developed the bond and rapport with them that other United managers have had, or indeed that he enjoyed at West Brom. I think fans are influenced by what they read or hear in the media and very few people in the media really knew Ron. He was always portrayed as flash Mr Bojangles, dressed in sharp suits and swigging champagne. He never denied or played down any of that because he had a sense of humour and didn't feel he had to defend himself.

It may have been that the United fans thought Ron's style was a bit over the top. They would have preferred a more obviously working-class type of manager and the new boss would fit that image perfectly.

7

ENTER SIR ALEX

A S SOON AS NEWS of Ron Atkinson's sacking got out, the question everyone asked was, 'Who next?' The answer came back pretty quickly. The players heard the name of Alex Ferguson coming through on the grapevine louder than any other. We didn't know of any approach to him, but within twenty-four hours of Ron's exit United confirmed that the Aberdeen manager was their man. Gordon Strachan's reaction was priceless. 'Och, no!' he said.

Alex Ferguson had a reputation for being both a successful manager and a strict disciplinarian. He'd led Aberdeen to the European Cup-Winners' Cup trophy and broken the Old Firm stranglehold in Scotland, but word was that he had a tough, uncompromising management style that didn't go down well with all of his players. Strachan had been part of Ferguson's outstanding Aberdeen team but left amid rumours of a personality clash with the boss. Gordon was certainly always his own man and things might not have been all that rosy between them, but I never heard him say he expected to be out of the Old Trafford door as soon as Fergie moved in, which is what some people reckoned.

Strach did tell us one story that gave us a bit of an insight into what we might be in for. The manager was going home in a taxi one night after a match when he overheard a message on the radio that a taxi was needed to take four of the Aberdeen boys to a nightclub.

Fergie, obviously fuming, turned his taxi around and went straight to the club. He marched in and threw the players out, telling them, 'Get yourselves home.' Once we got to know him, we could believe that story.

Alex and Gordon seemed to get on fine. In fact, we were all impressed with the new boss and his assistant, Archie Knox, at our first meeting with them. On the day they arrived, 7 November, they got everybody together, the young boys included, in the gym. The boss stood on the steps, with Archie next to him, and said, 'Good to see you, lads. I want to introduce myself and my assistant. Everybody will get a fair crack. You all start level and have a chance of getting into the team. So let's hope we enjoy it.'

That was it. He walked out of the gym and we got on with our work. There was no talk of rules or discipline at that stage. I'm sure he would have heard things about certain players, but he no doubt wanted to assess things for himself before laying down his law. He was as good as his word and started with a clean sheet of paper, taking it from there. He made clear his ambition to do what he had done in Scotland – end the domination of the country's number one football city at the time. In England that was Liverpool. His aim was to knock Liverpool and Everton off their perch and make United number one again.

I didn't have the chance to get to know him too well to start with because I was injured. I missed his first three matches in charge, but was named as substitute for the trip to Wimbledon. We'd gone a goal down late in the first half and went back to the dressing room to hear the boss's half-time team talk. It was the first time I'd heard him really let blast.

Sir Alex absolutely tore into the boys. None of this was coming my way because I'd not been on the pitch, but as he was ripping into the lads I had to get a grip to stop laughing. I'm thinking, 'Don't catch me even *thinking* about smirking.'

I'd never seen anything like this before. In fact, I've never seen another manager, before or since, rage like that. I'd seen Ron let go on the odd occasion, but not like Alex. It was pretty formidable, and we saw it a few more times down the years. I mean, he gets right up into the individual's face. It could be a general blast or personal, but usually it was personal – really up close and really personal, one on one. That day at Wimbledon it was the general treatment. More or less the whole team got it. I came on in the second half, but we couldn't get the equaliser and lost 1–0.

The only time he really went for me was in a match at Newcastle, the following season. Again it was half-time and we were losing 1–0 but this time I had been on from the start and I was having a poor game. They had Paul Gascoigne playing opposite Norman and me and we couldn't get near him. Gazza was different class. I could see Fergie was going to come for me and as soon as he started shouting and raging I got up. Before he could get across the dressing room to me, I was across to him, raging back.

'Do you think I want to play as badly as I am in front of all my family and mates? I'm trying, Gaffer, but the kid's not bad.'

'Well, get your finger out,' he shouted.

I'd seen him do it so often to the other lads that I was ready for him. I think by reacting the way I did, I drew a bit of his sting. I knew when I was playing badly and I didn't need him to tell me. Alex would use situations like that to find out about the character of his players. He reckoned that if you wilted and didn't stand up for yourself with an 'I'll show him' attitude, you weren't the type of character he wanted at his club.

All managers are different and I'm lucky that I've worked with some of the best in the business – Ron Greenwood, Bobby Robson, Terry Venables, Don Howe, Ron Atkinson and Alex Ferguson. There's not a bad one among them. They were all outstanding but they all had their own, individual way of working.

It was inevitable that comparisons would be made between Ron and Alex, so perhaps this is a good point at which to nail one or two myths and fallacies. Ron was very disciplined with his players and left us in no doubt about what he expected of us. I heard a little story about the day Paul McGrath joined the club that illustrates Ron's firm handling of players. Paul was apparently wearing an earring and Ron told him if he wanted to be a great centre-half at the club he'd have to get rid of it. He pointed out that John Charles never wore an earring! OK, it's only a little thing, but I think the little things can tell you a lot about people.

Alex certainly brought in more discipline in terms of how you looked after yourself. Around that time the importance of sensible diet was being recognised in football and he was very much aware of it. We had talks about nutrition and he gave us strict instructions on what we could and couldn't eat the day before games. We were to eat pasta, fish or chicken rather than red meat, the kind of thing that's taken for granted now. Some of the lads were still into steaks and fry-ups, but I'd been pretty disciplined about food since my early days at West Brom, so it wasn't a problem for me.

Our new boss was also stricter about nights out and drinking. I don't want anyone running away with the idea that Ron was happy for us to go out boozing every night, far from it. It was just that he would be a little more relaxed about the occasional drink than Alex was. Ron wouldn't mind if a player had a glass of wine with his meal on a Friday night. Some players did, a lot didn't. Fergie wanted players to stop drinking completely. He would tolerate us having a glass of wine with a meal on a Saturday night, but he made it clear he'd rather we had no alcohol at all.

I always had my own rule. I never drank for two nights before a match, so I didn't take Ron up on his offer of a glass of wine on a Friday night. Apart from training, I did virtually nothing else for the two days before a match. I didn't play golf as some players did. I put my feet up because I knew how important it was to rest.

If we had a midweek game, which was often the case, I drank only at weekends. Stories about a so-called drinking culture at United, and later at Middlesbrough, keep rearing their heads, so let's nail these, as well. The perception seems to be that Ron liked to glug champagne and let his players booze when they wanted to. For a start, Ron didn't really drink champagne at all. I've seen him sit round a table with friends and order loads of champagne, then keep topping up everybody else's glass but not his own. He would be quite happy having an occasional drink with players. This would be after a match, or away on a trip when we hadn't got a match for three or four days. He felt it was good for team morale. For some managers, though, that would be an absolute no-no. Ron put his trust in players and treated them with respect.

We didn't abuse that trust and I don't think our drinking cost us in terms of performances or results. If anything, you're even more determined to do well for a manager who trusts you like that because you don't want to let him down. We went out for a drink only at the start of a week when we didn't have a match until the Saturday or Sunday. So because we had so many midweek Cup matches, we'd maybe go out no more than once a month or even two months. Then we'd go out for lunch as a group of players after training on Monday and take it from there. The likes of Moran, McGrath, Whiteside, McQueen, Hughes and me would sometimes be out till two in the morning. Now and then we'd go to a nightclub, but usually we ended up at the Four Seasons, a hotel near Manchester Airport. The staff knew us there because we went regularly with our families for meals.

It was good to go out with your team-mates and get to know them a bit better away from the training ground. We'd talk about things other than football, have a laugh and relax. Mostly the lads would drink lager, never spirits. We never had trouble with punters, or got into scrapes. We were pretty good at looking after each other like that. If ever we saw one of the lads was getting a bit aggravated with a punter, we'd step in and calm the player down. If the punters were having a go at us and you could see things might turn nasty, we'd just leave and go somewhere else.

We enjoyed a drink, just like anybody else. I could drink loads of pints without falling over and making myself look stupid. It didn't take the edge off my game because if I'd had a session on the Monday, I wouldn't have another drop for the rest of the week. The morning after, I'd train hard and sweat it out. When you are comparatively young and fit, you can cope with it. I always made sure the drink didn't affect my job.

After Fergie took over, we had what we called 'team meetings' on Mondays. Again, we'd go off as a group for a bit of lunch and then on for a drink, but it was nothing like the sessions we had with the old school. I was a survivor of those days and the new boys included Brian McClair, Steve Bruce and Gary Pallister. Roy Keane and Lee Sharpe joined us later. Some of the players, mainly the foreign lads, were non-drinkers. Andrei Kanchelskis was one who didn't drink. Eric Cantona, on the other hand, did like a drink, mostly champagne, and he'd stay on. Eric was good company and enjoyed being out with us. Some went home after lunch, others around tea-time. A few of us would carry on till about ten o'clock and end up in one of the local pubs. We all lived in more or less the same area.

Alex had obviously heard stories about the drinking culture at the club, and spoke to me privately, saying, 'Look Bryan, I've heard you like a drink and I've no problem with that as long as it's not in the week. I don't want players coming in with alcohol on their breath.'

'Fair enough, Gaffer,' I said. 'If that's what you want, that's the way it will be.'

I think he wanted me, as captain, to relay the message to the rest of the players. The trouble was that fans would write or phone in if they had seen me or any of the other players out and that would wind him up. Of course, they tended to do that when we weren't playing so well, which was the case during the early part of Fergie's management at the club. He'd haul the player in, show him the letter on his desk, and say, 'What about this?'

This is where I had a fall-out with Alex – or at least, a disagreement. Kevin Moran had left to play in Spain with Sporting Gijon and came back to England during their winter break. Alex allowed him to train with us and he stayed at our house. Kevin had a couple of Birthdays shops – which Ronnie Wood and I had helped him set up – and he wanted to see Ronnie about the business. So one Thursday night Ron sent over his car to take us to his local pub for a meeting. Kevin, who wasn't playing for another week or two, had a few drinks. We got a taxi home and didn't think anything more about it.

We were playing away at Derby on the Saturday and were 1–0 down at half-time. Back in the dressing room, all of a sudden the boss started attacking me. Unlike that day at Newcastle, I wasn't expecting it because I was playing OK. He kept going on and on at me and I couldn't work it out. We won the match 2–1, but at the end it was still bugging me so I asked him, 'What was all that about at half-time?'

'I know you were out drinking on Thursday,' he said.

Now I've got a temper and I just exploded. I flung my boots across the dressing room in a rage and told him where he could go.

'I wasn't drinking on Thursday,' I told him.

Archie Knox heard what was going on and came into the shower room to try to calm me down.

'Bryan, come on . . .' he began.

'No, I'm not having it, Archie, using the drink to have a go at me.' I was really raging.

I was still angry on the following Monday morning. I was always one of the first players in for training because I used to drop the girls off at school and go straight on to the Cliff. Alex was good to me because he would let me sit with him and his staff and have a cup of tea. So on that Monday morning I said to him, 'Gaffer, can I have a word with you?'

It had obviously been preying on his mind all weekend as well because he threw down a letter that had been sent in by the taxi driver. It said Kevin and I were absolutely legless when he took us home. I explained what had happened. I told him Kevin had plenty with some of the lads in the pub, but I hadn't had a drink.

'Anyway, I've told you, that's enough of it,' he said.

Another time he heard I'd been out drinking, or it might have been that Archie smelt alcohol on my breath. We had a practice match at the Cliff and at the end of it, the boss said to me, 'If you're not going to put it in during the practice match, go and do ten laps.'

I didn't bother arguing with him and just said, 'OK.' I started running round the pitch and thought, 'Well, if I'm going to do this, I might as well get a right good sweat on,' and I just kept going. I'd got to about twenty laps when Archie started knocking on the window that looked out on to the pitch, waving at me to come in. I did another couple of laps and Archie came down to the side of the pitch.

'You, stop being stupid and get in,' he said.

'Oh, I'm the stupid one am I?' I replied.

I just walked in. I'd made my point. When I look back, I suppose it's quite funny. I must have looked like Forrest Gump, but I didn't like my commitment or professionalism being questioned. My metabolism was such that I could drink loads with the lads in the early days. I also knew that if we had a decent training session the next day, I could run through it. Some of the other lads would be struggling like hell at the back and no doubt cursing me, but I had no problem. When I got to the age of thirty-three or -four, I made a conscious effort to cut down on the drinking. I made sure I ate the right food all the time and kept my weight down. I realised I wasn't young any more and that if I wanted to prolong my career, I would have to look after myself.

I've tried to be frank about my drinking habits because I've had it thrown at me for so long now and there are times when I get really angry. Yes, there was a time when I drank a lot but, I repeat, I made sure it didn't affect my football. It was never the 'problem' that some players have had. In any case, I'd hope that my playing performances spoke for themselves. I never gave less than 100 per cent on the pitch.

Don't go thinking I was the only one to have run-ins with the boss over drinking. A few of the other lads did and some of those clashes were a lot more serious than mine. One player, an international but not one of the usual suspects, got shown the door after he drank a box of wine at the back of the team bus. We were on our way to a match at Southampton and Ken Merrett, the club secretary, sussed what the player was up to. He had a word in the gaffer's ear and when we checked in at our hotel, the boss made sure he got into the lift with the player and smelt his breath. He told him that was it – he was out.

You learn in football as you do in any walk of life. When I moved on to Middlesbrough, I was still playing and training with the boys there, so I tried to set the right example. As a manager, I won't have players drinking the night before a match. Maybe that's because I didn't when I was playing. Times have moved on. With the money the players can earn today, they've got to give themselves every chance of making the most of their careers for the benefit of their families. That's what I tell my players. I don't mind them having a couple of glasses of wine when they're out with their families, having a meal after a match, but the days when players went out and had a right good session have gone.

A manager has to give his players a code of conduct, but I think the more responsibility and self-respect you can give to the players the better. One of the first things I did when I got the West Brom job was to get the players to form a committee to set out their own rules and fining system. They decided for themselves what was acceptable and what wasn't about the place. We're not talking major points, but such things as taking off their boots and wearing flip-flops inside the training-ground buildings. They drew up their list of dos and don'ts and I was happy with that. Any fines went into the players' fund for an end-of-season trip. As a club, you don't want to be constantly stepping in and fining players for insignificant things. If any serious issues cropped up, I would obviously have to step in, but basically they had the responsibility of policing themselves and I think that gives the players a form of discipline they are more likely to appreciate and co-operate with.

I think managers have also got to be more disciplined about their own diet nowadays. OK, you don't have to be as fit as the players, but the fitter and healthier you are, the better able you are to do the job. I still like a beer and a glass of white wine with a meal, but I know I'm not going to be able to work properly, or get the respect of the players, if I don't show dedication and reasonable discipline.

The funny thing is, Sir Alex, as he became, and I now joke about my drinking. I was asked to say a few words about my old boss at a charity dinner and I recalled that every time I had a dodgy game he'd want to know if I'd been out drinking because he'd got letters from fans saying they'd seen me in a bar. I also reminded him that he used to tell me that if Gordon Strachan had a bad game it was because of his fish suppers.

Just like any other player, I had my skirmishes with Alex, but I think the fact that I was one of his old boys invited to join him on the top table that night shows what a good relationship we have. I have a lot to be grateful to him for and I have a lot of respect for him. I'd like to think the feeling is mutual.

Alex is disciplined and meticulous in all aspects of his work. Pre-season training under him was more structured than it was with

Ron. We didn't have so much long-distance running. It was shorter and more intense. I didn't feel we were particularly fitter, though. No matter what type of running we did I always tried to be at the front. I never felt comfortable in the middle of the group or trailing off at the back. I preferred to push myself at the front.

The major difference in match preparation was the way Ferguson studied the opposition. He would have reports drawn up on them, which he went through in great depth. He highlighted their strengths and weaknesses. In that sense, he was more analytical than Ron, but there was no difference in the way we played. Both managers liked us to be positive and impose ourselves on the opposition. We played some terrific, entertaining football under both of them. Fergie worked on playing one-twos, staying with runners, that type of thing. He wanted possession football and that was taught through-out the club, right from the kids. You could see it in their play as they came through the ranks.

The really big improvement at the club under Alex was with the kids. Ron would leave that work with his staff, but Alex was much more hands-on. He and Archie Knox would be out there on the training pitch in the afternoon, studying the young lads. Brian Kidd, who scored in United's 1968 European Cup final win on his nine-teenth birthday, was brought in to nurture that promising talent. All that work with the kids paid off when Ryan Giggs, David Beckham, Paul Scholes, Gary and Phil Neville and Nicky Butt broke into the senior squad.

Archie was a terrific partner for the boss. As a number two, you are a bit of a buffer between the manager and the players. The number two can be more like one of the boys than the manager and have a laugh with them. Archie certainly did. He was a great bloke and had good banter with the lads. That makes the work more enjoyable. It was never dull or too strict with Archie. His training routines were always varied, always interesting. That way you get a good response from the players. His light-hearted way of going about the job got the best out of us.

There was an Archie classic in 1991, when we were preparing for our European Cup-Winners' Cup quarter-final against Montpellier. The French club sent two spies to watch us at work. They turned up at the Cliff and were standing at the side of the pitch, with their charts and logs at the ready, as we came out to train. We thought it was strange that no balls, bibs or any of the other usual stuff were ready for us on the pitch. Archie came out with this big bulge under his tracksuit. He called us over to stand around the centre circle, with two players in the middle.

'Right,' he said, 'keep ball,' and dropped a rugby ball from under his tracksuit.

So we're trying to play keep ball with this rugby ball and it's bouncing all over the place. We're having a right good laugh, but the two French blokes are looking on, wondering what the hell is going on. I don't know what they were hoping to find out about us, but I think they had a wasted journey. It was typical Archie.

It wasn't always fun and games with Archie, though. I found that out that day when I was sent lapping the pitch. He had a short fuse and if you got the wrong side of him he would come down on you like a ton of bricks. Apart from when French spies were around, the training had to be done properly. If you mucked about in training and he got annoyed, he'd tell us to do it right. If he had to tell us a second time, he'd say, 'Right, the lot of you, I'll see you at three o'clock this afternoon,' and he meant it.

The first time he did it, I went to the gaffer and said, 'Come on, it was just a couple of the lads mucking about, nothing that much, and Archie's taken the nark and told us to be in at three. We just want to get on with our training and go home.'

'If Archie says three o'clock, it's three o'clock,' said the gaffer.

So we had to sit around from eleven o'clock till three before we could start training again. The lads would have to phone home and explain why they couldn't be back until much later. Then we'd have to go out and train at three.

Fergie's ambition and determination were obvious in everything he did but it wouldn't have taken him long to realise there was no easy fix to make us into a Championship-winning team. I thought once or twice that we were going to pull it off under Ron. Our team in the early to mid-eighties period had a real chance of toppling Liverpool and Everton. Then key players left, some of those who came in were nowhere near good enough to replace them and Fergie knew he would have to rebuild.

He gave a chance to a young goalkeeper, Gary Walsh, who had impressed everybody at the club. Gary Bailey was struggling with a knee injury and eventually had to retire. Walsh had a couple of spells in place of Chris Turner and most people reckoned he'd got a great future. I was sure he could have been a top keeper, but on a trip to Bermuda he got booted on the head in a horrendous challenge and I don't think he was ever quite the same again. I took him to Middlesbrough because I knew what outstanding ability he had, but the effects of that kick definitely gave him problems.

We were still capable of good performances during that 1986–87 season and a 1–0 win at Liverpool on Boxing Day showed that on any given day we could produce a result. Then the following day we lost 1–0 at home to Norwich. As if that wasn't bad enough, I had to go off with a hamstring injury that put me out for five matches. That just about summed up how it had been going for the team and for me. I was injured again at my jinx ground, Upton Park, and I don't think any of us were too sorry to see the back of that season.

We'd been knocked out of the Littlewoods Cup by Southampton in the third round and the FA Cup in the fourth round by Coventry. We finished eleventh in the First Division, so at least no relegation worries loomed at the end, but all in all, it was a pretty miserable season. Everton won the Championship – Merseyside still ruled.

Twenty years had gone by since United last won the title and, to be honest, we looked light years away from bringing it back to Old Trafford. Far from getting closer, we were falling farther behind. We were Manchester United and that just wasn't good enough. If Alex Ferguson had any illusions about the task when he took the job, he can have had none by that summer of 1987.

8
SILVER LINING

ALEX FERGUSON gave the squad a chance to show what they could do in his first season as manager of Manchester United and all we did was prove we weren't up to it. He probably couldn't wait to start work on rebuilding the team. Peter Barnes had gone back 'home' to Manchester City and many other players would make way for new signings. That summer he strengthened the defence by buying Viv Anderson from Arsenal and then returned to Scotland to land Celtic striker Brian McClair.

Tribunals fixed the fees at £250,000 for Viv and £850,000 for McClair. Both were excellent pieces of business for us and I wasn't surprised Celtic boss Billy McNeill thought they'd been robbed. I'd played with Viv for England so we were already mates. We roomed together at the 1988 European Championship in Germany and he later went with me to Middlesbrough as my number two. He was a really good defender, with bags of experience.

Brian McClair, known as Choccy, was a great signing for the club. I think he was one of the most underrated players in the game. His goal-scoring record was terrific and he became the first United player since George Best to score twenty League goals in a season. In fact, he ended his first term in English football with thirty-one goals in all, a fantastic total, but there was a lot more to his game. His best position was probably just off the main striker, yet he played much of his football for us in midfield. He was a worker and would do anything for the good of the team. If we were having a problem defensively and I felt I needed to go deeper to protect the back four, I'd tell him to come on to my midfield player. He'd do it without any moans or hesitation. He always put the team before himself.

We soon discovered he had a great sense of humour. He never missed a chance for a prank or a wind-up. He was always pratting around and coming out with the one-liners. I remember in a match against Aston Villa, one of their players called Choccy a 'Scottish tosser'. Quick as a flash, Choccy said, 'You couldn't even spell it.' There was always good banter with Brian around. He's still doing his stuff for United, working on the staff. He was in charge of the reserves and has now taken over the academy.

The new lads settled in pretty quickly and we made a much better start to the 1987–88 season, unbeaten in our first seven League matches. In fact, we lost only twice before Christmas. It was a very different year for me, as well. I steered clear of serious injury and made thirty-six First Division appearances. I remember getting a black eye in a Littlewoods Cup-tie against Crystal Palace and having to put up with some wisecracks from the lads, but I could take that. Even though I had to fill in at centre-back in some matches, I managed eleven League goals over the season.

When we had problems with injuries in the middle of the defence, the boss decided he needed to bring in another centre-half. I like to think I helped him find his man. I used to go through the players' marks in the *People* newspaper and I said to the gaffer, 'That lad at Norwich, Bruce, always seems to get star rating. Has anybody looked at him?'

The gaffer and his staff started talking about him, so whether my two penn'orth sparked their interest, I don't know. Obviously the boss was advised by his scouts, and that December, Steve Bruce joined us for £825,000. Norwich weren't a bad team but Steve had

117

probably gone largely unnoticed until then because he was playing out in East Anglia. It wasn't long before the rest of the country realised we had another great signing. Steve was a terrific defender, came up with some vital goals and was a real team man. There's no doubt he was one of the best English players not to be capped by his country. We became good pals and still are.

We let ourselves down in the Cup competitions, losing to our old tormentors Oxford in the fifth round of the Littlewoods Cup and going out against Arsenal at the same stage of the FA Cup. In the League we were much more consistent and at least had the satisfaction of finishing above Everton. We had two draws with Liverpool, including a 3–3 cracker at Anfield. We were trailing 3–1 and down to ten men after Colin Gibson was sent off, but we came back to grab a draw. I got a couple of goals and Gordon snatched the equaliser. He even had a chance to win it just before the end. It wasn't all over there, though. The gaffer and Kenny Dalglish, who had become manager of Liverpool and was also a Scot, of course, had a bit of a slanging match of their own. Kenny said his little daughter spoke more sense than Alex. You can imagine our gaffer's reaction!

The trouble for us was that Liverpool still had the last word in the Championship. We never really got close enough to them to make it an argument because we still dropped too many soft points. We lost 1–0 at Norwich and this time we were the ones who got the lashing from Ferguson. He was so angry he had us in on the Sunday for a bit more stick.

Still, we finished runners-up in the League, which was a big improvement on the year before. We had a really good run at the end of the season to secure that second spot, winning eight and drawing two of our final ten League matches. I remember saying to the lads before the game at Oxford that we ought to back ourselves to win that day. We were going so well and had everybody fit, and I'd read in the paper that they were going to try out a load of young

Norman Whiteside, Arnold Muhren and Ray Wilkins join in the celebrations after I scored against Brighton in the 1983 FA Cup final replay.

It's ours – lifting the FA Cup in 1983.

When I signed for Manchester United, flanked by Ron Atkinson and Martin Edwards, Les Olive, the club secretary, couldn't bear to watch!

Shaking the hand of a football god, Diego Maradona, before our great European Cup-Winners' Cup quarter-final victory against Barcelona in 1984.

Scoring my second goal on that never-to-be-forgotten night at Old Trafford.

New boys Jesper Olsen, Alan Brazil and
Gordon Strachan arrived for the start of
the 1984–85 season.

Alex Ferguson and Archie Knox delivered
their message loud and clear.

All smiles as we win the FA Cup again in 1985.

The 27-second goal that gave us a flying start in the 1982 World Cup finals.

Terry Butcher brings me back down to earth after that early strike against France.

Completing my hat-trick in England's 8–0 win against Turkey in Istanbul, 1984.

Taking a break in Mexico City on England's 1985 summer tour.

'You're Bobby, I'm Bryan!'

A challenge by Morocco's Mostafa El Biaz ended my 1986 World Cup.

With fellow goalscorers Tony Adams, Peter Beardsley and John Barnes after our 4–1 win against Yugoslavia in 1987.

Gary Lineker and I have something to shout about after my goal against Holland in the 1988 European Championship.

This time it doesn't look too serious – receiving treatment from England physio Fred Street.

It was a proud day when I collected my OBE at Buckingham Palace, accompanied by Denise, Claire and Charlotte.

players. The odds were good and I said we had to get on this. We won comfortably, 2–0. I told the lads we should back ourselves every week if it made us play better. I don't see anything wrong in betting on your own team to win. Betting on your team to lose is a different matter entirely.

We looked as if we were on the up again, especially with some of the signings we'd made. As well as Viv, Choccy and Steve Bruce, the gaffer brought in one for the future, a sixteen-year-old kid called Lee Sharpe, from Torquay.

Lee had to wait until his seventeenth birthday before he was officially our player, but it was a smart move to get him. He could play anywhere down the left side, he was quick and a great crosser of the ball. Apart from his terrific talent, he was also a lovely lad and became one of the most popular players at the club. He should have gone on to achieve a lot more than he did, both at club level and for England.

I think he allowed too many outside influences to affect him. A good-looking, easygoing lad, he had a really nice girlfriend. They liked going to nightclubs and he perhaps got drawn too much into that lifestyle. Eventually, his playing suffered. He didn't quite have the dedication to get the best out of his undoubted ability. It was a pity because he could and should have been a really top player. He was just too lackadaisical. He wanted everybody to love him – which they did – but you could see the difference in somebody like Ryan Giggs, who had not only the talent but also the discipline needed to succeed at the very top. Ryan could go on playing till he's forty because he has that dedication and hunger, as so many of the United players of his generation had.

Lee had just as much pace and stamina as Ryan when he came to the club – that's why he played in the European Cup-Winners' Cup final and had such a good game – but he wasn't as dedicated and in the end you can't blame anybody else for that. Once you start thinking it's easy at that level, the only way is down. He retired from League football at a relatively young age and was playing non-League on a part-time basis while he was still in his early thirties.

As you would expect, the gaffer soon worked out that Lee liked to enjoy himself, and watched him like a hawk. One day he got wind that Sharpey was having a bit of a party at his house. Lee had invited Ryan and one or two other young lads round, but the gaffer was having none of it. He'd found out that Lee and Ryan had been to Blackpool a couple of nights earlier, when we weren't supposed to go out, and now they were partying. So he went round to Lee's house, knocked on the door and threw them all out. He told them there was no way they were going to have a party. The thing is that this was four days before our next match. Now you could say it was over the top and plenty did, but that's Fergie for you and that's where his discipline came in, especially with the younger lads.

Lee has tried to make out that the boss victimised him and ruined his career, yet admits there were times when he was unprofessional. The fact is that we all knew what the gaffer was like and where we stood with him. If you weren't professional enough, didn't train and prepare properly and didn't perform, he didn't want you in the club – but he was fair and smart enough to give you a bit of slack as long as you didn't let yourself or anybody else down. Eric Cantona didn't always conform and people said the gaffer showed favouritism towards him, but no manager got more out of Eric because he knew how to handle him. That was good man-management.

He expected senior players to be responsible, trustworthy professionals. It was the young players he hammered to try to make them dedicated to their job. I don't think it was ever a case of bullying them. He genuinely wanted to get across to them the importance of discipline while they were still young and impressionable. He was on their case all the time and I'm sure that's partly why so many good lads came through the system at United.

A YTS boy would walk through the restaurant at the Cliff, where everybody was having a bite to eat after training, and suddenly hear the gaffer bark, 'What were you doing out last night?'

'I was only out for an hour or so, Gaffer,' the kid might say.

'Where were you?' Ferguson would persist. The kid would tell him – maybe he had been to a pub. The gaffer would then want to know, 'What were you doing there?'

Now, the gaffer wouldn't have a clue that this kid had been out. He was just testing him and if the kid had said, 'I was at home, Gaffer,' Ferguson would say, 'Well that's OK, then.' He'd do things like that and every now and then catch them out. It was his way of finding out about them and keeping them on their toes – all part of teaching them good discipline.

The younger players also had to learn some cruel lessons from the older players. When Giggsy broke into the first team, Brucie and I told him he ought to ask the gaffer for a club car. We knew what the response would be and listened from outside the door as the poor lad got a rollicking. A few years earlier we set up Graeme Hogg. A guy called Freddie Frost had a garage near the Cliff and he looked after the players' cars. He had an old wreck at his place that had been in so many crashes it was barely held together. So we put this old wreck outside the training ground and told Hogg that his club car had been delivered. He went out, rubbing his hands, only to see this pile of junk.

As well as Lee Sharpe, the boss had signed a proven striker – Mark Hughes. Bringing Sparky back to the club, for £1.8 million, was great news for us. He'd been to Barcelona, then to Bayern Munich on loan, and had clearly learned a lot about the game on his travels. He returned to United a more complete player. The club also forked out a world-record fee for a goalkeeper – £750,000 – to sign Jim Leighton from Aberdeen. He had a good reputation in Scottish football and I'd been impressed when I saw him playing for his country. He looked good for us. You felt you didn't have to worry about him. Mind you, he did have problems with his kicking. It was more of a slide-tackle than a kick! Jim was another piece of the boss's jigsaw, slotted in place.

One player the gaffer didn't get was Paul Gascoigne, which was a pity for us and for Gazza. I was into Gazza's ribs about coming to us because I thought he would have been brilliant for United and Old Trafford was the perfect stage for him. He annoyed the boss because he said he would sign for us and then went to Tottenham. I seem to remember he told the press at the time that he felt he would be overshadowed by me, which was rubbish. I'm sure we would have been great together. He would have got on with all the lads. There is also a suggestion that he felt intimidated by Fergie, but I don't think that was the reason he decided against United. As Gazza says in his book, he wanted to buy his mam and dad a house and the extra money Spurs offered up front enabled him to do that.

Gazza now admits to me that he should have joined United and his career would have benefited. He knows he missed out big-style. He would have been one of the main players in the side the gaffer built and he probably wouldn't have got into so much trouble off the pitch. He found the bright lights of London too hard to resist and, of course, it's easier to get lost in a city the size of London. You're more likely to get noticed in Manchester, as a few of us discovered! You knew that if the gaffer found out what you were up to, you were going to get hammered. I played with Gazza for England and had him at Middlesbrough, but I just wish we'd been side by side at United. He had fantastic talent.

With Steve Bruce established alongside Paul McGrath at the centre of our defence, Kevin Moran headed for a new life in Spain and left old pals who were full of optimism for the 1988–89 championship. I thought we would kick on after coming second the previous season, but instead we went backwards. We seemed to have difficulty blending all the new players into a team. Jesper Olsen went to France as the gaffer kept switching things around. Jesper played really well for us at home, but in the away games he went missing too often. You can't afford that, especially at the level we wanted to achieve. We just couldn't get it right and the Hairdryer was waiting for us after we let a lead slip at Wimbledon in the League. There was even worse for Viv Anderson following our defeat in the Littlewoods Cup at the same ground, a few weeks later.

Terry Gibson, one of those players who didn't make it at Old Trafford, dumped us out of the competition with his two goals. Viv, who went on as a substitute ten minutes from the end, was attacked by John Fashanu, Wimbledon's gangling striker, as he came down the tunnel. Fashanu hit him and then kicked him when he was on the ground. Viv jumped up and chased after him, but Fash locked himself in the dressing room. None of the other Wimbledon players could get in. Most of our lads and the gaffer saw it. Viv had to have three stitches in a cut eye. Fashanu was suspended for three matches and fined £2,000 by the FA over the incident. Viv was banned for one match and fined £750. The Commission blamed him for provoking Fash.

That was a bit rich considering the provocation you got playing against Wimbledon in those days. They were at best awkward to play against, at worst they were just bully boys – 'put it into the mixer' and that sort of thing. They would always try to intimidate you and talk to you on the pitch, telling you what they were going to do to you, how they were going to snap you in half and all that stuff. I didn't get much of that personally. They picked on opponents they thought they could bully. The main ones who went out to intimidate the opposition were Fashanu, Vinnie Jones and Dennis Wise. Alan Cork would also be at it, up front.

I never really got involved until I felt they were going too far with my team-mates. I did once try to snap Vinnie in half. I also got stuck into Fash. He moaned like hell about a tackle I made on him at Old Trafford. As captain, I felt I had to stand by my players and back then the referees didn't clamp down as hard on bad tackles as they do now. Roy Keane had the same attitude when he stood up for Gary Neville and warned off Arsenal's Patrick Vieira in the tunnel before a match at Highbury in 2005. Players and fans want to see that from their skipper. I think it's good for the game that a club such as Wimbledon can come from nowhere to the top division and win the FA Cup. To do that on their resources was terrific. It gives hope to all smaller clubs. I just didn't like their bullying tactics, but then that was the only way some of them could play. They did amazingly well when they had so many players with limited ability.

Another player who didn't make it at Old Trafford came back to haunt us a couple of months later. Peter Davenport, who moved on to Middlesbrough, scored the only goal in our match at Ayresome Park. This was after we'd beaten Forest and Liverpool in our other Christmas holiday fixtures and people were suggesting we could launch a bid for the title. That was never on and we knew it. We were going through a transition period and realised we might have a bit more pain to come.

I got my dose of it in a third-round FA Cup-tie against Queen's Park Rangers at Old Trafford. It was still 0–0 in the last minute and we were pushing for a winner. I went up and when the ball came in from the wing, I flung myself at it. It flew just wide, which was bad enough, but their defender, Danny Maddix, went for it at the same time and butted me on the side of the temple. The collision knocked me out and I swallowed my tongue. I was dead to the world. Eventually, I was carried off and came round back in the dressing room area. I needed stitches in my cut mouth and spent the night in hospital.

We got past QPR at the third attempt, but lost to Nottingham Forest in the sixth round and that was effectively the end of our season. The boss tried one or two younger players during the season and Clayton Blackmore was one of those who showed promise, but there weren't many consolations for us. We faded badly over the last few weeks, losing matches against teams we should have hammered. The fans showed what they thought of it when a crowd of only 23,368 – United's lowest at Old Trafford for eighteen years – turned up for the match against Wimbledon. Those who did come were singing 'What a load of rubbish' before Choccy scored the winner in injury time.

The Merseyside fortress finally fell that season, but no thanks to us. Arsenal were the new champions after Michael Thomas – a player I later had at Middlesbrough – scored an amazing late clincher at Anfield. They had to win by two clear goals to pip Liverpool and did just that. We were eleventh in the final table, sandwiched between Millwall and Wimbledon. It was a big blow to fall off so badly after finishing second the year before – a poor effort and way below our expectations.

The boss had made plenty of changes already, but there was a massive turnover of players in 1989. Gordon left before the end of that 1988–89 season to join Leeds United, yet another player who would come back to haunt us. Two of my pals from the old school went during the summer. Paul McGrath signed for Aston Villa and Norman Whiteside joined Everton. In came Mike Phelan, a Steady Eddie midfield player, from Norwich; Neil Webb, a stylish England international midfield player, from Nottingham Forest; Gary Pallister, a gangling centre-half from Middlesbrough, who cost a British record transfer fee of £2.3 million; Paul Ince, an aggressive midfield player, from West Ham; and Danny Wallace, a quicksilver winger from Southampton.

All sorts of speculation had been rife about Paul and Norman, as much because of events off the pitch as on it. Paul certainly had serious problems with the booze, as he readily admits. He came in for a match one day and we could tell he'd had a drink. So could the gaffer. He saw it straightaway and there was no way back after that. Paul had been given one or two warnings by the club about his drinking. He almost killed himself when he crashed his car just around the corner from my house. He went through the windscreen and was very lucky to survive.

It was a great shame we had to lose him because he was a genuinely great player, one of the most naturally gifted footballers I've ever seen. He played brilliantly at Villa for several years after he left us. He was also a really lovely man, a gentle giant, but the boss made it clear to everybody at the club that he didn't want people who drank too much and that's why he got rid of Paul. He'd also had his card marked by the medical people. They told him that Paul's knee injury was always going to be a problem. At Villa he hardly ever trained because of that knee, yet he turned out on match days and had a terrific career with them.

I was just as sorry to see Norman leave. He'd been at the club since he was a young lad and we became great mates. I think he looked up to me a bit and I kind of took him under my wing. Norman had his injury problems, as well. His knee started affecting him at an early age and he had to have an operation when he was still young. He ended up with arthritis in his knee joint. His kneecap was effectively eroding away.

Norman had been one of the best sprinters over in Northern Ireland, but the knee problems took a bit of his pace from him. He started out as a striker and had terrific ability. Some people compare the young Norman with Wayne Rooney, but for me he would have become the closest to a Kenny Dalglish if he hadn't suffered that injury. He was very similar in style to Kenny, fantastic with his back to play and a great finisher. He had good control for a big lad. He was also as tough as old boots – even as a lad. In fact, he seemed never to have been a lad.

He was absolutely fearless, scared of no one. I remember when we played Barcelona in the European Cup-Winners' Cup at Old Trafford. I said to Norman before the match that they'd got a couple of big centre-halves with reputations for being really hard, so don't go upsetting them early in the game. I told him just to play his football. Well, in the first five minutes he cemented one of them and sent him into the advertising boards. So that caused a mass brawl straightaway. That was Norman. He found himself in bother with a few referees down the years, but he was one of those players you'd rather have with you than against you.

Moving to midfield helped him because then he was facing the game and it was easier on his knee. He was able to play on longer than he might otherwise have done. Even so, his career was cruelly cut short. Everton never really saw the best of him. He had only a couple of years at Goodison Park before he was forced to retire. With a talent like that, he could have achieved so much more if it hadn't been for the injury.

The new arrivals were going to be under the microscope, but no one got more attention than the guy who was introduced to us at the start of the 1989–90 season as our new club owner. One or two people had been interested in buying control of United from Martin Edwards over the years and when Michael Knighton came down to the training ground with the chairman on the day before our first match to meet us, he seemed fine. He shook everybody's hand and made all the right noises. We were told he was a mega property speculator with a castle in Scotland. He was supposedly going to pay Martin Edwards £10 million for his controlling share of the club and find another £10 million to develop the Stretford End.

I think Martin had just had enough. He, and his father Louis before him, were never really appreciated by the fans. They were more likely to give Martin stick than credit for the way he built up the club and stadium, and always supported his managers with funds. I dealt with him directly quite a lot on behalf of the players and always found him fair and reasonable. The manager didn't particularly want the hassle of dealing with players over bonuses and promotional stuff, so we had a players' committee to negotiate with the chairman. It was never a case of, 'It's my club – like it or lump it.' He listened to our point of view and took it into account.

Anyway, on 19 August, when we kicked off the season at home to Arsenal, it looked as though the takeover was going through and Knighton would be in charge of United. We were sitting in the dressing room, getting ready for that opening match, and couldn't believe our eyes. We had a TV in the dressing room, showing pictures from out on the pitch, and there was Knighton, in our team kit, juggling the ball. Well, first we were amazed and then we were killing ourselves laughing, saying to each other, 'Who does he think he is?' As if that wasn't enough, he came into the dressing room just before we went out for the match. I was sitting next to Mark Hughes and we were wondering, 'What's he going to do next?'

Well, what he did next was to blow kisses at us! He said, 'Do it for me. I love you, lads.' Then we realised what he was really like – a head-case. We could see that he was just on a massive ego trip. Eventually, after a lot of toing and froing and excuses, the deal fell through, thank goodness. We were lucky. Some years later, Carlisle weren't so lucky, as they will tell you. Knighton moved in there and left them in an awful mess. His involvement with us was one of the most bizarre episodes I've experienced in the whole of my football career.

The signing of Gary Pallister, universally known as Pally, was a different matter altogether, although a few questions were raised about him in his first few months at United. He was still a bit weak and spindly-legged when he joined us. United put him on a weights programme, which helped his development and he suddenly started to mature. He and Steve Bruce went on to become a great partnership for the club.

It was like a breath of fresh air for the rest of us having Pally on board because for a while he got the hairdryer treatment almost exclusively. He did struggle to start with and the gaffer gave him some ferocious blasts, but he had ability, all right, and he had pace. Once his physique began to develop he became some player. Nobody could beat him in the air. He could see off anybody. After those first four or five months he settled in and the fans took to him – and again, he was such a great lad. We were bringing in players with ability and character, so we felt we had to turn things around.

Some might have had doubts about that when we were thumped 5–1 away by our neighbours, Manchester City. It was the low point, especially for the gaffer. Steve and I were injured and just relieved to be sitting in the directors' box that day at Maine Road. Any derby defeat is hard to take for the team and for the fans, but people still go on about that match – City fans, in particular. That's why I'm glad I wasn't playing.

I was back in the side when we went to Coventry, but I shouldn't have been on the pitch for the whole match. How I didn't get sent off for what I did to David Speedie, I'll never know. Speedie badly fouled Lee Sharpe in the first few minutes, then smashed Lee Martin, another young lad who had come into the team. Speedie went down his Achilles. In the second half he threw an elbow at Pally and split his head open. Pally had to have stitches. So I thought, 'I've had enough of him.' I absolutely belted Speedie with a tackle. I booted him so hard he must have gone at least five yards through the air. He got carried off and was on crutches at the end. All the Coventry players came running over, going crazy. I remember their captain, Trevor Peake coming towards me. I told him, 'You grab me and you're next.'

The referee eventually booked me, but that was the one day when I would have taken a sending off. I didn't intend to hurt him seriously. I just wanted him to know he couldn't get away with that kind of behaviour. We were two goals up and cruising with half an hour to go, so I knew it wouldn't have cost the team. We went on to win 4–1. Speedie was a decent player, no doubt about that, but he could also be dirty. When he'd gone in to three of our lads in the way he did and we'd got no protection from the referee, I felt I had to do something about it. Somehow I got away with it, but at least that balanced the books for the sending off at Sunderland.

It is a hard game and you have to take stick as well as give it, but players know what is acceptable and what isn't. Take our matches with Liverpool. They were always massive and still are. You had players with great ability but also aggression and determination. They had Jimmy Case, who went on to Brighton and Southampton, and then Steve McMahon, two terrific players but two of the hardest in the business as well. You knew what it was going to be like against them so you always tried to get in with the first hard tackle. They never complained because they were looking for the chance to come back at you. I caught Macca a few beauties over the years and he tried the same. That's the way it was and what you had to do to win your territory in midfield. You always wanted to put down your marker. You respected players like that. They were real pros. In fact, for all the hatred between United and Liverpool fans – and the occasional clash of managers – the players always got on really well. I think that's because there was that mutual respect. It was totally different with such players as Speedie and some of the Wimbledon players.

Brian Clough once had a go at me, saying I should stick to playing football and stop kicking people. I never knew Clough. To win the European Cup twice with Nottingham Forest was nothing short of amazing but it seemed to me that he ought to concern himself with one or two kickers in his own team. I own up to getting Speedie, but that incident apart, I played it hard and fair.

There was sadness at United that November when we learned that

Jimmy Murphy, Matt Busby's number two, had died. I had met him and heard all the stories about what a great job he had done, developing all those young players who became known as the Busby Babes. The way we were playing generally at the time was no sort of tribute to his memory. A 0–0 draw at Liverpool was probably the only decent result in a run of eleven League matches without a win – the club's worst for eighteen years. We slumped down towards the relegation zone and the manager took a battering from the fans and the media. Chants of 'Fergie out' were ringing around Old Trafford.

I don't think he was ever really in danger of getting the sack. The board had given him so much money to rebuild the team and they had to be patient. The team needed time to settle. The manager has said that he was puzzled at the time and asked himself whether he was doing things right. He felt he was and that it was just a case of getting the pieces to fit and the confidence to flow. We saw so often that players found it hard to cope with the charisma and expectations at United, and every year that went by without the title, the pressure became worse. The burden of '67 got heavier all the time and people were asking if the club would ever be champions again. One thing was for sure – we weren't going to be champions that season.

I missed part of that terrible mid-season spell with a groin injury and had to have an operation, but there was some good news for me. I was awarded an OBE in the New Year's Honours. We had a great day when we went down to Buckingham Palace. Denise, Claire and Charlotte went with me. The only disappointment was that we couldn't take our son Ben, as well. We were allowed to take only two of the kids so Ben, who was born on 2 September 1988, missed out. The girls loved it, getting all dressed up. The Queen asked me if I was going to be fit for the World Cup finals that summer and I said, 'Yes, hopefully everything will be OK.'

In the car, driving away afterwards, our Claire asked, 'Dad, what did the Queen say?'

'She was asking me who was my favourite pop group.'

'What did you say?'

'Queen.'

'Just shut up, will you,' Denise said.

Even though our form in the League was so bad, I never worried that we might be relegated. That wasn't arrogance or complacency. I just knew we had enough ability to get ourselves out of trouble. The papers were saying that if we were knocked out of the FA Cup in our third-round tie at Forest, that would be the end for Alex Ferguson. I still don't believe he would have gone, but the fact is we won at Forest and everybody now points to that match as the turning point. Mark Robins, a young striker who came up through the ranks, headed the only goal in that match, early in the second half. It was certainly a vital goal because of the positive effect it had. Sometimes it takes just one goal, one moment, to change the course of events.

We'd been knocked out of the Littlewoods Cup in the third round and we were at the wrong end of the First Division table, so the FA Cup was a lifeline. We kept on getting drawn away, but we kept on winning – 1–0 at Hereford, 3–2 at Newcastle and 1–0 at Sheffield United. We reached the semi-finals without the benefit of a single home tie. We also started doing enough in the League to stop the talk about relegation. Now all the talk was about a possible trip to Wembley.

Injury limited me to twenty League appearances that season, but I was back for our semi-final against Oldham Athletic. It turned out to be an epic. The Second Division side gave us a jolt by taking the lead at Maine Road. I equalised and we seemed to have it won when Neil Webb put us in front, but they drew level and forced the tie into extra time. Choccy gave us the advantage again and they went for broke. I think they had five strikers on by the end and it paid off. Roger Palmer made it 3–3 and earned Oldham a replay.

Choccy put us in front early in the second half of the replay, but again Oldham refused to lie down. They had some decent players, including Denis Irwin, who joined us that summer. Denis was one of two Oldham players who hit the woodwork before Andy Ritchie, a former United striker, equalised. We were six minutes from the end of extra time when young Robins, who set the ball rolling back in the third round at Forest, got the winner. Mark was an out-and-out goalscorer, although he didn't have a lot more to his game. That's probably why he didn't develop at United the way the manager and staff hoped, and eventually he moved on. People at the club said it was a similar story with Andy Ritchie.

We limped home thirteenth in the First Division – well behind Wimbledon, let alone Liverpool, who reclaimed the title – but at least we spared ourselves an embarrassing fight against relegation and were able to concentrate on the FA Cup. Our last League match was at home to Charlton. We won 1–0, with a goal by Pally. He was also presented with his supporters' player of the year trophy. That showed how he'd turned things around for himself at the club and it was also a pointer to the future for him.

The Cup final, against Crystal Palace, was our chance to prove we were taking the club in the right direction at last – and it was a cracker. We didn't have the best of starts against our old mate Steve Coppell's team, and they went in front. My header brought us the equaliser and Sparky made it 2–1. They brought on Ian Wright, who was coming back from injury, and he tilted the match in Palace's favour. He levelled the scores to take us into extra time, then put them 3–2 ahead when Jim Leighton failed to deal with a cross. Thankfully, Sparky came up with another goal seven minutes from time.

It's probably true to say Palace surprised us a bit, but when you look back now at the players they had, they shouldn't have done. Nigel Martyn was an excellent keeper and still is. Ian Wright and Mark Bright were outstanding individual players and formed a terrific partnership. They also had John Salako and Geoff Thomas. There was plenty of ability in that team.

The boss had another surprise in store for us when he named the team for the replay, the following Thursday. He dropped Jim Leighton and brought in Les Sealey. Jim did have a bit of a bad game on the Saturday, but none of us had any idea what the gaffer was planning. It was about the first time we saw the real, professional ruthlessness of Alex Ferguson. Jim was devastated. As far as I can remember, the gaffer pulled Jim to one side and told him before he announced the team. Jim was so upset he found it hard to sit through the replay. We all felt for him.

Les, who was a hell of a character, came to us on loan and couldn't have dreamed he'd play in the Cup final. He made a couple of important saves and played his part well – not that Palace produced much in the positive sense. They had done really well in the first match and deserved all the credit they got for that, but in the replay they resorted to desperate and cynical measures. Basically, they tried to kick lumps out of us. It backfired on them, though. We scored the only goal and took the Cup back to Old Trafford. We had an unlikely match winner in Lee Martin, our left-back. He brought down the ball from Neil Webb's pass and hit it into the roof of the net on the hour. I headed against the bar, but it didn't matter, just as the twinge from a jarred foot didn't bother me. A few minutes later I became the first United captain to lift the FA Cup for a third time.

That night made up for what had been a largely miserable season, not only for me but for everyone at the club. It was an especially important win for the manager. He'd had the fans and the press on his back, but now he had a piece of silverware to show his critics and I was sure he would have more before too long. It was also a crucial first trophy for Steve Bruce, Pally and Paul Ince. They now knew they could achieve success and would have the confidence to go on from there.

We had the usual lap of honour and celebrations after the match, but one man in our party was obviously finding it hard to get into the spirit of the occasion. Poor old Jim was still distraught. Les gave him his medal, which was a smashing, generous gesture. There was nothing anybody could do, though, to take away his pain. Les went off to his family in London, while the rest of us headed north. Had Alex done the right thing in dropping Jim? Well, we won the Cup so, based on the outcome, you have to say the manager got it right. It's all about the result.

The gaffer would have a few more difficult decisions to make in the seasons ahead, but he and the whole team had a fresh belief after that 1990 FA Cup triumph. It was time we started mixing it with the big boys. We needed a massive improvement in the League and the end of the ban on English clubs in Europe meant we had the incentive of a Cup-Winners' Cup competition to look forward to the following season.

9
EUROSTARS

ALEX FERGUSON'S MANCHESTER UNITED were on their way, although
I couldn't join them for the first three and a half months of the
1990–91 journey. I had ripped my Achilles tendon in England's
second match at the World Cup finals in Italy and had to have
another operation. It was bad enough having to pull out of the
tournament at that stage again, but then the long recovery period
meant I could only watch my club-mates try to follow up our FA Cup
success.

I also had to read and listen to more speculation about my future.
The papers printed my 'medical casebook' and questioned how many
more injuries my body could take. I needed no reminding about the
catalogue of breaks, tears, strains and knocks. I keep my original
medical notes and records, along with albums of press cuttings,
photos and mementos that my parents started collecting at the
beginning of my career. Hamstring and calf problems were added
to my casualty list that season, piling on the frustration.

The positive thing from United's point of view was that the squad
had become stronger and was still improving. Neil Webb showed
what an exceptional player he could be in midfield and it's just a pity
he snapped his Achilles tendon at the peak of his career. He had
surgery but was never quite the same player again. Another important player for us at that time was Clayton Blackmore, because he

was so versatile. He came in as a midfield player and had the touch and vision for that role. He was also a terrific striker of the ball and probably should have scored more goals than he did, yet that was his best season for us and he spent a lot of it playing left-back.

Denis Irwin joined us from Oldham for £625,000 during the summer, and proved to be a significant signing. He went about his job in a very quiet, understated way, yet when I talk to players and fans now, it becomes clear that they never underestimated him. Everybody appreciates what he brought to United. He had a bit of everything. He was terrific with either foot and could play right-back or left-back. He had pace, he could tackle, he read the game, and he had a great attitude. It's no surprise that he played into his late thirties. It says a lot for his ability that over the next few years, in a team that had so many gifted players, Denis regularly took free-kicks and penalties. He was a superb striker of the ball and very cool under pressure. He became a fixture in an excellent defence, alongside Steve Bruce, Gary Pallister and, later, Paul Parker.

A few years later I had an interesting trip to the Cork branch of the United Supporters' Club with Denis and Roy Keane, who were both from that part of Ireland. We had a night out with Denis's relatives and it reminded me of nights out with my family and friends in Chester-le-Street. It was great.

Our unlikely FA Cup final hero, Les Sealey, was another new recruit. The goalkeeper signed a permanent transfer deal and made the position his own that season. Jim Leighton had spells on loan at Arsenal and Reading before returning to Scotland to join Dundee.

Our League form was still up and down in the early part of the season and Liverpool thumped us 4–0, as if to let us know they were still top dogs. But we made a solid start in the European Cup-Winners' Cup and had no real trouble in the early rounds of the League Cup, which had become the Rumbelows Cup. Goals by Clayton and Neil Webb got us on our way in Europe against the

Hungarian side, Pecsi Munkas, and Brian McClair completed a 3–0 aggregate win. The lads cruised through the next round, beating Wrexham 5–0 over the two legs. In the Rumbelows Cup, Halifax made us work for our 3–1 victory before we got some revenge for that earlier League hammering by knocking out Liverpool, also 3–1.

The Rumbelows Cup draw then paired us with Arsenal, always a tasty fixture. Our League match against them at Old Trafford the previous month had made headlines for what was described as a '21-man brawl'. As usually happens in these situations, most of those supposedly involved were trying to pull players away and it wasn't as bad as it looked – more handbags than real fighting – but there was a huge outcry and both clubs ended up in front of the FA. Arsenal were docked two points, United one. The two clubs were also fined £50,000 each. There was always bad blood between the two teams and it's much the same to this day. Trouble would start with an incident involving a couple of players, not necessarily the same ones every time, and flare up. We traded goals instead of punches down at Highbury in the Cup-tie and they couldn't handle us. We murdered them 6–2 – Arsenal's biggest home defeat since 1921 – to reach the quarter-finals. Lee Sharpe scored a hat-trick and was unstoppable.

My first League or Cup appearance of the season was still a few days away, but I did play for eighteen minutes as a substitute on 20 November in my testimonial match against Celtic. A crowd of 41,658 at Old Trafford made it a fantastic and emotional occasion for me. Our Claire, Charlotte and Ben, dressed in different kits, were with me as I walked out on to the pitch, carrying the FA Cup. Celtic played it like a proper match and their fans were brilliant. They were regular visitors to our ground for testimonials and were always magnificent. Our fans responded and the atmosphere was amazing. I was mobbed at the end, but I never minded that. You always treasure that kind of bond with supporters. For the record, Celtic won 3–1, but that was one defeat that didn't bother me too much.

I suppose it would have been natural on a night like that to have thoughts about life after playing, particularly as I'd been out for so long with injury, but at the age of thirty-three I felt I had plenty more to give and achieve as a player. Management didn't figure in my plans. I was convinced I could recover my fitness and just as certain we would put other trophies alongside the FA Cup. My comeback match was at home to Leeds on 8 December. I came on twenty minutes from the end to another fantastic reception from our fans. We drew 1–1, but I felt OK and was just relieved to be playing again.

We began our defence of the FA Cup with a 2–1 win against Queen's Park Rangers and then made it to the last four of the Rumbelows Cup, thanks to Mark Hughes' goals against Southampton. He scored the equaliser at The Dell and then got a hat-trick as we won 3–2 at home. Sparky was on target again to get us past Bolton in the fourth round of the FA Cup, but we couldn't keep our hold on the old pot much longer. We went out 2–1 at Norwich after I missed a late chance.

That made our Rumbelows Cup semi-final against Leeds even more important. Both teams were on the up and the first leg, at Old Trafford, was predictably tight and tense. This is another fixture with 'previous' and there is no love lost between the two sets of fans. Our supporters were celebrating after a late goal by Choccy gave us a 2–1 advantage to take to Elland Road. Lee Sharpe scored even later in the second leg to give us a 3–1 aggregate win and book another Wembley Cup final. Mind you, we also had Les to thank. He made a great save when we were still only a goal in front. He liked his Cup football, did Les.

Next on our Cup agenda was a meeting with the French team, Montpellier. They may not have learned much from Archie Knox's bizarre training routine at the Cliff, but they thought they had the measure of us after the first leg of our Cup-Winners' Cup quarter-final at Old Trafford. They equalised Choccy's first-minute goal when Lee Martin put the ball in his own net and they celebrated at the end as if they were already through to the semis. They were jumping in the air and hugging each other in delight. We didn't play as well as we could in the first match, but put that right in the second leg. Clayton smashed in a free-kick that their keeper couldn't hold and Steve Bruce made it 2–0 on the night, 3–1 on aggregate, from the penalty spot.

The only downside for me was a second booking in the competition, which put me out of the first leg of the semi-final, against Legia Warsaw. I made up for that by finding perhaps my best form of the season to that point in a 3–0 win at Norwich and then scoring my first goal of the term in a 3–1 victory against Derby. After all the problems it was good to be playing regularly and playing well again. I was coming to the end of my seven-year contract and the club showed their faith in me by offering a new two-year deal. I had no hesitation in accepting. As for the European tie with the Poles, I needn't have worried. The lads virtually put us into the final with a 3–1 win in Warsaw.

The squad couldn't have been in better spirits as we headed to Wembley for the Rumbelows Cup final against Sheffield Wednesday and a reunion with our old boss, Ron Atkinson. But at the end of what was a hugely disappointing day for us, it was the familiar smile on Big Ron's face that the cameras wanted to capture. We were beaten by a smashing goal from John Sheridan and had no complaints about the 1–0 win for Wednesday. They were a reasonable side and played pretty well on the day. Ron obviously enjoyed the result, but he didn't gloat. He shook hands with us and I congratulated him. I've no doubt he let himself go later. That was the only semi-final or final I lost with United.

Just three days after that defeat, we had some semi-final business to finish against Legia Warsaw. A 1–1 draw at Old Trafford was more than enough, giving us victory by 4–2 on aggregate and taking the club to their second European final. This was the Cup-Winners' Cup rather than the Champions' Cup, and we may not have been rated as highly as the team that won the premier prize for United in 1968, but we all felt it was a hugely significant landmark for the club. Our opponents in Rotterdam were Barcelona, the Spanish champions and one of the great clubs in world football, managed by Johan Cruyff, one of the greatest players of all time.

We weren't in contention for the Championship, so the gaffer concentrated on trying to make sure he had his strongest possible side available for the final. Some players were injured, some were rested, so not surprisingly we lost our last two matches before going to Rotterdam. I got a whack from Anders Limpar in our match away to Arsenal, the new champions, and went off as a precaution after twelve minutes. I was also struggling with a hernia problem right up to the Rotterdam game and couldn't do any shooting practice. I knew I needed an operation but was determined to put it off until after the final. Gary Pallister gave us another scare when he limped off against Crystal Palace. Fortunately, though, the boss was able to name a full-strength team to face Barcelona.

We played like a full-strength team, as well. We performed really well that night. In fact, we battered them in the first half without managing to score, but we were so confident I had no doubt we'd get the breakthrough. It came midway through the second half, from my free-kick. Brucie headed towards goal and Sparky, against his old club, was on hand to make sure. There was some debate at the time about whether the goal should have been Steve's, but it was Sparky's. So was the second, six minutes later, and this time there were no arguments. I sent Sparky through, he went round the keeper and, from an ever-narrowing angle, drilled the ball into the far corner. It was classic Sparky and our hundredth goal of the season. They pulled one back when Les Sealey made a rare mistake ten minutes from the end and put us under a bit of pressure. Clayton had to clear one off the line, but we deservedly held on.

Six years after English clubs were thrown out of European football because of the Heysel tragedy, an English club had won a European trophy. It was a great night for our country, but in particular for United and our fans. They made up two-thirds of the crowd and created a tremendous atmosphere. To go back into continental competition after all that time and win a cup at the first attempt spoke volumes for the progress of the club and our potential to go even further.

It was a proud and satisfying moment for me when I collected that trophy. I felt I had genuinely earned the honour. A lot of people say my performance against Barcelona at Old Trafford in 1984 was my best for United, but I honestly believe I played better that night in Rotterdam. I didn't score a couple of goals, as I had done seven years earlier, but I felt I controlled the final and was right on top of my game. It was an especially good feeling after having so many injury problems and people writing me off. I knew I wasn't finished and I proved it that night. The older you get the more you appreciate opportunities and occasions like that. I had no intention of letting it pass me by. You don't get to win a European trophy every year. United brought over the players' wives and girlfriends for the final and we had a big party at our hotel afterwards.

We still had a League match to play, so that gave us the chance to celebrate with all our fans at Old Trafford. In fact, it was a double celebration because our opponents, Tottenham, brought along their newly won FA Cup to show off as well. Gary Mabbutt, the Spurs captain, and I paraded our silverware in front of a capacity crowd. Not surprisingly, given the carnival atmosphere, we also shared the points in a 1–1 draw.

That point confirmed our sixth place in the First Division. It wasn't bad, considering our recent finishing positions, but not good enough. Two cup wins in two seasons had given us all a lift and it was time we had a serious go for the Championship. We definitely had the makings of a title-challenging team, but the gaffer was still aiming to strengthen it. Interestingly, he played a young Australian goalkeeper, Mark Bosnich, in that match against Spurs. Bosnich went back to Sydney the following month because he couldn't get a work permit, but he later returned to United after establishing himself with Aston Villa.

In the meantime, Fergie brought in a giant blond Danish goal-keeper called Peter Schmeichel. It wasn't long before that challenging name was on the lips of football fans all over the country. None of us realised how good Pete was when he arrived at the club, but he became vital to the team. At around £600,000, he has to go down as one of United's bargain buys. To win major competitions you need a top-class goalkeeper. You only have to look at successful clubs down the years to see that. Schmeichel wasn't only a great goalkeeper because of his ability to save shots, he also had presence. When you have a big goalkeeper and big defenders, you are less likely to concede soft goals against teams chasing the game and hitting high balls into the box. We already had Pally to deal with such players as Duncan Ferguson or Lee Chapman. Now we had a big keeper.

Pete was brilliant in one-on-one situations. He made himself even bigger with those star saves, arms and legs stretched out. A great goalkeeper gives confidence to a defence. Ray Clemence did that for Liverpool and Peter Shilton did it for Forest. Schmeichel and Shilton were the best two keepers I ever played with and I wouldn't like to try to split them. Schmeichel also became known for his shouting, especially at Pally and Brucie, the two players in front of him, but that really wasn't a problem. It was Pete's way of winding them up and keeping them on their toes – and they gave Pete plenty back, don't worry about that. It was good for the three of them because it kept them alert all the time. They demanded maximum effort of one another and if you want to be successful, you've got to have that. Pete wasn't a prima donna, he just wanted to be good and win trophies. I think it shows how good Pete was that it proved so difficult for United to replace him adequately.

Another big signing for us that year was Andrei Kanchelskis, a Ukrainian flying machine. He actually made his debut for us as a triallist in the League match at Palace, just before the Cup-Winners' Cup final. He joined us on contract at the end of the season. As soon as he arrived you could see what a threat he carried. He had such quick feet. He impressed everybody in training. He was also a really nice person and a good professional, but he had a nightmare trying to pick up the English language. It took him years to get anything like a grasp of it.

The week before Andrei played his first match for us, the gaffer gave a debut to a kid who had come up through the ranks. Ryan Giggs marked the occasion by scoring the winner against Manchester City. One of the major strengths of United over the following few years was the pace and penetration of their wide players. Kanchelskis provided it down the right, Sharpe and Giggs down the left. That opened up the play and made space for our other players who had great ability on the ball. The boss also brought in Paul Parker, a nimble and versatile defender who eventually settled in at right-back, behind Kanchelskis.

There was a change on the coaching staff, too. Archie Knox, Ferguson's number two since he took over at Old Trafford five years earlier, left to become assistant manager at Rangers. He was replaced by Brian Kidd, the former United player who had returned to the club as youth-team coach. Brian was very similar to Archie in his ways. He had that enthusiasm and he got on with the players. He also brought in more modern training techniques, the sort of things they were probably already doing in Italy and Spain. He had worked in America and picked up on different aspects of training and physical conditioning. It was based on modern technology and understanding of the body.

Kiddo was excellent at one-to-one fitness work and was very good with me. I think he helped me prolong my career with his advice and routines. For instance, he advised me on the sort of exercises and running I should do, rather than go through the same routines as the younger players. He told me to do shorter running stints, stressing the importance of understanding your body and its needs. He was into that in a big way and tailored training to suit the needs of individual players. As with Archie, you could have a laugh with Brian, whereas the manager was the more serious one. I suppose I have a similar situation with Nigel Pearson, my number two at West Brom. That's the way it works.

You could sense everything was coming together – ability and commitment running right through the team and staff, people with that bit of edge. We showed it in different ways. I had my way, Steve had his, and when Roy Keane arrived, he was different again. Some were more aggressive than others. Pete's shouting was his way. It worked for him. Denis and Sparky were quiet, but they still had that will to win. Sparky seemed to change personality on the pitch. He was a fierce competitor. Pally was a really smooth passer of the ball. He could take it down and deliver it. Brucie could bring it down and also score goals, and the pair of them were great defenders. We had just about everything in that team, from back to front – technique, pace, fight and determination. There were tacklers and creators, and strong characters right through the team. It was a great team to play with and was bound to have more success.

One of the widely misunderstood characters we had was Paul Ince. He was what you might call a typical Cockney wide boy and I think he quite liked that image – brash, noisy, in your face – but there was never any harm in him. It was almost as though he felt he had to play the part. After he came to United he did quieten down a bit. He got booked quite a lot in the early stages and I think his reputation went before him, but make no mistake, Ince was a good player and very serious about his football. He wanted to better himself as a player and was willing to learn. He took things on board and did calm down.

People go on about him calling himself 'The Guv'nor', but that was just his way. He didn't mean anything by it. He wasn't trying to say he was the boss or number one. It was a bit of fun. It certainly didn't upset or bother any of the other players. Those players weren't bothered by much at all. They were all solid professionals. We all got on well and Incey and I still keep in touch. It is no surprise to me that he has gone on playing for so long.

Incey liked to come across as tough and aggressive, which he was on the pitch, but he was also a good laugh and got up to some daft pranks. One classic story is about the time he and Sharpey were negotiating new contracts and weren't happy with what they were being offered. So one day, when the boss was in his shower at the training ground, Paul and Lee crept into his office and hid behind his desk. Incey had an airgun and held it on top of the desk, pointing towards the shower. When the boss stepped out of the shower, wrapping his towel around him, Paul shouted, 'Pay us what we want or you're dead.' The boss, not surprisingly, jumped back into the shower in fright and the two lads ran off, laughing. Once Alex realised who they were, he went after them, yelling, 'I'll kill you two.'

In the end, I think Incey and the gaffer did have a bit of a personality clash. One thing that no doubt stuck in the gaffer's mind was an incident during a match at Norwich, at an important stage of the season, when Paul stood up to him more than any other player had done. The boss had one of his rages and Paul went back at him really aggressively. It wasn't just that he stood up to him, as maybe I had done – Paul tore into him. I don't think the boss respected him for that and he held it against him.

That may have been a factor behind the gaffer's decision to sell him in 1995, when he was only twenty-seven and still had a lot of football left in him. Then again, Fergie always wanted to do what he felt was best for the club and as soon as he detected that a player had an injury that was going to affect him, he would think about getting rid of him. Everybody at United was concerned that Paul had arthritis in his big toe and had problems with it. The gaffer felt the deal with Internazionale of Milan was a good one for United and sold him. So I think it was more than just a clash of personalities.

No one at the club had a stronger personality or greater winning mentality than the gaffer, even at sports quizzes and when playing cards. We used to play on the team coach. The boss never allowed serious gambling, so we played for fivers and tenners at the most. He liked to join in with the regular school. Norman and I were two of the original players, then Brucie and Pally came in. If one of us was injured, Incey would take over. I always took money off the boss playing cards and on the way home I'd pop into a shop to buy our Ben a treat. I got Ben to call the boss Uncle Alex because of the sweeties I'd buy with the winnings. Every Saturday after an away game I'd get home and say to our Ben, 'Uncle Alex has been buying you sweets again.'

Now and again, though, the boss wasn't such a nice uncle. He'd say, 'You three are ganging up on me, you don't play the game fair,' and sling the cards across the table. Whatever he did, he'd want to win.

A good example was an incident on a pre-season trip to Japan. The rain was absolutely bucketing down, so he and Archie took us under the stadium stand to do a bit of training. We fixed a rope between two girders for a game of head tennis. It was Alex's team against Archie's. I was on Archie's team and we won. So of course we're all winding up the gaffer and laughing and joking as we climb back on to the coach, but he wouldn't have it. He shouted, 'Get off that coach. We're having another game.' He wouldn't let us go until he'd had another chance to beat us. He threatened to fine us all unless we got off and played again.

Alex, like Ron, was good at quizzes. I think what happens is that when you reach the top of your profession you take an interest in all sport, because your life revolves around it. You store up all sorts of information in the memory bank. Add to that the competitive element and you get keen quiz players. We're back to the winners.

The other element our team had at the beginning of the 1991–92 season was the confidence derived from winning cups in consecutive years. And after winning a major European trophy I felt sure we would be genuine contenders for the Championship. We had real momentum.

I had my usual appointment with the surgeon's knife that summer, this time to sort out that nagging hernia problem, but I was back for the start of the season and headed our equaliser against the Republic of Ireland in a testimonial match for Sir Matt Busby. I scored another late equaliser against Leeds to keep our unbeaten start to the First Division Championship going. We were top of the League, playing with the belief and consistency of potential champions. The players who had come in over the previous couple of years were settled. The team had gelled and the blend looked just right. We felt we were capable of beating anybody. Most teams couldn't live with us.

We weren't at our best against the little Greek club, Athinaikos, as we began our defence of the European Cup-Winners' Cup, but we went through, 2–0 on aggregate. We also got past our first-round opponents in the Rumbelows Cup, Cambridge, with a 4–1 win over two legs. We fancied ourselves in every competition, but came unstuck twice in four October days. We lost 3–0 to Atletico Madrid in the first leg of our next Cup-Winners' Cup-tie and suffered our first League defeat of the season, 3–2, at one of our bogey clubs, Sheffield Wednesday.

We had a nightmare in Madrid. We were trailing 1–0 in the eighty-second minute and would have taken that, even though I had a header blocked on the line and we had a goal disallowed. Then in a madcap final few minutes, we conceded two more goals. When you lose by that margin to a Spanish or Italian team, you know you've got virtually no chance of coming back. Even the Liverpool players can't have fancied their chances after going three down to Milan in the 2005 Champions League final. Anyway, all we could manage in the second leg was a 1–1 draw. We were out of the competition, a big blow after winning it a few months earlier.

It was around that time that I announced I was out of international football for good. I decided my ninetieth appearance for England, in a 1–0 win against Turkey in a European Championship qualifier, would go down as my last. It's fair to say that the gaffer wasn't unhappy about the turn of events. He felt that I could contribute more to United without the demands of international football, the risk of injury and the travel fatigue. At the age of thirty-four, I knew it was important to get as much rest as possible.

One bright spot on the international front was our 1–0 European Super Cup victory against Red Star Belgrade. That play-off match, which in those days was contested by the winners of the European Champions' Cup and the Cup-Winners' Cup, and now by the winners of the Champions League and the UEFA Cup, has never really taken off as it perhaps should have done. We had a crowd of only 22,110 that night, less than half Old Trafford's capacity at the time. The Super Cup still doesn't get much recognition, which is a pity.

Most people in the game recognised that United were going to be genuine challengers for the title that season. We had a good December, drawing away to our main rivals, Leeds, winning 3–1 at Chelsea, beating Coventry 4–0 and banging in six at Oldham. We also beat Oldham in the fourth round of the Rumbelows Cup.

Kanchelskis just cut through them. Some years later, I was on a coaching course with Andy Barlow, who'd been the Oldham left-back in those games. He told me Kanchelskis was the one player he hated playing against because he ripped him to shreds. It was our turn to be torn apart on New Year's Day, losing 4–1 at home to Queen's Park Rangers and with it the top spot in the table. A few snidey suggestions surfaced about New Year's Eve celebrations, but it was just one of those games. In any case, I wasn't playing!

We had two more big matches away to Leeds in the first half of January and won both. We beat them 3–1 to reach the semi-finals of the Rumbelows Cup and 1–0 in the third round of the FA Cup. I missed those games but returned for the 1–0 win against Aston Villa that took us back to the top of the First Division. I also played in our FA Cup fourth-round tie against Southampton. We drew 0–0 away and were level at 2–2 in the replay when I had a perfectly good goal disallowed. The ball was about two yards over the line. We went out on penalties.

Around that period Brucie needed a hernia operation and was out of action for a while, but we managed to keep our noses in front of Leeds in the League and made it to the final of the Rumbelows Cup. Middlesbrough, then a Second Division side, held us to a goalless draw at Ayresome Park in the semi-final first leg and took us to extra time in the second leg before Giggsy secured a 2–1 win and another Wembley date.

I was out injured again when we met Nottingham Forest in the final, but it was satisfying for all of us at the club that we won 1–0 and made amends for our defeat twelve months earlier. It was the first time United had held that trophy and, thirteen years on, they still hadn't reclaimed it. I was particularly pleased for Choccy when he scored the decisive goal, but even as the players and fans celebrated at Wembley, the gaffer was making it clear that our priority was the League.

It all came down to our last six matches. We had lost only three of the thirty-six played up to that point, but our Cup run had left us with a ridiculously congested fixture schedule in the First Division. Four days after the final, a smashing goal by Kanchelskis gave us a 1–0 win against Southampton and a two-point advantage over Leeds, with a game in hand. Two days later, we were held 1–1 at Luton, two days after that we lost 2–1 at home to Forest and another two days on we lost 1–0 at West Ham. I was injured, powerless to help a team running on empty.

Leeds led us by a point and both teams had two matches left. We had to win at Liverpool, four days after the trip to West Ham, to keep our hopes alive. Paul Ince and I still weren't fully fit, but the boss decided we had nothing to lose. Leeds had won earlier in the day so we just had to go for it. We hit the woodwork a couple of times, but sensed it wasn't going to happen for us. We lost 2–0 and Leeds were the champions. Winning our last match, 3–1 at home to Tottenham, was no consolation.

Missing out on the Championship hurt. I'd been close to the title a few times, but this was the worst feeling because there's no doubt in my mind that we should have won it. It hurt even more when the smart alecks were going on about how we still weren't up to the job after twenty-five years of waiting. We had to listen to more droning about the ghosts of the past. The plain fact of the matter is that we would have been champions but for the backlog of fixtures and the injury toll with which we had to contend. If we had been allowed to finish our programme after the FA Cup final, as had been the case in previous years, it might have been different.

Experience of winning championships – or lack of it – had nothing to do with it because Leeds had not won it for a long time, either. Leeds had a good team with some outstanding individuals, including Gordon Strachan, Gary McAllister, Gary Speed, Lee Chapman and an influential Frenchman – Eric Cantona. Even so, it was more a case of our losing the title than their winning it. We lost three of our last four matches because we were dead on our feet. The irony is that we effectively helped Leeds' cause by knocking them out of the two cups and giving them the chance to concentrate on the League. We were convinced we were the best team in the League and were even more determined to prove it the following season.

10
DELIVERANCE

T HE BIG CHANGE in English football for the 1992–93 season was the breakaway of the leading clubs to form the Premier League. What had been the Second Division became the First Division of a restructured Football League. Top clubs were inevitably accused of greed as they demanded more opportunity to cash in on their market value in the modern era of Sky television and wall-to-wall media coverage. At Manchester United, though, we were driven by the same old desire to win that elusive Championship and rid ourselves of the increasingly heavy burden.

We felt we should have been the last champions of the old First Division and knew there wasn't much wrong with our side, but the boss decided we needed another option up front, preferably someone who could provide more of a physical presence and goal threat. The player he targeted was Alan Shearer, the young Southampton striker who had been terrorising defences. He had the lot – power, pace, fierce shot, great in the air and brave as a lion. He was made in the classic centre-forward mould and he was a Geordie. Yet instead of joining the biggest club in the country, Alan went to Blackburn Rovers, a decision that has baffled me to this day.

United apparently said they wouldn't get into an auction against Jack Walker and his millions, but I don't know what the ins and outs of the precise reasons were. I do believe, though, that Alan made a massive mistake in not going to United. There's no getting away from that. Even though he had a fantastic career with England and a good career with Blackburn and Newcastle, his cabinet would have been full of all kinds of trophies and medals if he had gone to Old Trafford.

From 1992, when Alan first turned down United, to 2005, Ferguson's side won eighteen trophies. Alan won the Championship with Blackburn in 1995, but then had a succession of disappointments. He could and should have been part of United's eighteen-trophy success. In fact, he might have won more than eighteen because United might have won more with a player like him in the team. They would have been even better. There's just no knowing how many goals he would have scored and how many records he would have broken with United, given the chances they create. I know Alan. He's a strong character and Manchester United wouldn't have fazed him. He would have been perfect for the club.

Alan is a brilliant professional and has a great work ethic to go with all that ability. I look at him as a player and wonder why he made that decision. Why leave Southampton to go to Blackburn rather than Manchester United? That's the question as far as I'm concerned. I don't understand it. Money may have been an issue, I don't know, but if I was offered £100,000 more to go to Blackburn than United, I'd go to United. He would have made more money at United, anyway, because money follows on success, and there's no doubt he would have had far more success at United.

There were stories that he hoped to go to United when he left Blackburn and eventually signed for Newcastle in 1996. At least you can see the reasons why he would want to move to his home town and be a hero up there. Again, there were suggestions that Jack Walker wouldn't sell him to United. You never find out the whole truth behind these deals. Ultimately, though, a player will go where he wants to go and I think that if Alan had really wanted to go to Old

Trafford, at some stage of his career, he could have done. I think Alan, deep down, will probably regret that he never joined United.

In the end, the gaffer brought in Dion Dublin, a big, raw but promising centre-forward from Cambridge United. Dion gave us that something different because he had tremendous aerial power. Sparky and Choccy were very good at build-up play and running beyond people. Both could score goals and Sparky always had an eye for the spectacular. Dion's great strength was his ability in the air, as he has proved over the years. He was also smashing to have about the club, but he was unlucky to break his leg and damage ankle ligaments in only the third game he started for us, and he never really got another chance at United.

Dion scored our only goal on his debut, at Southampton, to give us our first Premier League win at the fourth attempt. I wasn't involved in the early games and realised I would, more often than not, be used as a substitute. I accepted that. I believed I could contribute when needed and as long as I got the chance to do that I felt I was still an influence at the club. I came on in the second leg of our UEFA Cup first-round tie, away to Torpedo Moscow, and did my bit in the penalty shoot-out after a goalless three and a half hours' play. Sparky had been sent off, so the 'dummies' had to step up to the mark. I managed to put mine away, but Brucie and Pally missed, as did Choccy, and we were out of Europe. We didn't last much longer in the competition that we had won the season before. Our defence of the League Cup, which had now become the Coca-Cola Cup, survived a tie against Brighton but ended in a 1–0 defeat at Aston Villa.

That might not have been a bad thing, bearing in mind what had happened to us in the League run-in a few months earlier. Our priority was the title and a 2–0 win against the champions, Leeds, gave the team a timely boost. Even so, with Dion injured we still seemed to be lacking something up front. I played from the start against Oldham and we beat them easily enough, 3–0, but generally we were struggling to score goals and the gaffer was trying to do something about it. He made a few bids for Sheffield Wednesday's David Hirst, but they wanted £3.5 million for him. He was a good player and could have had an outstanding career if he hadn't been so unlucky with injuries.

The boss's luck eventually changed towards the end of that November. A lot of people reckon the signing of Eric Cantona was a fluke but I'm not sure that's fair, although circumstances did work in his favour. The story I heard from inside the club was that the Leeds manager, Howard Wilkinson, came on to Fergie for Denis Irwin. The gaffer wouldn't go for that, but asked Wilkinson about Cantona. They did the deal for £1.2 million. The boss had turned the approach around to his advantage.

The players weren't convinced at the time that it was such a good signing. Eric had a reputation for flitting from club to club, staying nowhere very long and generally causing trouble. He'd had bust-ups in France and got the hump at Sheffield Wednesday when they wanted to give him a trial. Now Leeds were willing to get rid of him. We had a great set of lads, things overall were looking good and we didn't want anyone coming in and upsetting things.

Of course, Eric did nothing of the sort. I don't know whether he made an effort to change his ways or rein in his emotions, but he fitted in really well. He was nothing like the guy we feared he would be. He became one of the lads, going out with us and enjoying a drink and the banter. He didn't speak all that much English to start with, but he understood more than he let on to people outside the club. Most importantly, he could play. He was the final piece in the jigsaw.

I don't think Eric was as good as a lot of United fans make out. I wouldn't bracket him with Pele and Maradona – players in the very top league – but he had fantastic ability and the move was perfect for him and for us. The team we put around him suited him down to the ground. We had pace on the wings, the strength of Sparky up front, the running power of Choccy, the tackling of Paul Ince, myself and later Roy Keane in midfield, and a solid, settled defence in front of a magnificent keeper. The balance of the team was just right and he finished it off. Eric had great vision to pick and judge the pace of a pass. When we were banging our heads against a brick wall, trying to break down a team, he would do something out of the ordinary to create a goal or score himself. He scored all sorts of goals, many of them unbelievable, a lot of them match-winners. He was a big-time player.

Eric was a great professional and not just a natural talent. He worked at his game. He'd go out and start warming up for training before the other players went out. Afterwards, he'd practise free-kicks. He always trained seriously, never in a half-hearted way. He expected preparation to be spot on and expected his team-mates to be just as professional, but then they were all good trainers. That's probably another reason why he settled so well with us.

He was terrific with the fans and they took to him. On the pitch he gave them what they wanted and off it he always had time to sign autographs and pose for pictures. He loved the adulation they gave him. He played up to the fans like the showman he was, but unlike some showmen who don't contribute to their team, Eric gave us an awful lot. He has been criticised by some for not producing his stuff in Europe, but you can't blame Eric alone for that. We under-performed as a team in Europe, especially after winning the Cup-Winners' Cup. We should have gone on from that and done far better than we did.

As a team, we responded to Eric's arrival straightaway. He watched us win at Arsenal and then slotted in. We beat the surprise League leaders, Norwich, drew at Chelsea thanks to Eric's first goal for the club and came from three goals down to earn another point at Sheffield Wednesday. We thrashed Coventry 5–0 to end the year on a high, we hammered Tottenham 4–1 and won 3–1 at Queen's Park Rangers to go top of the Premier League. We had taken 23 points from a possible 27 and were just about everybody's favourites for the title. Our confidence had also grown. When you are winning, and winning well, it builds to the point where you're sitting in the dressing room, thinking you're unbeatable.

That can be dangerous, of course, and we slipped up at Ipswich, another of the season's surprise packages. The Merseyside stranglehold had been broken at last. Liverpool and Everton were starting to fade, whereas we were getting stronger, but the opposition was good. Both East Anglian sides could play, while Aston Villa were a real threat and Blackburn were on the up. Going out of the FA Cup against Sheffield United in the fifth round may have been another blessing in disguise. After that we focused totally on the Championship and had the benefit of a manageable fixture schedule.

It wasn't all plain sailing and, three days after winning at Liverpool, we lost at Oldham. We were also held at home by Villa, who were beginning to look like our main rivals after we won at Norwich. It became a test of will-power as much as ability and if any match typified our determination that season it was the 2–1 home win against Sheffield Wednesday.

John Sheridan, an old thorn in our side, scored from the penalty spot in the sixty-fifth minute after Chris Waddle had been brought down. The boss sent me on a couple of minutes later and my experience possibly helped us get a grasp of things. Brucie equalised with an eighty-sixth minute header and then headed the winner, six minutes into stoppage time. A lot was made of the time added on, but the referee had been injured and replaced, and then Wednesday started wasting time. That result put us back on top and everybody went potty, Kiddo especially. He jumped on the pitch like a maniac and he never lived it down. It showed what those three points and the title meant to the club. That was a massive win for us, and satisfying for me because it demonstrated that, even coming on for the last quarter, I could still make a real contribution to the team effort.

I came on again as substitute when we won 3–0 at home to Chelsea and 2–0 at Crystal Palace. We led Villa by four points with two matches left for each team. Big Ron's side had to beat Oldham to stay in it. Even then, we would have the chance to wrap it up in our home match against Blackburn, the following day. I was sitting at home, watching television, when Villa were playing Oldham. I think we all expected Villa to win and put a bit of pressure on us. Then the score came through – Aston Villa 0, Oldham Athletic 1. That was it. They couldn't catch us. We were champions.

Soon Steve was on the phone, inviting me round to his place to celebrate. He rang everybody in the team and every single player turned up. We had a great time and yes, we downed a few – but it was only a few because we still had to play the next day and the manager would have killed us if we hadn't performed. Not surprisingly, Steve didn't invite him. In fact, we didn't let on about our party until after the Blackburn match. It certainly wasn't an anti-climax, winning it like that, because it meant so much to us, and the game against Blackburn was such a fantastic occasion, anyway. The fans made sure of that. Old Trafford was shaking.

Mind you, I did worry that our celebrations would backfire on us when we went 1–0 down after eight minutes. I'm sitting on the bench thinking, 'Oh no, here we go!' Then Giggsy, to all-round relief, brought us level with a cracking free-kick and I was happy to get on for the second-half fun. Incey put us in front and Pally rounded it off by scoring from a free-kick in the last minute. He was the only regular outfield player who hadn't scored that season, so it capped a brilliant day perfectly. We won 3–1 and owned up to the gaffer about the night before.

We'd talked about the presentation of the trophy and I'd said that although I was club captain, Brucie had captained the team for most of the season and he should receive it. He and the gaffer suggested we should go up for the trophy together and when it came to the moment, Steve insisted I join him. So that's what happened and I'm grateful for that gesture because it was an unforgettable experience. This was what we'd all been working for.

It wasn't just about the pleasure of winning the title. As much as anything, it was the massive sense of relief. We'd had to put up with the constant reminders about how long it had been since the club were champions and there's no question, it was a burden for us. Now, after twenty-six years, the Championship was back at Old Trafford. We had finally delivered and I was pleased for everyone involved – chairman, manager, staff, players and fans, and also for those behind the scenes, the many people at the club who never got a mention. Of course, it was great for Sir Matt Busby, who was there to enjoy it with us. I can still remember his beaming smile. That said it all.

From a personal point of view, I felt a sense of fulfilment. I had left West Brom for United to try to better myself and win trophies. Over a decade I had enjoyed a lot of success. I had a collection of medals and I had the honour of captaining both my club and my country, but the Championship had become more important with every passing year and now it was ours. I felt we should have had it the year before and winning it in 1993 showed we weren't just making excuses. That wasn't being disrespectful to Leeds. There were genuine reasons – the injuries and backlog of fixtures – for what happened in '92. Those circumstances made our win all the sweeter.

So did the distinction of being the first winners of the Premier League. It was the beginning of a new era in the English game and United had put down a marker. We were number one and intended to remain number one. The response from the fans was amazing, because once we had become champions the interest mushroomed. United had always been recognised as England's biggest club, but suddenly we were swamped. During the school holidays it was mad down at the Cliff. Instead of the usual twenty or thirty autograph hunters at the training ground, hundreds would turn up. The club had to put up barriers to keep control, but at least the fans could still get to the players. These days fans aren't allowed anywhere near the new training ground and, because there is such a trade in signed pictures, the players are told not to give their autographs. It's a shame it's come to that.

Eric was always in big demand and took it all in his patient, laid-back style. Not much fazed Eric. He had a casual attitude to material things. He was typically French when it came to cars. We Brits spend hours polishing and caring for our cars, but he didn't bother. His car had scrapes and bumps down the side and if he got another one he would just shrug his shoulders. I never went to his house but I can imagine he would be perfectly happy with something quite modest. He came from a family who lived in a cave house near Marseille and that all added to the mystique of the man.

He wasn't one for standing on ceremony, as he showed when we went to Manchester Town Hall for an official reception after winning the Championship. The boss stipulated collars and ties and Eric arrived sporting some sort of country and western-style rope tie, the sort of thing you might expect Frank Worthington to wear. I was standing with Sparky and Choccy and we were looking at the boss, wondering, 'What are you going to do about that, then?'

I had a word with a few of the boys and we agreed that we weren't bothered that Eric had stepped out of line on this occasion. So I said to the boss, 'Gaffer, the boys aren't bothered. You can't be fining him for that, on a night like this,' and he said it would be OK this once. We'd got him off the hook, but that was Eric.

I was in the starting line-up for our last match of that season, at Wimbledon, which we won 2–1, and I scored my League goal for the campaign to make it the perfect finish. We were all on a high and enjoyed our summer break. Denise and I went on holiday with Steve and his wife, Janet, to Portugal. There was a feeling in the club that we could take our game to another level yet. With the pressure lifted, we would be more relaxed and play with greater freedom, but although I believed I could still contribute, I realised my days at the club were numbered – especially when, that summer, the club paid Nottingham Forest a record £3.75 million for Roy Keane.

Funnily enough, I possibly had a bit of an influence on that signing. I was in with the staff one morning when they were talking about Keane. The boss was asking whether they should pay that sort of money for him. I was sitting, having a cup of tea, and said, 'For what it's worth, Gaffer, I'd pay whatever it takes to get him.' I'd played against him and thought he was a really good player who would get better. Kenny Dalglish thought he'd got him all tied up for Blackburn but, unlike Alan Shearer, Keaney jumped at the chance to join United.

People go on about Keane being my natural successor and the similarities between us. He certainly went on to prove his worth as a central midfield player and captain, but every player has his own style and personality and has to be judged as an individual. I could see a top-class player and that was all that mattered. You could see his potential when he was a kid. I knew I was shooting myself in the foot. The first-choice combination in midfield would probably be Ince and Keane because I was getting on, but that didn't bother me as long as I could still be part of United and come in whenever I was needed.

I didn't even mind losing the No. 7 shirt to Eric. I knew I would be used a lot as a sub in the 1993–94 season and Eric had already shown his value to the club. We'd won the League in his first season with us and it was obvious he was going to be an important player for quite some time. He'd always liked to wear the No. 7, so that summer, when the boss was working out his squad numbers for the new season, I told him I didn't mind having a different number. I'd had a great World Cup in 1982 wearing 16, so it wasn't a problem having 12, 14 or any other number. I was, after all, now a bit-part player for United. I'd made fourteen League appearances the previous season. In 1993–94 it would be fifteen. As long as I could make an impact for what had become a terrific side, I felt I was doing a worthwhile job.

During the summer of 1993 the club made a more than worthwhile visit to South Africa. We went to the Soweto township to give the local kids a coaching session. We signed autographs, posed for pictures, all the usual stuff. They loved it and I think we got just as much out of it. It was a real eye-opener to see the poverty of that township. I had travelled all over the world in my career with West Brom, United and England, but normally on football trips all you see is airport, hotel, training ground and match. Now and then you would go on a sightseeing trip, and in China I had been to a rice commune and the Great Wall, but generally, you don't get to see the real world, the slums and terrible poverty. I have since been to Nigeria and seen areas where hygiene is virtually non-existent. The more you become aware of such conditions the more thankful you are for our standard of living at home. For the United players in Soweto, spending time with those enthusiastic kids was a humbling experience.

I suppose from my point of view it helped make up for getting sent off in a match on that trip. We played Arsenal and the South African club, Kaiser Chiefs. In the match against Arsenal, the Irish referee turned out to be a rugby man. He gave some unbelievable decisions against us, including ignoring a couple of blatant penalties. All right, so it was a summer tour and the result wasn't vital, but it became ridiculous and I'd had enough. I just said to him, 'You're a cheat.' In rugby they don't stand for that from players, so he sent me off. Then, after the match, he had the gall to come up and ask if he could have his photo taken with me. I gave him his marching orders in more colourful language. What really bothered me was that he could make the sending off official and report it, which would mean a suspension when the English League started.

Someone else who annoyed me on that trip was Paul Merson, the Arsenal and England player who later joined me at Middlesbrough. We went into a bar and the Arsenal lads, who had played earlier, were already in there, a few drinks ahead of us. Merse, who was standing with Ray Parlour and Tony Adams, was flicking his spittle at this girl's back and because they'd had a drink they all thought it was funny. I like a laugh as much as the next man, but that wasn't funny. It was disgusting and the girl hadn't a clue what was going on. I told Merse to pack it in but he did it another couple of times, so I went up to him and said, 'Next time you do that, I'll knock your lights out.'

'Ah, what's your problem?' he said, or something like that.

Anyway, he did back off. I said to Ray Parlour and Tony Adams, 'You two should know better.' They didn't really answer, but that was the matter closed as far as I was concerned.

Apart from the time we had with the kids, the other highlight of the trip was meeting Nelson Mandela, or at least having our photo taken with him. He watched us play and then came to a reception afterwards. The players didn't get to chat with him that much, although he spent some time talking to the boss, but it was enough to realise what a charismatic and inspirational figure he is.

We came up against my old sparring partners from Arsenal in the Charity Shield match, drawing 1–1 and then beating them on penalties. I put mine away, and scored again in a 2–0 win at Norwich as we made a good start to our title defence. Little did I realise at the time that I'd scored my last League goal for United.

I was kept busy in that opening phase of the season, playing in a midfield three with Paul Ince and Roy Keane. People go on about

4–5–1 as if it's something new, but we often played that way. Eric or Choccy played off the front man rather than alongside him. As we feared, our rugby friend reported my sending off in South Africa and I had to serve a two-match suspension. I hope he was satisfied.

We lost at Chelsea, our first defeat in seventeen League games, but were still top of the table as we began our European Cup campaign. We were away to the Hungarian side Kispest-Honved in the first leg and before our match we stood at the side watching a pot-bellied old man playing in some sort of exhibition game. He was unbelievable. He was pinging balls sixty yards, straight to feet. He had an amazing left foot. I had seen only bits of black and white footage of Ferenc Puskas, but after watching him that night I could well imagine what a fantastic player he was in his prime. We won our match 3–2 and went through to the next round after completing a 5–3 aggregate victory.

We seemed to be comfortably on our way to the third round after I scored within a couple of minutes and an own goal gave us a two-goal lead against Galatasaray of Turkey at Old Trafford. They came back with three goals, though, and we had Eric to thank for a late equaliser that preserved United's unbeaten home record in Europe. We knew we would be in for a hot reception when we went to Istanbul for the return leg and, sure enough, the 'Welcome to Hell' banners were there to greet us. It was the same at the stadium, but most of our lads were fairly experienced and weren't easily intimidated. Nothing, though, could have prepared us for the diabolical treatment we received during and after the match.

They were a decent team and had their moments, yet we felt we did enough to get the goal we needed. Lee Sharpe had a goal disallowed and long before the end it was obvious they had settled for the 0–0 that would give them the tie on the away goals rule. Their time-wasting was blatant. It wasn't just the players. Even their coaching staff and security personnel kicked the ball away from us when it went out for a throw. Eric was getting more and more annoyed. As the referee blew the final whistle I could see in Eric's eyes that he had gone. He gestured to the referee and was shown the red card. I ran straight across to Eric because it was obvious he was ready to fight anybody. I linked my arm in his and said, 'Come on, the game's gone. There's nothing you can do about it now.'

I'd got a firm grip on him because I just wanted to get him to the dressing room before there was any more trouble. He walked with me towards the tunnel, which was at a corner of the pitch. We'd walked a few yards when a policeman appeared at the other side of Eric and I thought he'd come to help us. At the entrance to the tunnel there was lots of police with riot shields. We came to the top of the steps, which led down to the dressing room area, and I was just about to thank the policeman when he punched Eric on the back of the head. Eric stumbled down a couple of steps, so I turned to throw a punch at the copper. As I did, a shield smashed into the back of me. I fell down a few steps, bashing my elbow against the wall. Eric wanted to go back up and fight, but by then the other lads were coming down the steps and calmed us down. They led us back to our dressing room. I had six stitches put in my gashed elbow.

UEFA people came in and interviewed us about what had happened. Then Eric came out in the press with comments claiming that referees could be bought. The referee that night gave us nothing and let their staff kick the ball away. Nothing came of our statements to UEFA, yet Eric was banned for four European matches. Our coach was bricked as we left the stadium and there were attacks on our fans. The whole thing was a disgrace. The net result was that we were out of Europe and I realised I probably wouldn't get another chance of playing in the continent's number one club competition. The boss was criticised for leaving out Sparky, but UEFA regulations limited the number of foreign and 'assimilated' players. The fact is that we could and should have done better in Europe during that period.

All we could do was go home and show we were still the best in English football. We'd made United champions again, so why not go one better? The club had never won the double – the League and FA Cup. We felt we were good enough to do that, and while we were at it, we could have a go at the Coca-Cola Cup, as well. We honestly believed we could mop up the lot. The gaffer came in for more stick when he rested some of his first-team players for the Coca-Cola Cup-tie at Stoke. Nowadays, the rotation of players, especially for that competition, is accepted. We squeezed past Stoke, 3–2 on aggregate, then beat Leicester 5–1 at home and Everton, away, 2–0.

Eric put Istanbul behind him with two goals in our 3–2 win away to Manchester City. There was never any serious danger of our losing the League that season and when we beat Sheffield United 3–0 at Bramall Lane, on 7 December, we had a lead of 15 points. Ladbrokes stopped taking bets on the title. Oldham were on the wrong end of another five from us, but at least Andy Barlow wasn't in the firing line this time. I was substitute that day and again for the 3–3 draw at Liverpool. The match got rave reviews, but we weren't happy because we had led 3–0.

Sparky's goal at Sheffield United was enough to send us on our way in the FA Cup, although he got himself sent off for kicking one of their players up the backside. It was unlike Sparky to retaliate like that. He was a hard nut who could take stick as well as dish it out. Portsmouth gave us a bit of a wake-up call before we beat them in a Coca-Cola Cup replay at Fratton Park, but that tie, like everything else around the time, was overshadowed by the death of Sir Matt Busby on 20 January 1994, at the age of eighty-four.

The sadness was felt not only within the club but throughout the football world. The response from fans, the tributes and media coverage reflected Sir Matt's standing in the game. Supporters laid out shirts, scarves and flowers at Old Trafford in reverence and thanks to the great man. United's first match after he died, at home to Everton, was a sombre occasion. A piper led the teams on to the pitch and the minute's silence was observed immaculately. These days such tributes are usually respected, but that wasn't always the case. The silence was often broken by louts whistling or shouting. On that day, you could have heard a pin drop. The Everton fans were brilliant. I wasn't in the squad because I had problems with my sinuses and went into hospital the following week for an operation, but I discharged myself so that I could go to the funeral. I felt privileged that I'd got to know him better than most players of my generation. Thousands turned out to pay their respects, lining Sir Matt Busby Way as the Father of Manchester United was driven past Old Trafford for the last time.

I believe we gave him our tribute by winning the championship in 1993 and playing football the way we did into 1994. We won matches in style, just the way he wanted his teams to do. Talk of a unique treble increased as we beat Norwich and Wimbledon in the FA Cup and thumped Sheffield Wednesday 4–1, away, to complete a 5–1 Coca-Cola Cup semi-final victory. Chelsea, the last team to beat us in the League, ended our thirty-four match undefeated run in any competition with another 1–0 scoreline, but we came back with a 3–1 win against Charlton to reach the FA Cup semi-finals and a 5–0 battering of Sheffield Wednesday in the Premiership.

Schmeichel was sent off against Charlton, the first of four red cards we were shown in five matches. Eric was dismissed in consecutive matches, at Swindon and Arsenal. He did have a volcanic temper but sometimes his reputation went before him. We were held in both those matches and our lead over Blackburn was cut to six points. Then Kanchelskis had to go in our 3–1 Coca-Cola Cup final defeat by Aston Villa – again the opposing manager was our old boss Ron Atkinson. I wasn't involved that day but we all felt the blow because the treble had been a realistic target. Ron's team played well, though. We had another setback when two goals by Alan Shearer – who else? – gave Blackburn a massive win against us and slashed our advantage to three points.

We met Oldham in the FA Cup semi-final at Wembley and I was substitute, even though Keane, Kanchelskis and Cantona were suspended. We were nowhere near our best and I came on in the second half. Sparky's equaliser saved us in the last minute of extra time. The replay was at Maine Road and, with Keane and Kanchelskis back, I thought I had no chance of being in the starting line-up. I'd not been in the Wembley team and yet the boss picked me for the replay. I scored and was happy with my performance. Kanchelskis, as usual against Oldham, was unplayable. We won 4–1, the double was still on and I thought I had to be in for the final.

I was particularly keen to be involved because I knew by then that I would be leaving United at the end of the season. My future had been taking shape for some weeks. I'd asked the gaffer whether I figured in his plans for the following season and he made it clear that I didn't. He said that with so many good young players coming through he would have to move on a few of the older ones. I was thirty-seven and said that was fair enough, as long as I knew where I stood. I wasn't going to get another contract with United, so I had to think about what I would do next. I wondered about management, but at that stage it was only a percentage consideration. I felt I could still do a good job playing, maybe in the First Division, and help a club get promoted. That was my aim.

Then when two clubs, Wolves and Middlesbrough, approached me about becoming their player-manager, it was a different matter. Suddenly management did interest me. Jonathan Hayward, the Wolves chairman, came to my house one Sunday to interview me and he left saying he would recommend appointing me. That job appealed to me because Wolves had the tradition, the stadium, the support and, in Sir Jack Hayward, an owner prepared to make funds available for new players. The problem was that they wanted me to sign before the transfer deadline, in late March, and I still had a Championship medal – and possibly an FA Cup final medal – to play for at United, so I told them I couldn't join them until the end of the season. I read in a Sunday newspaper, a couple of weeks later, that they'd given the job to Graham Taylor.

I heard about the Middlesbrough job when Alex told me he had been approached by Lennie Lawrence, who was their manager at the time. Lennie knew he was moving on and said he wanted to speak to me about taking over from him. It sounds a bit odd, but that's the way it happened. Lennie came to a midweek match at Old Trafford and we met in the gaffer's office. Lennie told me that Middlesbrough's chairman, Steve Gibson, wanted to know if I'd meet him for an interview. So I went up to see Steve and he told me about his ambitions for the club and asked me about mine. We were obviously thinking along the same lines. He said he had a short list of candidates and would be back in touch. He phoned me a little later and said he'd like another meeting because he wanted to offer me the job.

Middlesbrough finished ninth in the First Division that season after being relegated the year before. Crowds were as low as 6,000 for some matches and Ayresome Park was looking a bit dilapidated, so they weren't in a great state. But I knew the feeling for the game in the North East and the chairman had great hopes for the club. He had plans for a new stadium and he promised me £2 million to start with for new players. Steve was only a young bloke – four or five years younger than me – but he was a successful, self-made man. He was in the tanker business. We hit it off straightaway and I felt I could work with him, so I took the job.

Back at United, meanwhile, our League form picked up after a slip at Wimbledon, and Blackburn couldn't stay with us. We were champions again and, just as in '93, we'd done it with a couple of matches to spare. Our final League match of the season, at home to Coventry, took on a particular significance for me because it was my last for United. Everyone knew I was leaving the club to be player-manager of Middlesbrough, and it became a very emotional occasion. The reception from the fans was tremendous. The boss rested a few players with the Cup final in mind and brought in a couple of kids, including a right-back called Gary Neville.

The match itself was a bit of an anti-climax and ended 0–0. Choccy tried like a beast to set me up for a goal because I was on ninety-nine for the club. I had one good chance, late on, but overdid the bend. It wasn't that big a disappointment for me. I'm not one for records – I'd sooner win medals. Steve called me up to receive the Championship trophy with him, and Old Trafford enjoyed another knees-up.

I hoped I would end my thirteen-season career at United with an FA Cup final appearance against Chelsea, six days later. The boss had everybody back from injury and suspension, but after playing my part in the semi-final I felt I ought to be picked for Wembley, at the very least as a substitute. I didn't get a look-in. That was a dampener to my last week with the club. On the day before the final, the boss called me in to see him.

'You can have a drink tonight if you want,' he said. 'I've got to look after the young lads who are coming through and make them feel part of it, so I'll be leaving you out of the squad. Here's a few quid. Get yourself a drink.'

'I don't want your money, I don't want a drink,' I replied.

I felt more angry than insulted. It was his way of trying to deal with an awkward situation. He obviously thought it was best to try to get me relaxed about it. I can appreciate even more, now that I'm a manager, how hard it can be in these circumstances. It's never easy to tell a player he's out of a big game and I had been at the club a long

time. The disappointment for me was that having played an important role to get us to the final I felt I deserved to be involved. A
place on the bench would have been a fair compromise, but then
that's my biased take on it.

I found it a little strange and uncomfortable at Wembley because I
was with the squad, wearing my club gear, on the sidelines, so close
to the action. I knew what it was like to be out there. I'd lifted that
trophy three times. The fans helped me. They were brilliant. They
appreciated what I'd done over thirteen years at the club. They
chanted my name and made me feel a lot better. Difficult though it is
in a situation like that, of course you get behind your team-mates. I
was lucky to have won so much. I wanted the lads to do it. It was
important for them and the club to complete the double, and I was
still part of the club, if only for a short time.

Chelsea had beaten us 1–0 in each of our League fixtures that
season and they held the lads for an hour. Then Eric tucked away a
couple of penalties and the contest was effectively over. Sparky and
Choccy, who went on as a substitute near the end, made it 4–0.
That equalled our record win against Brighton, eleven years earlier.
It was United's eighth success in the competition and, most
importantly, made them only the fourth club to win the double
in the twentieth century.

It was a funny feeling, watching the lads go up to receive the
trophy and their medals. I was happy for them, but it would have
been the perfect way to sign off with another medal of my own. The
club offered to have a medal made for me, but I said I didn't want
one if I'd not been involved in the final. I felt I had to be in the team
or one of the substitutes for it to mean anything.

That night the chairman presented me with a framed picture of
Old Trafford and thanked me for my time at the club, which was a
nice gesture, but it still rankled with me that I'd missed out on the
final. You wouldn't be human if you didn't feel the way I felt. It was

a natural reaction to feel a little let down and annoyed with the manager. I was sorry to leave the club on that note.

I had hoped I might have another year at United, playing the sort of role I'd had for those last two seasons. I had been brought in when I was needed and I also felt I'd helped in the development of young players such as Paul Scholes, Gary Neville, Nicky Butt and all those others coming through the reserves. I had played quite a lot of games with the reserves and was happy to encourage those boys along. They won their league and didn't just beat teams, they murdered them. So I felt there would have been a useful role for me at the club.

Instead, it was time to move on and, despite my disappointment over the 1994 FA Cup final, I could look back on a fantastic career with United. I joined the club to win trophies and more than achieved my ambition. I had three winners' medals in the FA Cup, two in the Championship and one in the European Cup-Winners' Cup. I played my part in taking United back to the top of the English game, where they would remain for many more years. In my last season, the club won the double and not even the great United sides of the fifties and sixties managed that. I had been captain of this fantastic club, as well as captain of my country. I'd played in front of great fans, with some great players, under two great managers in Ron Atkinson and Alex Ferguson at United.

Alex and I had one or two rucks over the years, but that takes nothing away from his ability as a manager or my admiration and respect for him. You're going to get disagreements and fall-outs, as you do in any business or walk of life. We worked together for eight years and I realise even more since becoming a manager that it can't run smoothly all the time, especially when you've got two determined characters. I accept I can be strong-minded at times but, like the gaffer, I care about what I do. Overall, we got on well and I believe that together, and individually, we served the club well. I'm grateful for all he did for me at United, and has done for me since I left the club. I like to think we have come through it all as real friends.

I was about to start a new football life as player-manager at Middlesbrough and an assistant to Terry Venables, the new England manager. Terry had asked me to be part of his coaching staff, on a part-time basis. It was a terrific opportunity for me and wouldn't cut across my work at Middlesbrough, and Steve Gibson said he had no problem with it. So much happened so quickly I didn't have time to reflect or reminisce too much about my United days. I had things to do for Boro – and England.

11
ENGLAND PRIDE

R EPRESENTING YOUR COUNTRY is the ultimate honour and the chance to join Terry Venables' coaching staff effectively took my international career full circle. I had played for Terry and Dave Sexton – who also joined him in 1994 – at Under-21 level and knew all about their abilities. The broken legs I suffered at West Brom limited me to seven caps at that level, but Terry and Dave still helped prepare me for promotion to the senior England squad and that debut against the Republic of Ireland on 6 February 1980.

A player takes pride in his shirt every step of the way, but nothing compares with the feeling when you walk out for the first time in your country's colours. It's a cliché to talk about a dream coming true and such stuff, but that's what it is. Every young footballer sets out aiming as high as he can and on that night at Wembley there was no prouder Englishman than me. Except, perhaps, my dad.

Kevin Keegan was the star against the Irish and his two goals sent England on their way to the European Championship in good spirits. I felt I had done OK in my first appearance for the full side, but if I thought my senior England career could be up and running I soon had to think again. I injured my ankle in training and was ruled out of the home internationals against Northern Ireland, Wales and Scotland. So I virtually had to start again and prove my fitness before

Ron Greenwood named his squad for the European Championship, held that summer in Italy.

My fitness test was a friendly match against Australia, played in Sydney at the end of May. I was one of five players competing for two remaining places in the squad. The other players were Terry Butcher, Glenn Hoddle, Paul Mariner and Peter Barnes. A lot was made of my 'duel' with Glenn for a midfield spot. It was almost a re-run of the paper talk before my debut. We won the match 2–1 and I was satisfied I had played well, but I put so much effort into trying to impress Ron Greenwood that in the last ten minutes I got cramp. It was the only time I ever had the problem.

At the airport, the manager told us which two players would be going to Italy. I wasn't one of them. He said that because of my injuries he didn't think I was fit enough for the European Championship. He thought I needed more fitness training. I was gutted because my form with West Brom had been good. My ankle was fine. I'd just tried too hard and I was sure I would have been OK for Italy, but he'd made his decision and that was it. The two players he picked were Glenn and Peter Barnes. It was so frustrating that summer because I was sitting at home watching the tournament on telly thinking, 'I should be there.'

It didn't really make me any more determined for the following season. I already had all the determination I needed and when I was given another opportunity, I made sure I didn't waste it. I played in the World Cup qualifier against Norway, at Wembley, in September 1980, and from that point my England career did take off. We won that match 4–0, but didn't exactly cruise through to the 1982 finals in Spain. Romania beat us in Bucharest and held us at Wembley. My first experience of playing against Brazil ended in disappointment, as well. We lost 1–0 to them at Wembley. The old stadium wasn't a happy hunting ground for us at the time. I was in the side that drew 0–0 against Wales and was beaten 1–0 by Scotland at home.

The main concern was World Cup qualification. A 2–1 defeat in Switzerland at the end of the season put us under pressure. We came back with a 3–1 win in Hungary, but then lost 2–1 in Norway, a match remembered for the taunting rant of the host broadcaster. Norway were definite underdogs and we got off to a good start. I scored my first goal for England and there seemed no way we would blow it, but so-called smaller countries have better players than people give them credit for and can rise to the occasion. They played like a team with nothing to lose and we conceded a couple of bad goals. It hurt to lose that match, but I've got to admit the Norwegian guy's commentary was priceless. He was near hysterical as he reeled off a list of famous English people, including Lord Nelson, Sir Winston Churchill, Sir Anthony Eden and Maggie Thatcher, and told them, 'Your boys took a hell of a beating.'

We couldn't begrudge the Norwegians their pleasure, but I was amazed at the reaction of the English media. I remember picking up one of the Sunday papers on the following weekend and every England player had been crossed out. The paper said we should never represent our country again. I was still fairly new to the hype that surrounds the England team and over the years I got used to the highs and the lows. It didn't knock my confidence because I was pretty hard-skinned, but I think some younger players can be affected by that kind of treatment. You learn not to get carried away by the praise or depressed by the criticism.

Certain sections of the media can get out of order and England managers, especially, have had to put up with some diabolical attacks. I respect a journalist's right to have an opinion and as long as he presents a balanced view, that's fair enough. The great thing about football is that everybody can have an opinion. Reporters, like fans, may have their favourite players and favour a particular style of play. The trouble is that some papers go over the top and don't necessarily reflect the opinions of the general public or people in the game. I'd seen the two extremes with the press campaign to get me selected for England and then being written off, along with the rest of the team that lost in Norway.

The good thing about a qualifying group is that one defeat – even an embarrassing one – might not spell the end. We knew that if we beat Hungary at Wembley we would go through. We managed it, 1–0, and all that mattered was that we were heading for Spain. Our form picked up during the build-up. This time we stamped our authority on the home internationals, beating Northern Ireland 4–0, Wales 1–0 and Scotland 1–0 in Glasgow. We also had good wins against Holland and Finland in friendly matches. We went into the World Cup finals on a roll and full of optimism.

We had been drawn against France, Czechoslovakia and Kuwait in the first group stage and set up camp in Bilbao. Security was inevitably tight because the more extreme Basque separatists had a reputation for kidnapping footballers and members of their families. There were particular concerns for our safety because the World Cup finals were held just a few months after the Falklands War and we were aware that Argentina had a lot of sympathisers among the Spanish people. Once we arrived at our base, a small, family-run hotel, any worries quickly disappeared. We couldn't have been treated better anywhere. Despite the security, it was just brilliant. The accommodation, the food and the attention were terrific, and we had a beach right outside. Most importantly, the training ground was just up the road and the facilities there were perfect.

The mood in the camp was good. Ron Greenwood, who made me feel welcome from day one, had a calm, composed air about him. He was an excellent manager, supported by an equally excellent coach in Don Howe. Everything about the set-up put the players in a positive frame of mind. We thought we were good enough to have a long run in the tournament. The only concern was the injuries to two of our main players, Kevin Keegan and Trevor Brooking. We thought they would be fit for the start, but their progress was slower than we'd hoped. Kevin had back trouble and saw a specialist in Germany. Unfortunately, he wasn't 100 per cent fit for our opening match and didn't play until the second-round game against Spain, when he came on as a substitute.

Even so, we got off to a great start. It was particularly good for me. I scored twice in our 3–1 win against France, the first coming after twenty-seven seconds. It was officially the quickest goal in World Cup history and remained so for another twenty years, until Turkey's Hakan Sukur scored after 10.8 seconds against South Korea. I was presented with a gold watch, which I still wear from time to time.

That goal came about through a chance remark on the day before the match. We were on the training pitch, practising our routine from Kenny Sansom's long throw. Kenny had always given us that threat from the left. Terry Butcher or Paul Mariner would try to flick the ball on for me to make a late run and get in behind the defence. As we walked off the pitch, Steve Coppell, who was sitting on the ground with Ray Wilkins, having a drink at the end of the session, said to Don Howe, 'I can do that, you know, Don.'

'Well, we're not going to put the lads in again because we've done enough,' Don said. 'Just show me how far you can throw it.' So Steve picked up a ball and threw it. Sure enough, he had a terrific throw, which nobody had realised. Don said, 'That's fine. You take them from the other side.' It meant we could work the routine from the right as well as from the left.

In the match, we got a throw down the right and Steve took it. He threw the ball in to the near post, Terry flicked it on and I met it on the volley to hook it in. My second goal was a header and Paul scored the other.

As if that wasn't enough, the next day, 17 June, Denise gave birth to our second child, Charlotte. Denise wasn't sure whether it was the excitement of the match, which she watched on TV, but our Charlotte arrived the following morning, and ITV stitched me up big-style – but in the nicest possible way.

I did a load of after-match interviews and when we got back to the hotel that evening, I did a one-to-one with ITV's reporter, Jim Rosenthal. Then in the morning, everybody found out about the baby and after training Glen Kirton, the England press officer, came up to me and said, 'Bryan, there was something wrong with the camera. Could you do the interview again this evening, after you've all eaten?'

I thought that would be a bit late and asked Glen why we couldn't do it straightaway. He said they'd got no other time and it would take only ten minutes. Jim was a good lad, he said, so I'd better do it. I was thinking that I'd done lots of interviews after the match and again that morning, and all I wanted to do that evening was relax and have a game of cards with the lads. In the end, though, I said I'd do it and they set up a room with all the TV equipment to do the interview. I looked at the camera and Jim said, 'Well, Bryan, you thought you were here to do an interview, but we've got a little surprise for you.' They'd brought in a TV and there, on the screen, were Denise and Charlotte. They'd been round to the hospital and filmed them. Denise was in bed, holding our baby and answering a couple of questions. The interview with me was going out live and Jim asked me, 'What do you think of that?'

To be honest, I was thinking, 'What can I say?' I was gobsmacked. I managed to splutter something, but I don't know what. So that was the first time I saw our Char. It was a great touch by the ITV boys.

Getting back to the football, you can imagine what a high I was on. In our second game we beat the Czechs comfortably enough, 2–0, but I felt my thigh muscle a bit. So, as a precaution, I missed the Kuwait match, which we won 1–0. We were through to the next phase and had got there convincingly.

The only slight disappointment was that we would have to leave Bilbao and head for Madrid. We were sure nothing would match the accommodation and hospitality we'd received in Bilbao. The owner of the hotel had really taken to the lads and on the night before we left he took us down to his wine cellar. He had an unbelievable collection of about 2,500 bottles. He gave each player a bottle of the year of his birth. I've still got my bottle of 1957 red.

There was no drinking during the tournament. The camp was teetotal. All the England managers insist on that. You wouldn't even be allowed a glass of wine with your evening meal. The only possible exception would be after a match, when the manager might let the players have a couple of beers. We had a good laugh on our last night in Bilbao. Half a dozen of us grabbed Ted Croker, the FA secretary, and threw him in the swimming pool. He didn't have a clue who'd done it because we'd put pillow cases over our heads. Ted took it in good part. He was good fun and got on well with the lads. Ron Greenwood was a good, decent man, but straight as a die. He took everything quite seriously. He may not have appreciated a dip.

We were going to miss Bilbao, but we had no complaints about Madrid. The facilities and training ground were very good. It was just that it didn't have the homely feel of Bilbao. I was back for our match against West Germany and felt great, possibly because I'd missed the Kuwait game and had a rest. Karl-Heinz Rummenigge hit the bar for them and we had a couple of chances. Their keeper, Harald 'Toni' Schumacher, who later 'cemented' the French player, Patrick Battiston, made a good save from my header. I thought we edged the play but couldn't get the goal and it ended 0–0. Looking back, I think that even though Trevor Francis and Paul Mariner did well for us up front, Kevin, who was European Footballer of the Year, might have given us that little bit extra to score a goal. Trevor Brooking was fit again, but Graham Rix played so well it was difficult for him to get back in the side.

The pressure was on us in our second and last match of the phase, against Spain, because the Germans had beaten them 2–1 in their game. A real howler by the Spanish keeper had given them the decisive goal, so we were chasing the game right from the start. Kevin and Trevor came on as substitutes and both had chances. Maybe if Kevin had been fully match sharp he would have scored with a header from my cross. We again drew 0–0. We were unbeaten and had conceded only one goal in five matches, yet we were out of the tournament.

We couldn't help but feel there was something wrong with a system that eliminated a team with a record like that. We were also unlucky to be in such a tough second group. Winning our first group worked against us because if we'd been runners-up we would have had Austria and Northern Ireland rather than West Germany and Spain, but then nothing is certain in football. Who would have expected Northern Ireland, with my young United team-mate Norman Whiteside in the side, to beat Spain in Valencia?

Our goalless draw with Spain left both sides unhappy and the Spanish fans took it out on us as we left the Bernabeu stadium. They were banging the side of the coach and throwing anything they could lay their hands on at us, chanting: 'Argentina, Argentina.' That was a bit of afters from the Falklands conflict. We ducked down inside the coach in case something came through the window. It was a sour note to finish on, but we'd had a good tournament and I felt I could be happy with my first World Cup. As I explained earlier, the confidence I gained from that experience raised my game to another level.

I thought the manager had to be satisfied with his performance, as well, yet as we returned home he announced he was quitting. The senior players, including Kevin, the captain, and Mick Mills, the vice-captain, tried to talk him out of it and convince him he should stay on, but his mind was made up. We had no idea it was coming.

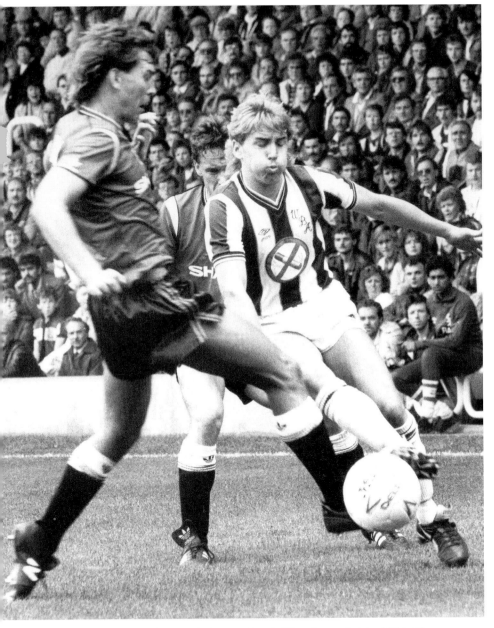

There was no brotherly love when we beat our Gary's West Brom 5–1 in 1985. That got me into trouble with our mam, who said we should have stopped at two!

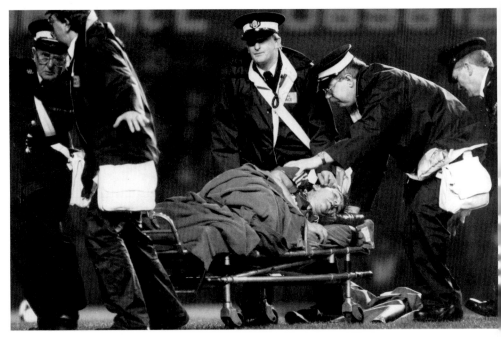

I was stretchered off after being knocked out and swallowing my tongue in a third-round FA Cup-tie against Queen's Park Rangers in 1989.

Charlotte, in Celtic hoops, Ben and Claire, in United strips, with me at my testimonial match. Pat Bonner is the Celtic captain, Roger Dilkes the bearded referee.

Right: Saluting our fans with Alex Ferguson after we beat Crystal Palace in the 1990 FA Cup final replay.

Below: My finest hour for United – leading the team to triumph in the 1991 European Cup-Winners' Cup final against Barcelona.

No one was happier than Sir Matt Busby to see the title return to Old Trafford in 1993 after twenty-six years.

Not sure about the headgear, but Steve Bruce and I were just glad to get our hands on the Premier League trophy.

What drink culture? We all deserved a lager after we beat Blackburn and were crowned champions.

Different game, same aim – lining up a putt on United's 1993 tour of South Africa.

We met the great man, Nelson Mandela, in Johannesburg.

Spending a little time with these youngsters from a South African township was a wonderful and humbling experience.

An all-star cast join me at Old Trafford to support the Bryan Robson Scanner Appeal – Robbie Williams (with ball) and the other members of Take That, radio presenter Susie Mathis and entertainer Frank 'Foo Foo' Lamar.

Lee Sharpe helps me try to keep the peace as two Galatasaray players confront Eric Cantona in our European Cup-tie in Istanbul, 1993.

Recording our 1994 FA Cup final song, 'Come on you Reds', with Lee Sharpe and two real music men, Status Quo's Rick Parfitt and Francis Rossi.

I think that's a congratulatory slap on the head from Gary Pallister for my goal against Oldham in the 1994 FA Cup semi-final replay.

I lead out United for the last time, against Coventry City, on 8 May 1994.

A final farewell after the 1994 FA Cup final.

As far as I can remember the press hadn't had a go at the manager over his selections or tactics. The main talking points had been the injuries to Kevin and Trevor and how different it might have been if they'd been fit from the start.

Bobby Robson replaced Ron Greenwood as manager and that wasn't the only significant change at the outset of England's next European Championship qualifying campaign. Bobby left out Kevin, which was a big story at the time. It surprised me, but I was never sure whether Kevin wanted to retire from international football or Bobby pushed him aside to try younger players. Whatever the reason was, Ray Wilkins took over as captain and I became vice-captain.

Jesper Olsen scored both goals for Denmark in our 2–2 draw in Copenhagen and, when I next lined up for England, I was captain. Ray's fractured cheekbone cost him the job for club and country. It was difficult for me because of the way it happened. Ray came back to be told I would be keeping the captaincy of England, as well as United. He would be vice-captain. It was a double blow for Ray, although he never really showed it. He took a lot of pride in the appointment and I could understand how he felt. We spoke about it because we were good pals and roomed together. He told me not to worry about it, that it wasn't a problem. He said that as long as we were playing, that was all that mattered. We're still good pals.

I think Ron Atkinson and Bobby Robson felt they had two leaders out there, but perhaps they chose the one who'd got more aggression to be captain. Ray would shout at people, but I was more likely to clatter into opponents who were laying into one of our team-mates. That may have swayed them into sticking with me rather than giving the armband back to Ray.

I led out the national team for the first time against Greece at Salonica in a European Championship qualifying match, on 17 November 1982. I know I've said playing for your country is the

ultimate, but to skipper England tops everything. Thankfully, I
didn't fluff it. We won 3–0, and then thrashed Luxembourg 9–0,
the kind of score you would be very unlikely to get these days.

I had to wait until 1 June for my first international of 1983 because
of injury and, apart from leading the team on the pitch against
Scotland, I found myself leading the players behind the scenes, as
well. When Bobby took over, he decided we should stay at Bisham
Abbey, a purposely adapted training facility, rather than a hotel.
Bear in mind that this was at a time when players were beginning to
earn reasonable money and becoming used to a decent standard of
living. At Bisham the rooms were pretty basic, with small beds, one
wardrobe, no TV and no phone. This was before the days of mobile
phones so the lads had to queue to use a pay phone. There was a
television lounge but so few chairs that some of the lads had to sit on
the floor.

So the players had a meeting about the facilities and agreed that we
should do something about it. As captain, I went to see the boss and
told him that the accommodation and set-up were not good enough
and that we weren't happy. We weren't asking for anything luxurious, just a level of comfort we were used to at home. Bobby listened
and said he would have a word with Ted Croker. We soon heard that
we'd be going to a hotel in High Wycombe and eventually moved to
Burnham Beeches, which became England's regular base. The epi-
sode was reported in the press as a 'players' revolt', but it was
nothing as dramatic as that. It was all sorted out in a civilised
manner.

Bobby was very good to deal with and I developed an excellent
understanding with him. In terms of the football, he wasn't particularly different from Ron – they both played 4–4–2 – but they had
very different personalities. Ron was much deeper and tended to hide
his feelings. Bobby was a lot more animated. He wore his heart on
his sleeve. Bobby loved to see the players having a laugh and a bit of

banter. He was always asking me if the players were happy. He showed genuine concern for everybody.

He was the manager who allowed us to bring our wives and partners out for a week during the preparation for major tournaments. You can be away for a couple of months, playing warm-up games, training and then playing the tournament matches. I went to see him on behalf of the players and asked if there was any chance of bringing the girls out for a few days, just to break things up a little while we were preparing for the tournament. He said he had no problem with that and it has become established practice in the build-up to tournaments. Bobby took the view that a happy team was more likely to be a successful team.

Bobby also played Peter Shilton – Ron Greenwood's first choice in Spain – regularly in goal rather than have him alternate with Ray Clemence. He gave Ray the odd match, but Shilton was his number one. I put Shilton and Schmeichel right up there on a par. Schmeichs had the presence because he was a lot taller and could command his area on crosses better, but Shilts was better on angles and making saves. Shilts wasn't that big for a keeper, hardly six feet tall. Teams nowadays want keepers of six foot four or more, but Peter was such a strong bloke, with a massive upper body and shoulders. He worked at his angles, technique and reflexes all the time in training. He was the hardest trainer I've ever seen among goalkeepers – a perfectionist and always very proud about maintaining his level of performance.

I was again out injured when we met Denmark in our deciding European Championship qualifier at Wembley. I had played just twenty-three minutes of England's previous eight internationals and was a helpless TV panellist as we lost the match 1–0 and with it any hope of going to France for the finals. I was back for our convincing wins against Hungary and Luxembourg, but that was no consolation. Good though Denmark were, we had been confident of qualifying, especially on the back of our 1982 World Cup, but instead of heading for the European Championship in the summer of 1984, we went on a tour of South America.

We played Brazil in Rio de Janeiro's famous Maracana stadium, which had become a bit run down. Their team weren't too special against us, either. We beat them 2–0, John Barnes scoring that great solo goal and Mark Hateley getting the other on his first full appearance for England. Our next stop was Uruguay, where things went less smoothly. We woke up at our hotel in Montevideo one morning to find three armoured tanks and troops carrying machine guns outside. We didn't have a clue what was going on. An official function had been laid on that evening and Bobby Robson said a representation from the team would have to go to it. Players are never keen on these receptions, which can be a bit stuffy and boring, and in any case, the players' main concern is to prepare for, and play, football matches.

The lads voted that, as captain, I should go on behalf of the team and the rest stay at the hotel. Ted Croker came with me and we had a conversation with a couple of British Embassy people about the tanks and troops. They told us a bomb warning had been received and a decision had to be made about whether the match was played or cancelled. They were clearly concerned, but eventually it was decided to go ahead with the match and trust the security forces. I was not to tell the rest of the players about the bomb threat.

A massive military presence lined the route as we travelled by coach to the stadium, and I had to look cool and tell the players I was sure it was just normal security procedure. Inside, though, I wasn't so cool. Anyway, nothing came of the threat. We played the match and lost 2–0. I wasn't too sorry to get out of there. I don't know who the so-called terrorists were or what their cause was, but the Embassy obviously had their intelligence. It was only a couple of years after the Falklands War and we were close enough to Argentina to be wary. We wrapped up the tour with a 0–0 draw in Chile.

Such trips give players useful experience of playing against different styles and in different conditions and we were already setting out our stall for the next World Cup, in Mexico. Back on the qualification trail early in the 1984–85 season, we were determined to make up for our European Championship disappointment. We beat East Germany 1–0 at Wembley and played Finland, also at Wembley, in October. The newspapers reported that I was in the middle of a club v. country dispute and that United insisted I had to prove my fitness in a game against West Ham. This is an issue with a lot of clubs, and players do get pulled out of friendly internationals with the slightest niggle, but I never had a problem with United over playing for England. If I was fit, I told the gaffer I would be playing and that was it.

Players are constantly being told they need rest and, as they get older, maybe they do, but then look at the example of John Terry and Frank Lampard, who hardly ever had a rest for Chelsea or England during the club's Championship-winning 2004–05 season. I think some players believe too much of what managers and the media say about rest. When you play at the highest level, you need a reasonably strong character and mentality. Once I got myself established in the England team, my ambition was to win one hundred caps. I felt it was a realistic aim and I wanted to play whenever I could. Unfortunately, I fell ten short. Glen Kirton worked out that if it hadn't been for injuries I would have had another thirty-five caps.

A lot was made of United and England being one-man bands and how much they missed me when I was injured. Comments like that and the 'Captain Marvel' stuff were a bit embarrassing and awkward for me because it demeaned my team-mates. No one player can have that much influence and you have to have good players around you to be a good player yourself. I was lucky to have exceptional players around me.

I did play against Finland, and with a 5–0 win we were building the sort of momentum we needed to take us to the World Cup. An 8–0 thrashing of Turkey, in Istanbul, wasn't bad, either. I scored my only international hat-trick in that match. I missed the qualifier against Northern Ireland after dislocating my shoulder for the first time, but was back for the later stages of that season and the 1985 summer tour of Mexico and the USA. It was a test run ahead of the 1986 World Cup finals in Mexico, a chance to get used to the heat and the altitude.

We lost our two opening matches in Mexico City, 2–1 to Italy and 1–0 to the host country. Our third match was against West Germany, who decided on a different strategy to deal with acclimatisation. They flew in the day before the game, apparently working on some theory of beating the effects of jetlag, heat and altitude. I don't know where they got that idea but the poor sods were out on their feet. We walloped them 3–0. We rounded off the tour with a 5–0 win against the USA in Los Angeles.

Another big win against Turkey, 5–0, helped send us on our way back to Mexico and, although I missed a chunk of that winter through injury, I was fit to win my fiftieth cap in Israel. In interviews at the time, I made the point that the heavy football schedules in England put our players at a disadvantage in internationals. I felt our players didn't have enough time to rest and prepare adequately for major tournaments compared with players in other countries and that made it unfair. It's interesting that this is still a bone of contention. Sven Goran Eriksson had to fight to get his England players the four-week break he wanted ahead of the 2006 World Cup finals. We went behind against Israel, but I scored my seventeenth and eighteenth international goals to give us a 2–1 win.

I know some people think it's a bit rich when players complain about playing too much football. The argument goes that top players are well paid, usually have afternoons off and seem to find plenty of time for commercial work. Point taken and don't get me wrong. I wouldn't have changed my profession for any other. I have been very lucky in my football life and had even more endorsement offers at the height of my United and England career. Under Harry Swales' strict guidance, I agreed deals with Guardian Royal Insurance, Robson's Choice (a range of clothes) and Easy Jeans. I had a modelling contract with them, and another contract with the American running shoe company, New Balance. I suppose my promotional earnings at the time were around £250,000 a year. That may seem modest by the standards of today's leading players, but in the mid-eighties it was big money. I didn't take it for granted. I knew it was all down to success on the field. Football was always the priority.

Footballers do, in general, have an image problem. People get the impression they are greedy, selfish, spoiled brats and in one or two cases that may be true, but I think it's fair to say that most players give up at least some of their time for fans and charity work. A lot of that is never reported in the media. Players, especially those at the highest level, know how lucky they and their families are. That's why so many of them try to give something back and do as much as they can in the community. Visits to hospitals and supporters' clubs, appearances at charity functions and signing sessions are part and parcel of a footballer's life.

I still support the Wallness Charity, which we carried on from the Bryan Robson Scanner Appeal at Pendlebury Children's Hospital. They were desperate for a scanner and needed to raise £1. 5 million, so I put my name to the appeal and we reached our target in two years. It meant a lot of effort, going to presentations of cheques and making personal appearances, but the public were unbelievable with their support and the sense of achievement was brilliant. I've been working with them for more than twenty years. Many footballers make similar commitments.

My fan mail shot up when I became an established United and

England player. In fact, I still get lots of mail from United fans, mostly asking me to sign photos. Over the years most of the mail has been great, from genuine fans, although you do get one or two cranks. One in particular frightened Kath Phipps, the United receptionist who sorted my post for me. Someone started writing to me, saying I was his dad and he was going to kill me. The letters got gradually more threatening. He sent photos of himself and he was obviously a big bloke. He made no attempt to hide his identity, including his address, which was in Ireland, on the letters. We contacted the police, who said there was nothing they could do. In the end we spoke to his mother, who was very apologetic and explained that her son was schizophrenic.

Many fans no doubt think footballers deserve menacing letters for all the lousy songs they record. The worst one I was involved with was 'World in Motion', England's 1990 World Cup song. That was the video with Tony Adams and a bunch of other lads in a car. The best England song has to be 'Three Lions', which became the anthem for the 1996 European Championship, but then that's probably because the players didn't have a lot to do with that one. I brag to the kids that I've been in the top ten five times with United and England. 'Glory, Glory, Man United' got to number one and sold loads. United fans still sing it. The royalties from these songs go into the players' pool and the main thing is that the lads always have a good laugh over them. Mind you, one or two of them fancied themselves – remember Gazza and the Hoddle and Waddle duo? There was never any danger I would go that far!

We weren't always in tune as singers, but there was a real togetherness with almost all the England teams I played with and that '86 side grew in confidence as the finals approached. The problem for me was that I dislocated my shoulder again on 5 March and an operation then would have left me with no time to train or prepare properly for Mexico. I decided against having surgery and was playing again by the end of that month. It was a hamstring injury that kept me out of the Scotland match in April. The shoulder felt fine and I flew out with my England team-mates to our training camp in Colorado Springs convinced we were genuine World Cup contenders.

12
CRUEL FATE

T HE ENGLAND PLAYERS were happy campers at Colorado Springs. The team had gone ten matches unbeaten and morale was high. We had good players and good management. The team had a nice balance, a mix of abilities and strengths, and great character. Shilton was in goal, Terry Butcher was a genuine centre-half, brave as they come, and Kenny Sansom, Gary Stevens of Everton and Terry Fenwick were also outstanding defenders. Ray Wilkins and Glenn Hoddle were with me in the middle, Chris Waddle and John Barnes were our wide players, with Peter Beardsley and Gary Lineker up front. The other Gary Stevens, of Tottenham, Alvin Martin, Peter Reid, Steve Hodge, Trevor Steven, Paul Mariner and Mark Hateley gave us terrific options.

The Beardsley-Lineker combination allowed us to play a bit like foreign teams. Peter was great at dropping off the front, into the midfield area, and sliding those balls through for Gary. Peter was an intelligent player who could create opportunities for others as well as scoring himself. He could also tackle and would come back to nick the ball off an opponent and send us on the attack again.

Gary was an out and out finisher. He made no bones about it. He used to tell us, 'I'm not getting involved in any of that physical stuff. Just give me the ball and I'll score,' and more often than not, he did. All he was interested in was scoring goals. He left the rest to his team-mates. He will tell you now that he was like that. He went through his entire career without getting booked, let alone sent off. That takes some doing, even for someone who doesn't tackle, fight or argue with referees! He ended his career with forty-eight international goals, one short of Bobby Charlton's record for England. People sometimes underestimated the timing of his runs and the intelligence of his play. He would guide the ball into the net and always sensed where to pick up the bits and pieces. He was a genuinely great goalscorer.

I got terrific support from those England players and the manager, who inevitably had to face questions about my fitness. Apart from dislocating my shoulder a second time, and having hamstring problems, I also had an Achilles injury late in the season, but I was convinced I would be fully fit for the start of the tournament and Bobby Robson backed me all the way. That faith was put to the test after I dislocated my shoulder for a third time, during a pre-World Cup friendly against Mexico in Los Angeles. I fell on it and there were obviously concerns in the camp, but the shoulder went back in and I came through a series of rigorous fitness tests. I continued with my thousand press-ups a day regime in Colorado to strengthen the shoulder and my overall fitness had never been better. Gary Stevens – the one from Everton – and I were miles ahead of the others on the running machines and bleep tests. The squad took long walks up to a reservoir, about 5,000 feet above sea level, to help our altitude preparations and we had all the usual training and practice sessions. I felt fine.

During one practice match, against a Monterrey XI, we had a nasty scare when our doctor, Vernon Edwards, had a heart attack. I was sitting next to Doc Vernon on the bench when he suddenly went yellow. I called over the physio and the Doc was whisked off to hospital. Fortunately, he recovered, but it was distressing for him and for everybody else. He'd been with the players on one of those long walks up to the reservoir and perhaps it was a bit too much for him.

Wives and girlfriends joined us for a relaxing week before we got down to the serious business. We were always sure of a laugh with the manager around. All those stories about Bobby being forgetful and mixing up names – they're spot on. He called Graham Rix Brian Rix, while Mark Hateley was always Tony – his dad. Bobby's mind was always racing and I think that's why it happened so often. One morning when Denise and I came down to breakfast Bobby was on the phone. He was deep in conversation but half caught a glimpse of us through the corner of his eye.

'Morning, Bobby,' he said.

'*You're* Bobby. I'm Bryan!' I had to tell him.

It's amazing how many older people call me Bobby. Loads of people used to think he was my dad and of course the lads had a running joke about my dad, the manager, and me, the captain. If Bobby said something complimentary about me at team-talks, the lads would start smirking and say, 'Ah, Dad's picked you again.' There was always lots of banter about us. The boys hammered me, saying I could never do anything wrong for my 'dad'. We certainly got on well and have done ever since. Mind you, it drives you daft trying to keep in touch with him because he's forever changing his number. That's probably because he keeps losing his phone!

Bobby put his trust in me and I had no intention of letting him down. I knew I had a responsibility to him, the other players, the country and myself. If I'd had any doubts about my fitness for our first match, against Portugal, in Monterrey, or the rest of the World Cup, I would have held up my hands and pulled out. I believed I could play my part in helping England go all the way. I was twenty-nine, at the peak of my career, and ready to lead my country into the World Cup finals.

We were favourites to win our group, with Portugal second favourites. The other countries in our group were Poland and

Morocco. I had no problems with my shoulder in that opening match, but our football could have been better. We were disappointing and lost 1–0. We had to get something from our second match, against Morocco, but again things didn't go to plan and for me they went wrong in a big way.

For forty minutes, everything was OK. I felt fine, playing my normal game. Then I knocked the ball past one of their players and ran on into the box. As I went past him he grabbed me by the right shoulder and pulled me back. I fell in agony. The shoulder had come out again. Everybody thought it was the fall that did the damage but it wasn't, it was their player pulling my shoulder. You can see exactly what happened in the photograph of the incident. The thing that is overlooked in all the attention given to my injury is that we should have had a penalty, but I was in so much pain I couldn't even think about appealing and I suppose the other players were just concerned about my shoulder.

I was led away, clutching my shoulder, and the tears were of frustration and annoyance as much as pain. When I got back to the dressing room Fred Street, our physio, put the shoulder back in, but I knew it was almost certainly the end of my World Cup. That's what really hurt – the thought of all the work, training and planning that I, like all the players, had put into it. It had all been a waste of time and effort.

Things got worse still for us in that match. Ray was sent off for throwing the ball at the referee. It was totally out of character for him to do anything like that, but frustration got the better of him. He was distraught about it afterwards because he felt he'd let everybody down. That's what can happen in the game. Nothing was going right for us. We'd lost the first game, I'd gone off injured in the second, decisions were going against us and the build-up of frustration tipped him over the edge. It was too much, even for Ray. It meant also that he had a two-match ban.

We drew 0–0 against Morocco, so we had to beat Poland in our last group match. Like Ray, I wouldn't be playing and there was a lot of debate and speculation about what I should do next. Ron Atkinson wanted me on the first available flight home to have an operation as soon as possible, so I could try to be fit for the start of the new season. The newspapers quoted Martin Edwards and Bobby Charlton as saying much the same. I spoke to Bobby Robson about it and he said he'd like me to stay on with the lads. He thought it would help the camaraderie to have me around. My thinking was that there was no telling how far we might go in the tournament. If we went out after the next match, I'd be home in a few days, anyway. I told Ron I wanted to stay. Not surprisingly, he wasn't happy.

There was no way I could have played again in Mexico, though. That was obvious a couple of days after the Morocco game, when the boys were having a fun game of cricket. I tried to join in but couldn't raise my arm to catch the ball or do anything. I ran around, holding my arm into my side, and if I let go of it I felt that the shoulder would come out again. I just wanted to be involved and although I could only sit and watch our match against Poland, I was as happy as anyone when we beat them 3–0. Gary Lineker scored a hat-trick. We had another 3–0 win, against Paraguay, in our second-round match at the Azteca Stadium, which put us through to the quarter-finals, to play Argentina.

The lads were confident, and rightly so after back-to-back 3–0 wins. We knew it would be tough against Argentina, who were one of the World Cup favourites, and that was mainly because of one player – Maradona. That was when I really started to feel sick. The lads had done well against Poland and Paraguay, but I thought I just might have been able to make a difference against Maradona. I'd played against him before, I knew his game and I felt I could have done a job on him. He liked to drop off into midfield and you always had to be aware of that. When he came into your midfield area the one thing you couldn't afford to do was allow him to turn and start running at your defenders. That was when he was most dangerous.

Nobody, though could have done anything about his 'Hand of God' goal – except the match officials. I was sitting on the bench and we all stood up, appealing for hand ball. We could see it clearly. He put his hand in front of his head and knocked the ball in as Shilton came out. The only two players on the pitch who reacted with any conviction were Shilts and Terry Fenwick. They sprinted to the referee. I think most of the lads were stunned. It was a bitter blow to be cheated like that in a World Cup quarter-final, but also to be let down by the referee and linesman. One of them should have seen what happened. There had been nothing in the match before that goal. Maradona's other goal was a different matter. He just cut through us with his pace. He did it again when they played Belgium and that goal might have been even better than the one against us. They were both fantastic goals and showed what a great player he was. Argentina beat us 2–1 and went on to win the World Cup. Maradona was the difference.

To my mind, there is a category of players who are a cut above the rest. Maradona has been one of those unbelievably brilliant players. I can't judge players before my time. I saw enough of Pele to know how great he was and that he belongs in that top category. The others I would put with them are Zico, Michel Platini and Johan Cruyff. People may wonder why I don't put George Best in with them. He was brilliant, no doubt about that, but he was really a winger, whereas the other five played in that vital area, just drifting off the front into the midfield. They were basically the classic No. 10s, the main men, playmakers who could also strike. They were all such incredible players that they regularly won matches on their own. None of them was a giant physically. Four of them were five foot eight to ten. Maradona was tiny, about five foot four, but they all had great strength and balance. Maradona was so solid, physically, and his quickness over the first ten yards, running with the ball, was devastating – and that left foot of his was fabulous.

It was a heartbreaker for England to go out like that, but the lads flew home from Mexico knowing they had done themselves and their country proud. Five days after the Argentina match, I was in hospital. Staying on with England had delayed my operation a couple of weeks and although I hoped to be back for the start of the season, that wasn't possible. Do I regret not having been back for United sooner, to help Ron when he was struggling to keep his job? Of course I wish I'd been there. As I have already said, players have to share the blame when their manager is sacked, but I feel the club made the wrong decision when I dislocated my shoulder in the first place. That was when I should have had the operation. If I'd had it done straightaway, there would have been no further problems.

I didn't find things difficult or unpleasant with Ron when I returned. As a manager you try to be strict with your players and adamant on certain issues, but as football people you understand that you can sometimes be at loggerheads because of circumstances. Ron knew me as a person and I don't think he held any grudges against me. Deep down, he realised what it meant for me to be out there with the England team because he was a football man.

One of the crazy suggestions going around at the time was that I didn't want to have an operation because it would leave a scar on my shoulder. I didn't give a monkey's about that. I had plenty of scars anyway. All I wanted was to be fit and playing football. I told the girls I had a scar on my shoulder because I'd been bitten by a shark. They thought I was really brave.

I was back for England's European Championship qualifier against Northern Ireland, at Wembley, in October, which we won 3–0. We were off and running again. The shoulder was absolutely fine, but a hamstring injury put me out of the match against Yugoslavia on 12 November. Not for the first time, I heard from someone offering me a 'miracle cure'. I was always getting letters from people who claimed they could end my injury problems. As soon as I had anything wrong with me, I could be sure I'd have somebody on with a potion or treatment that would sort me out. It's the same when you are down towards the bottom of the League as a manager. You hear from psychologists who say they can do great things to your players' minds. I got plenty of offers when we were fighting relegation at West Brom in the 2004–05 season. I believed in myself, my assistant Nigel Pearson, my staff, the fitness coach, nutritionist and physio. So no, I didn't see the need to bring in a psychologist.

I was playing for England again in a friendly in Spain the following February. Lineker scored all our goals and Tony Adams made his international debut in a 4–2 win. The nucleus of the '86 World Cup team was still around so I felt we would not only reach the 1988 European Championship finals in Germany, but also be one of the strongest there. We were held 0–0 away to Turkey but hammered them 8–0 at Wembley in October 1987 and had an excellent 4–1 win against Yugoslavia, in Belgrade, the following month. We'd qualified again for a major tournament – yet were major flops in Germany.

We got off to the worst possible start, losing 1–0 to the Republic of Ireland. I never saw Gary Lineker miss as many chances as he did in that match. He had four or five really good opportunities and on any other day he would have stuck them away. We battered them but couldn't score, and then Ray Houghton scored a goal out of nothing. That was a massive blow for us because it put us on the back foot against the two other countries in our group, Holland and the USSR. They were two of the best teams in the tournament, as they proved by going on to reach the final.

Next up for us were Holland, who took the lead through Marco van Basten. Then I played a one-two with Gary Lineker, got there just before the keeper and dinked it over him to get us back in the game. We looked as if we had a chance at that stage, but they had three world-class players in van Basten, Ruud Gullit and Frank Rijkaard and in the end they made that ability tell. Van Basten completed his hat-trick and they won 3–1. He later scored a fantastic volley as Holland won the final. He was a great finisher and, for me, in the class of players just below the very top category.

We had no chance of going through after losing to the Dutch, so Bobby Robson changed the team around for our last match, against the USSR. We lost 3–1 again and went home without a point to our name. We knew we had underachieved and I was particularly hacked off because I never went through a tournament fitter than I was in Germany '88.

That wasn't my only cause for feeling bad after that trip. I got involved in an incident that I've regretted ever since. It was an argument with Peter Shilton that went too far. Shilts was a good mate, we got on really well and I've made it clear how highly I rated him as a keeper, but after a bad result he had an irritating habit of blaming somebody else and telling them they weren't good enough. It would get to the point where the other lads asked me to take him out of the way and have a word. He had a go at a few players. I remember Ray Wilkins, John Barnes and Mark Chamberlain having to take it from him. Terry Butcher was going to kill him on a flight from Los Angeles until I stepped in and told Terry I'd sort it. I told Peter he couldn't say things like that to his team-mates because it caused bad feeling in the camp.

Anyway, after we'd been knocked out of the European Championship, one or two of us were having a drink at the hotel bar and Peter started having a go at me. It shocked me because he'd never turned on me before. He went on and on, taunting me about the 'Captain Marvel' stuff and saying he was number one. I said, 'Fine, you be number one. Now leave it alone. I know what you're like,' but he couldn't leave it alone. He went on and on. I kept my temper for about half, three-quarters of an hour. Then he said I was a 'bottler' and that was when I snapped. He was sitting at the bar so I told him, 'Get up and I'll show you who's a bottler.'

He wouldn't get up, but I was so angry I punched him. He just sat there and went quiet. I was fuming, but as soon as I went for him I knew I shouldn't have. The following morning, at breakfast, I walked straight up to him and apologised. It was usually Shilts saying he was sorry to one of the other lads, but this time I was at fault. I told him I was out of order. He said that it was forgotten already.

I've still not forgotten and still not forgiven myself for what happened that night. You get bust-ups in teams and Peter could be argumentative after a couple of drinks, but he was also a great goalkeeper and the players knew that when he reacted like that he was really showing how much he cared. We're all human and sometimes our emotions get the better of us. All you can do is move on, which is what we did. Peter and I played together for a few years more with England and we're mates to this day.

Shilts and I were very much the senior professionals as we set off on our next England campaign – Italia '90. Our World Cup qualifying group brought us up against one of our old rivals, Poland, in two crunch games. We beat them 3–0 at Wembley and drew 0–0 in Katowice. That draw was down to Peter. It was a backs-to-the-wall effort. We defended well and Peter made a couple of fantastic saves. We needed a point, got it and were off to Italy. I missed a couple of warm-up internationals following a groin operation, but played the later stages of the domestic season and felt match sharp for the World Cup.

As well as Shilts and me, we had plenty of experience with Terry Butcher, Gary Stevens, who had moved from Everton to Rangers, Trevor Steven, Gary Lineker and Peter Beardsley. There were also some good younger players in Des Walker, Mark Wright, Paul Parker, Stuart Pearce, David Platt and a kid who really was a bit special – Paul Gascoigne. He'd embarrassed me playing for New-castle against United and I was glad to have him on my side. Despite a 2–1 defeat against Uruguay in a friendly at Wembley, and a 1–1 draw away to Tunisia in our last warm-up game, I felt we got stronger as we approached that World Cup. With the finals being in Europe, I thought we had an even better chance than in '86.

As usual, Bobby Robson kept us entertained with one of his gaffes. We were on the team coach, driving to our training ground one day, when Bobby suddenly said, 'Stop the bus. I've forgotten my boots.'

'Gaffer, what size are you?' shouted Chris Waddle.

'I take an eight or a nine.'

'You're OK, then, Gaffer,' said Chris. 'I've got a spare pair of brand new nines. You can borrow these.'

So Bobby borrowed Chris's boots and we went training. After-wards, we were sitting having a drink when Bobby came across, having a right go at Chris.

'Waddle, these boots have given me blisters.'

'They can't have, Gaffer. They're size nines.'

Bobby took them off and threw them over to Chris. When Chris looked inside, he found the paper stuffing still inside the toes. The gaffer had worn them all through training like that, curling his toes to get his feet in. We just fell about laughing.

Apart from being good for a laugh with the players, Bobby was always willing to listen to us and take our thoughts into account, and we did influence him that year. We had a chat with him and said we felt that a sweeper system would suit us. We played for some time with what was more or less a 4–4–2 system, yet the Brazilians and Germans had been winning World Cups down the years with three or five at the back. Managers and coaches tend to let their experi-enced players have a say like that. I'd worked with Bobby and Don

Howe for eight years and they respected the input of their senior players. Anything that helped was valued, although of course the final decision was always the manager's.

The gaffer was less impressed with his players – and this one in particular – after a bit of messing around left me with a bloody big toe. This was an incident that Gazza claimed in his book ended my World Cup, which he now accepts was a load of rubbish. We were at our training camp in Sardinia, and our first match was still several days away. A few of us fancied a last drink before the tournament started, so we went to a local bar. Gazza says that Bobby found out we were missing and sent the police after us. Well, we did hear police sirens as we walked back to the hotel, but that was nothing to do with us. There must have been some trouble in the town.

When we got back, we went to Gazza's room and started larking about. I tried to tip Gazza off his bed and caught my big toenail on the corner. I had no shoes on and it ripped the top off my toenail. It was bleeding badly so I went into the bathroom to try to staunch the flow. I had to have an injection in it to kill the pain to play in the first game. Bobby went mad at me and rightly so. He comes over as nice Uncle Bobby, but he could be tough if he felt he had to be and he had a right go at me for pratting about that night.

Gazza says in his book that we were absolutely legless, which isn't right. He also says I broke my toe, which I didn't. Worst of all, he says that it was after the second match and was the real reason why I went home from the World Cup. It happened, as I've said, before our first match and I had to pull out of the tournament because of an Achilles injury, which I got in our second match. I have told Gazza he got it totally wrong about that night and he was distraught. He said, 'I just didn't know what was going on then, Bryan. If I got the story wrong, I'm sorry.'

As we all know, Gazza has had his problems. He has been in such a mess at certain stages of his life that there was a lot he couldn't remember clearly. We've not fallen out. We've managed to stay pals even though he's given me a few headaches over the years.

Gazza was one of my accomplices in a brilliant betting scam we pulled inside the England camp. At the '86 and '90 World Cups we had a film room, with a video library, set up at the team hotel. We could go in and pass the time watching as many films as we wanted. We also had videos of horse races, which Fred Street brought in. Gary Lineker had a relative who was a bookie, so he and Shilts said they would run a book and the lads could have a bet on the races.

The tapes were sealed so that nobody could cheat, but Neil Webb and I persuaded Fred to let us have a look at them before they were shown to the rest. Gazza was also in on it with us. We told the other lads to stay off such and such a horse because it had no chance. Then we'd go in and bet on the horse we knew was going to win. Neil wasn't a big gambler, but Gazza and I put on a couple of hundred quid, at 16 or 20–1. Gary and Peter took the bets, no problem.

Then, of course, our horse came in first and Peter went white. It was the perfect race, as well, because our horse was at the back, came on the outside and eased its way in front. I've never seen Peter so pale. He looked sick. Gary just shook his head in disbelief. When we did it again in the next race they said that's it, they couldn't do any more. We'd cleaned them out. About half an hour or so later, we owned up and told them what we'd done. Fred had got the whole set-up on camera. We had to give them their money back but it was worth it. Poor old Shilts eventually got his colour back, as well.

You need a bit of fun like that in a camp, especially on the long tours, because boredom can be a problem. People wonder what footballers are on about, saying they are bored, staying in five-star hotels and leading a pampered lifestyle, but when you're preparing for tournaments you're not on holiday and can't do anything you like. You can't play golf because the management don't want you on your feet. You can't play tennis because that takes too much energy out of you. You can't sit in the sun for more than half an hour because that burns and drains you. They want you to rest and put your feet up between training sessions, and that doesn't leave you with much to do.

A few of the lads were readers, a lot liked watching films and some got into Space Invader machines. I quite liked reading real-life stories, especially about gangsters such as the Kray twins. I could sit and watch films all day – and did. My record during the World Cup was five in a day. My favourites are 'The Sting', 'Butch Cassidy and the Sundance Kid' and 'The Godfather'. More recently I've enjoyed 'Gladiator' and 'Troy'.

I liked a game of cards, but towards the end of my England career the games started getting out of control. In the early days we said we wouldn't be daft and played for fivers or tenners. At United it always stayed sensible. With England, the kitty built up to fifty or a hundred quid, which was OK, playing seven-card brag. By the time I finished playing for England the lads were playing shoot pontoon and were losing up to a thousand pounds. I felt it was getting too high and too dangerous. You're mates and you don't want bad feeling in the camp, which can happen with shoot pontoon. The stakes can rocket.

We fancied our chances as we again opened a tournament against the Republic of Ireland, in Cagliari. We missed a couple of decent opportunities but at least we didn't lose this time. We drew 1–1. The injection in my big toe did its job and I came through the match with no problem. The Irish have done well over the years for a small nation. Mind you, they do recruit anybody with the slightest Irish connection! Their fans are terrific. They follow their team in great numbers, enjoy themselves win, lose or draw and never cause any trouble.

I hate to admit it, but in the eighties England had too many fans who were more interested in looking for trouble than supporting their team. It has taken a lot of effort to get rid of that bad reputation and thankfully most of the thugs have been weeded out. As a player, you're not affected by hooliganism or anything else that goes on around you because you are concentrating totally on the game. But as an Englishman, you want England supporters to behave properly, enjoy the football and follow their team with pride instead of tarnishing the name of the country. Our fans have been great over the past few years, but we know we can't afford to be complacent. It takes only an isolated incident for other countries to say, 'Ah, it's the English.'

We were confident when we met Holland, another familiar team. They weren't the force they had been two years before. They had struggled to score goals, but we had the same problem that day and drew 0–0. At least England were still in the tournament. I wasn't. A second successive World Cup ended for me in the second match. I suddenly felt a click in my left Achilles tendon as I was running. No one kicked me, there was no collision or strain to get the ball. I tried to carry on, but couldn't. The pain was terrible and I knew it was serious. I had to go off. I'd torn about three-quarters of the fibres, so it was near enough a rupture. I had jarred my foot in the FA Cup final replay against Crystal Palace a month earlier and my heel and Achilles tendon were sore for about a week. Whether that had something to do with the problem I don't know. Anyway, my World Cup was over and this time I went straight home for surgery. It was a different type of injury from the one I had in Mexico and there was no point in hobbling around.

When I came round from the operation, the surgeon told me the injury was a result of wear and tear over the years. It could have given way in another two weeks, two years or ten years. If you tackle a lot, you're bound to get kicks on the Achilles over the years. The surgeon explained that he had cleaned up the damage and sewn it up again. There are no guarantees with Achilles operations, but he said I shouldn't have too many problems, and I did carry on playing for a good few years after that. I just feel I was unlucky with the timing of the shoulder and Achilles injuries. I could have had them the year before Mexico and Italy. Instead, they had to happen in the second match of each World Cup. That's the annoying thing. At the same time, I realise I was fortunate to be able to get over those injuries and continue my playing career. I see a lot of lads I played with who are near enough crippled.

After the operation I joined the BBC World Cup panel, working with Terry Venables and Jimmy Hill. It was hard to watch England from a TV studio and not be involved in the action, but it was still good to see the lads do so well and reach the semi-finals. Once it gets to a penalty shoot-out, as it did with the Germans, you need some luck to go your way. It went against us that day and we were out of the tournament, but that was the second best achievement by an England team in a World Cup, and all credit to the management and players for that. They did tremendously well – none more so than Paul Gascoigne.

This was the tournament where Gazza announced himself to the football world. He was sensational and you could see it coming in the warm-up friendlies. He was just a naturally gifted footballer. When I talk about the Maradonas of that top category, I have Gazza in the group just below. He never progressed to the next stage because of his injuries. He knows he has only himself to blame for the rash tackle on Gary Charles in the 1991 FA Cup final that tore his cruciate knee ligaments, one of the worst injuries you can have. He also broke his kneecap. Serious damage like that inevitably takes a percentage from a player's game.

Despite that, he was still able to play to a fantastic standard. Very few are blessed with that gift. He was also a great trainer. He worked hard because he had a passion for the game and wanted to be a winner. That's also why he had this angry head to him. People loved him not only because he was so good, but because he was a character and had that bit of aggression to go with the skill. Your average Joe Public will pay to see a player like Gazza.

It would have been outrageous if England had got through to the '90 final and Gazza had missed it, but that was the scenario facing him after he was booked against the Germans. He knew it as soon as he saw the yellow card and one of the abiding images of the tournament was Gazza in tears. Obviously, you can't allow players to get away with rash challenges, but I think there should be flexibility in the rules when a player could be denied the chance to play in the biggest match of his life. Roy Keane and Paul Scholes missed United's 1999 European Cup final through suspension. Maybe there should be a distinction between a red and two yellows for minor offences. You shouldn't have to pay such a heavy price for a couple of petty indiscretions.

That said, players have to be sensible and not get themselves booked too often. Gazza was easy to lead on and wind up. There were times when he needed to be calmed down. It's not always easy, as a footballer, to stay calm. I didn't always control myself. You get your angry head on now and then and push the referee to the limit, but you have to know when to pull back. If you go over the line, you're going to get punished and I knew how far I could push it. Then you have to calm down. I had just one suspension through picking up too many bookings. It comes down to common sense.

It didn't need too much sense to work out that I had played in my last World Cup. I would be thirty-seven by the time the 1994 finals came around. But I did feel I could carry on with England for another couple of years and try to help my country to qualify for the 1992 European Championship. That was, of course, providing the manager wanted me.

─────── 13 ───────
BITTER SWEET

T HE ACHILLES INJURY and operation meant I missed the start of the 1990–91 season, but the reassurance of the surgeon encouraged me to believe I had plenty of football left in me for club and country. Sure enough, I made a full recovery and had a good season for United, topping it with that European Cup-Winners' Cup success. As far as England were concerned, though, things had changed. Bobby Robson had been replaced as manager by Graham Taylor and I sensed through my early dealings with the new boss that he didn't particularly want to involve me in his plans.

As he points out, I wasn't fit when he took over and he was looking ahead not only to the 1992 European Championship but also the 1994 World Cup, so he needed to try out some of the younger players. If I hadn't played well for United, I would have been able to accept that my international career was over, but I was happy with my club form and thought I could still do a job for England. I wanted to play for my country and help us reach another major tournament. That's why I accepted the chance to play for Graham Taylor that December in a B international in Algeria. He said he wanted me to be in the team, alongside a few of the younger lads. It seemed to me that he'd had a change of heart about me so I went along with his proposition. Alex Ferguson wasn't best pleased when I told him I wanted to go on the trip. He felt I didn't need to prove myself at that stage of my career because everybody knew what I could do. He felt it was a fixture the manager should use to look at new players, not seasoned internationals.

'What the hell do you want to go there for?' he said. I was asking myself the same question when we got there.

There was a hailstorm and a half during training, the night before the match, and we had to stop the session. That just typified the whole trip for me. In his team-talk, Taylor went on about people working down pits and in factories, and I was thinking, 'What's this got to do with the game? Any chance of hearing about the Algerian team?' I realised there and then that we weren't on the same wavelength.

I started the match at centre-half and moved to right-back when he switched things around. I seem to recall we went to a back four. He says I was on the left side of a back three, then on the right. Either way, I couldn't see the point of playing where I did. The match ended 0–0 and Alex was right, it proved nothing. It gave the younger players experience, and that was fair enough, but for me the whole trip was a waste of time. I didn't say anything to Taylor at the time. I thought it would be best to go back to Old Trafford, get on with my job at United and see what happened.

Fortunately, my form with United was pretty consistent and I was recalled to the full England team for the friendly international against Cameroon at Wembley on 6 February 1991. It was a freezing night and they couldn't move. We won 2–0. I played again in our 1–1 draw with the Republic of Ireland in a European Championship qualifier at Wembley, on 27 March. Injuries and United's summer tour cost me the chance of winning more caps that year, but I returned for another European Championship qualifying tie, against Turkey, on 16 October 1991.

The day before the match Taylor and I had a chat on the pitch and he asked me why I had been playing so well for United. I told him it was because the manager played me in front of the back four, where I could use my knowledge and reading of the game. I could double up with the centre-halves when necessary, keep possession, switch the play, set our moves in motion and use the legs of the young, quick lads on the flanks. He gave me the impression he understood but then when he picked his team I found myself on the left side of midfield. I'd not played there since I was about nineteen, in West Brom's reserves. I couldn't believe it after the discussion we'd had. Taylor now says I was on the left of a midfield three, with David Batty in the holding role. I just remember playing left-wing – it's imprinted on my mind – and I didn't enjoy it one bit.

Playing in that position, and especially at my age, just didn't suit me. You need pace as well as a good engine to get up and down the wing. I still had the stamina to run all right, but at the age of thirty-four I had maybe lost a yard of pace. That wasn't a problem when I played in my proper position. We'd talked about my role at United the day before, yet he played me wide. I couldn't understand it. He didn't tell me why he played me there, he just named the team in formation.

I had a poor game and didn't need anybody to tell me. As I walked off the pitch I knew, deep down, that I had played my last game for my country. We'd won 1–0 and I was pleased about that. England were on their way to the European Championship finals, which had to be the main objective for all of us, but I couldn't see myself being with the squad. That wasn't the way I wanted to play for England. The position didn't suit me and the manager didn't suit me. You have to be big enough to take media criticism, but it's hard to take it when you're played out of position.

I'd set myself a target of a hundred caps, but I didn't want to stick around, just hoping to get another ten, somehow, some way. If I couldn't have a role where I would be able to play to a standard I expected of myself, there was no point in carrying on. When I went back to United I told Fergie I didn't think the England set-up was for me any more and that I thought I should pack it in.

For the first time in my international career I sensed it was getting a bit cliquey in the camp. You could see it as we were sitting around in the hotel and going to the matches. Ever since I'd been involved with England, going back to the days of Phil Thompson, Terry McDermott, Kevin Keegan and Trevor Brooking, then with Terry Butcher, Gary Lineker, Peter Beardsley and Gazza, there had been a good atmosphere. Terry McDermott wasn't a club-mate but we became good pals outside the England set-up. We went to the races together. He gave me advice on shooting and how to dink the ball over the keeper. He was great. They all were and we got on well as a group. Suddenly, I didn't feel the same togetherness. I don't know whether that was because so many new faces were coming into the squad and they needed time to gel, but to me it appeared the players formed cliques. Times had changed and it seemed the time had come for me to move on.

I knew Fergie would be happy for me to stop playing for England and save myself for United, but he suggested I should wait until Taylor picked his squad for the next match, against Poland, before taking things any further. Ten days before that match, Taylor spoke to Alex and told him he wasn't selecting me. Taylor then phoned me to tell me. I think I was pretty calm about it. I wasn't surprised and told him I wanted to retire from international football, anyway. The announcement was made on 4 November 1991.

Taylor has explained that he thought my legs were going and that he had to look to the future. He also says he risked upsetting Gary Lineker by taking the captaincy off him and giving it back to me for the match against Cameroon. I don't believe Gary had a problem with that. I had been captain sixty-three times before Graham Taylor was manager and I'd missed only a few matches, so I think Gary probably expected me to have the armband back. Gary and I always got on well and still do. We never had a problem over that. We bump into one another every now and then and whenever we do we'll have a drink and a laugh together.

I could have had another cap because I was offered a farewell international at Wembley, but I realised that the FA just wanted to generate some money. It was a time when England international crowds were dropping off and they were looking at ways of bringing in extra cash. I wasn't impressed with the proposition and told them, 'No thanks.'

I see Graham Taylor occasionally and we'll say 'hello', but we don't have long conversations. I've never mentioned the England situation to him. He had a job to do and he did it as he saw fit. I accept that. England finished bottom of their group at the 1992 European Championship finals and failed to qualify for the 1994 World Cup finals.

It's fair to say Graham Taylor wasn't my favourite manager, but then I can count myself lucky to have worked with so many great managers at club and international level. Although it was disappointing to end my England days like that, I'm grateful for a fantastic career with my country. I won ninety caps, sixty-five of them as captain, and scored twenty-six goals, but the bare facts don't begin to tell of the experiences, friendships and memories from those eleven years.

The real pity is that the England teams I played for didn't fulfil their potential. At the 1982 World Cup I was still comparatively young and learning the international game. Then, when I was at my peak and perhaps could have had an influence on tournaments, I had injuries. We certainly had the ability, individually and collectively, to have achieved more than we did. I'm convinced the team we had in 1990, especially, was good enough to have won the World Cup. But I still have the satisfaction of having played in three World Cups, with some excellent teams and fantastic mates. The spirit in the camp was brilliant, with no petty jealousies, no back-stabbing. That camaraderie stays with you forever.

We had a lot of outstanding wins and some big wins – Luxembourg 9–0 and Turkey 8–0 twice, once when I scored a hat-trick. My only hat-trick with United was against Portsmouth in a testimonial match. I did get a competitive hat-trick for West Brom, against Ipswich. Another England game that stands out for me was our 4–1 win in a European Championship qualifier against Yugoslavia, in Belgrade, in 1987. I scored in that match, but the real pleasure was in the team performance. We were tremendous that day. I scored against the same country in 1989 after thirty-eight seconds – the fastest goal in a professional match at Wembley.

I always looked forward to playing Scotland. That traditional fixture really had an edge to it. In those days the top English clubs had a number of Scottish players, so the banter in the build-up to England-Scotland internationals was constant. I have to admit that the Scottish fans made it such a great occasion, especially at Wembley – 90,000 of them seemed to be in the ground. I don't know how they got the tickets but the atmosphere was always great. People say the Scots, Welsh and Irish have more passion than the English but I know from the group of English lads I played with that those matches meant just as much to us. We loved them even more when we won. One of the most memorable was a 2–0 win against Scotland in Glasgow in 1989. John Fashanu and Steve Bull played up front for us and the Scots just couldn't handle their sheer, physical power.

We played all the leading football nations during my career with England, but were never hammered. That's not bad going. You would have thought that somewhere along the line luck would have gone against us big-style and we would have been really turned over. Thankfully, it never happened. We never lost by more than a couple of goals. We lost 2–0 to the USSR at Wembley in 1984 and in truth it could have been much worse. They murdered us. Then there were those two 3–1 defeats at the 1988 European Championship finals, by Holland and the USSR, but generally any defeats were narrow. Even Brazil only ever beat our team by the odd goal.

England duty took me to just about every corner of the world. The experiences were fascinating and educational but I suppose one of the most enlightening trips was to a European country, Albania. It struck me as a strange, almost unreal place. People didn't have their own cars. The only traffic was government buses and taxis. It's difficult to imagine that a country like that is just two or three hours away from Britain.

As far as the organisation for England tours and home matches was concerned, nothing more could have been done. When it came to arrangements for the players, the FA were top class. This is where Roy Keane was trying to draw comparisons when he had his big bust-up over the Republic of Ireland set-up in 2002. Roy and I would go out and have a drink and a chat and he'd tell me what it was like in the Irish camp. Then I'd tell him what it was like with England, how we had the best facilities, medical attention, travel, accommodation, food and so on. The FA lay on cars, there's no delay or arguments over expenses, everything is spot on. The differences were mind-blowing.

I can understand Roy's frustration. When you've been involved with a top club, winning trophies for so many years, you appreciate the importance of good organisation and preparation. That's probably what set him off. I spoke to other former Ireland players when I was in for the Ireland manager's job and they made similar observations. I can understand why Roy got so annoyed. He is a perfectionist and he felt Ireland could go on from where they were to become even better. He wanted the best for his country.

I got the opportunity to do a bit more for my country as assistant to Terry Venables in 1994. He realised I could work for him only on a part-time basis because I had been appointed player-manager of

Middlesbrough, but said he was keen for me to join him. I think he felt that with Don Howe and me alongside him he had a good age balance on his coaching staff. Don was a fantastic, experienced coach, but Terry probably thought I could relate more closely to the players. I had played with a lot of them. From my point of view it was great not only to be back on the England scene, but also to have the chance to learn and gain valuable experience as quickly as possible.

Terry and Don were wonderful to work with. Terry's man-management of the players was terrific. He knew what he wanted and how to get the best out of players. We worked hard but Terry liked to see smiles about the place. The players enjoyed their work. He was good at working with players one to one, explaining exactly what he wanted from them. Tactically, he was excellent. He covered every little detail on the pitch. The training sessions were carefully structured. Every morning when we were together with England we had a meeting in Terry's room to discuss the day's training and how we were going to plan for the team we were playing in our next game.

He welcomed input from Don and me. Terry was thinking about playing the Dutch way, with two wide players and Teddy Sheringham dropping behind Alan Shearer. Don thought we didn't have enough time to get it right, but I argued that the best players in the country were good enough and intelligent enough to adapt to the new system. That's what we did and it worked well.

Our objective was the 1996 European Championship, which was held in England. I'm convinced we should have won that tournament. As the host country, we didn't have to qualify, and although that meant we had no competitive matches in the two-year build-up, I thought our preparation benefited. We were able to concentrate fully on the finals rather than on individual qualifying ties. We had quality, strength and character with David Seaman in goal, Gary

Neville, Tony Adams, Gareth Southgate, Stuart Pearce, Darren Anderton, Paul Ince, Paul Gascoigne, Steve McManaman, Sheringham and Shearer. We also had Sol Campbell, David Platt, Nick Barmby, Steve Stone and Robbie Fowler in the squad. The more we worked together, the stronger we looked.

We completed our preparations with a tour of China and Hong Kong. We had a comfortable 3–0 win against the Chinese, in Beijing, and then beat a Hong Kong Golden Select side 1–0. The mood in the camp was terrific. We were to have a few days' break when we flew back and then meet up for Euro '96. Things could hardly have been better, but then came the nightmare of the 'dentist's chair'.

After the Hong Kong match we had to attend an official dinner. The following day was Gazza's twenty-ninth birthday, so he asked Terry if he and the other players could go on to a club later to celebrate. Terry said that would be OK, but only for a couple of hours. He sent me with them to make sure they were back by two o'clock. The club cordoned off an area for our party and I stood chatting with Paul Ince and a bouncer, who made sure they weren't given any bother. The barman put a big glass bowl of what looked like punch on a table in front of the players, but Gazza said they'd have a bit of that later. He wanted a go in the chair. They were saying, 'Come on Robbo, come on the chair,' but I said I'd stay where I was. Gazza and about six of the other lads went over. I didn't see the chair, but I gather it was basically a case of being strapped in and having vodka or tequila poured down your throat.

About half an hour later they came back to the bowl and started sipping the stuff through straws. Within twenty minutes they went from near enough sober to absolutely wrecked, but funny wrecked. I've never seen anyone go so quickly. They were all in really good humour and just having a laugh. Then they had bottles of beer and started spraying each other. Next thing, one of the lads was tearing birthday boy Gazza's shirt. So then they're ripping each other's shirts, mine included. There was no trouble, just boisterous fun. At that point I said we'd call for some taxis and go back to the hotel. All the squad had gone to the club and, apart from Gazza and the other six players who went over to the chair, they each had just a couple of beers.

We flew back the following day and I went straight out to Portugal to join Denise and the kids on holiday. As I walked around the pool, I could see pictures and headlines in the English papers – 'England Stars' Shame' and all that sort of thing. The thing was that every time a player went to the toilet in the club he was asked to pose for a photo, and by then some of them didn't look too clever. We didn't have a clue that the pictures had got out. It was mainly Gazza and Teddy who were spread all over the papers. I just hung my head in my hands and thought, 'Oh, no!' Then I had some explaining to do to Denise. I got some real earache over that.

We got slaughtered in the press and they presented it as if the trip had been a piss-up, start to finish. You'd have thought we'd all been out on a bender. I couldn't believe it. The truth is that we were out for a couple of hours at the end of the tour and with a fortnight to go before the European Championship. Terry naturally wanted to know from me what had happened. After all, I was supposed to be looking after the players. I told him the full story, that they were just having a daft carry-on among themselves, and he was satisfied with the explanation.

Despite all the fuss about Hong Kong, the players were totally focused on the job when we met up again. If anything, something like that draws a squad closer together. It was tremendous to have a major tournament in this country – the first since the 1966 World Cup – and the response was everything we hoped it would be. There was a fantastic buzz at all the matches, not just England's. The fans really got into it and the whole thing was a terrific spectacle. Of course, it helps to stimulate interest when the host nation does well, but we didn't get off to the start we wanted. Switzerland held us 1–1 in our first match, while the other two teams in our group, Scotland and Holland, drew 0–0.

Our next match was against the Scots. Shearer gave us the breakthrough early in the second half and Gazza got the second goal with a brilliant solo effort, flicking the ball over Colin Hendry and then firing it in – pure Gazza. Then he lay on his back on the ground with his mouth wide open so that the lads could squirt liquid down his throat, like they did when he was in the chair in Hong Kong, only this time it wasn't booze! That was the players' way of answering their critics. Gary McAllister missed a penalty for Scotland and there was a lot made about the ball moving on the spot just as he was running up. Whether it did or it didn't, we won 2–0 and were looking forward to playing the Dutch.

That game against Holland proved to be our outstanding team performance of the championship. We played brilliantly and hammered them 4–1, Shearer and Sheringham scoring two apiece. Wembley was rocking that day. The atmosphere was unbelievable. It seemed everybody in the country was singing 'Football's coming home . . .' We topped the group, setting up a quarter-final tie against Spain, who always had good players yet tended to underachieve in major tournaments. They gave us our toughest game and we were a little fortunate to beat them, on penalties, after drawing 0–0.

In the semis against our old rivals, Germany, we had our chances and looked the better side, but again we drew, this time 1–1, and so faced another penalty shoot-out. Our penalty-takers were Pearce, Anderton, Teddy, Shearer and Gazza. I took them for penalty practice at the end of every training session. They had five each. When I look back, perhaps I should have had a couple of reserve takers, as well. The other lads usually started mucking about if they were still around when we were practising penalties, so I always sent them away. I wanted the five takers to practise properly. You don't think about the sixth – and now I kick myself that I didn't. Both teams scored a perfect five out of five at the end of that semi-final, so we needed a sixth taker, and you don't usually get a queue of volunteers in a situation like that. I think Terry asked Paul Ince if he fancied it and he said, 'No.' Gareth Southgate stepped forward bravely, but he didn't manage to score. The Germans won the shoot-out 6–5.

The lads were gutted, especially for Gareth. We were out of the championship, but felt we should have beaten Germany and I was just as sure we would have beaten the Czech Republic in the final, as the Germans eventually did. Even so, we'd done the country proud and the tournament as a whole went down well. It gave me fantastic experience because, as well as helping Terry with the coaching, I went to other matches to compile scouting reports. It was a busy but thoroughly enjoyable championship. In fact, those two years were very important in my coaching and management career, combining England duties with my full-time job as player-manager of Middlesbrough. I was paid only expenses for my England work, which I had no problem with. The knowledge I gained and the contacts I made along the way made me better equipped for my club work.

Euro '96 marked the end of my coaching role with England. Terry had been hoping for an improved and extended contract, but the FA were obviously not so keen and had already appointed his successor. All sorts of rumours about Terry's business dealings were being reported, but he insisted he had nothing to hide and I don't think anything was proved against him. In any case, he left and Glenn Hoddle arrived on what I believe was a far higher salary. Terry had done a great job for England and I've no doubt would have gone on doing a great job. He was the perfect man to lead our country.

Whatever decision the FA came to regarding Terry, I had made up my mind that I couldn't carry on with England, anyway. Much as I'd learned over those two years, the workload involved in doing two jobs had become too much. I just didn't have a family life and Denise was rightly unhappy that I was spending so much time away from home. I'm glad I had that spell with England and I know how lucky I was to be given the opportunity, but enough was enough.

There was a suggestion that I might have taken over from Terry as England's number one. In fact, I had a meeting with Jimmy Armfield, who was the FA's head-hunter, but although the approach was very flattering, I told Jim that if I was ever going to be the England manager, I wanted it to be when I had the vast experience necessary to do the job well. I was too inexperienced at that time. I'd had only two years in management with Middlesbrough and coaching with Terry. I knew the international set-up but that wasn't sufficient to take over the top job.

My coaching stint with England had been brilliant. I'd enjoyed every minute, working with Terry and the best players we had, but as a coach, you're not in the firing line. You're with the lads, joining in the training and banter without the pressure and flak that the manager has to contend with. The manager is the man who makes the final decisions and takes the ultimate responsibility. I knew I wasn't ready to step up front for England. Besides, I had a big job to do back at Middlesbrough.

14

BUZZING BORO

LIFE HAD BEEN FRANTIC in the two years after I left Manchester United. I didn't have time to reflect on my years at Old Trafford or even think about missing all my old mates when I moved on. Leaving United was a wrench but I had more than enough on my mind. My challenge was to rebuild Middlesbrough and take them back to the Premiership.

There was no chance to sit back and analyse my approach to management because I had to get stuck into it straightaway in that summer of 1994. I didn't have any coaching qualifications when I went to Boro, which shows how much the game has changed since the mid-nineties. Now the requirements for managerial jobs are much stricter and I have since qualified for all the necessary national and international badges. It was a big step, from being a player to being the player-boss, with all the responsibility that carries, but when you have been in the game as long as I had been, at club and international level, you learn what it's about. Over the previous couple of years I'd spent a lot of time with the United coaching staff, watching and listening as they prepared for training sessions. In those last few weeks, when I knew I was going to Middlesbrough, I took an even closer interest in their work.

I also learned from the managers I worked under, although I didn't necessarily adopt all their techniques. For instance, I felt sure I would never go in for the hairdryer treatment. I can lose my temper and my teams have had a few blasts over the years, but never to the extent that I've witnessed with Alex Ferguson. He used to break tea cups and anything else that was within range when he went into one of his real rages. Whatever was in front of him on the table would go flying. That was his way and you can't say it hasn't been successful. We're all different.

He does have a softer, human side that the public don't see and probably wouldn't believe. He's not all iron fist. Just when you expect a rollicking, he'll be very sympathetic and supportive. He cares about his players and all those who work for him. You can't be a good manager if you don't understand people and don't have good man-management skills. I'd recognised that in all the great managers I'd worked under.

Alex was prepared to be hard, though, and move players on when he felt it was necessary. After I left, so did Ince, Hughes and Kanchelskis. I tried to sign Kanchelskis, but Everton were a bigger club at the time and on the doorstep, so he went there. United had all that terrific young talent coming through and Fergie realised they were going to be exceptional. His changes weren't ruthless, they were good management. You have to strike the right balance of youth and experience. You can't allow your team to get too old, which is perhaps what Liverpool did in the eighties. It's virtually impossible to make seven or eight changes all at once and maintain your level of success.

Two of his more controversial sales were Jaap Stam and David Beckham, who were key members of his 1999 treble-winning team. The one that surprised me was Stam because he was, and still is, a top defender. I heard at the time that Sir Alex – as he became following the Premiership, FA Cup and Champions League victories – was worried Stam would never be the same player after he snapped his Achilles tendon. There were also suggestions that Stam had upset the manager and players with comments in his book. Whatever the reason was, I think United missed him. Becks was a different case. Sir Alex thought all the media hype and promotional interests were taking over Becks' life and threatened to overshadow the team. Real Madrid's offer of £25 million for a twenty-eight-year-old was too good to turn down.

These are the difficult decisions a manager has to make and you have to say Sir Alex has got most of those decisions right. His record speaks for itself. He is one of the best British managers, if not the best, there's ever been.

I was armed with all I had taken in from my managers as I assessed the playing and coaching staff at Boro as quickly as I could. John Pickering, an excellent and experienced coach, was on the staff and I was more than happy for him to stay on. I brought in Viv Anderson, my old England and United team-mate, as my number two. We also registered him as a player. He was manager of Barnsley at the time and we had to pay them £50,000 in compensation, but I felt it was money well spent. I respected Viv's knowledge of the game and his judgement of players. I knew that we would have a good relation-ship, which was important when we were going to spend so much time together. I gave the reserve team coaching job to Gordon McQueen, another former United colleague. He'd had management experience at St Mirren and was eager to get back into the game. He, again, had the knowledge and enthusiasm I was looking for. I was satisfied we had the backroom staff we needed.

Boro weren't exactly a glamour club or a big attraction for the stars at the time. They'd had a modest season in the First Division and were struggling to get decent gates. I knew what the score was. Even so, it was a bit of a culture shock when I arrived. We had no training ground so we had to change at Ayresome Park and drive either to one of two college pitches we used – it depended which surface was better – or to the local prison where we were also allowed to use the pitches. The dressing rooms at Ayresome Park were unbelievably dreary. The paintwork was a dark mustard colour. You felt depressed as soon as you walked in. I looked around for a water dispenser. There wasn't one.

On my first day with the players, John Hendrie was going round the lads, asking for money.

'Ah, Gaffer, you're player-manager, aren't you?' he said to me. 'Two quid then.'

'What's that for?' I asked.

'Tea and biscuits before training.'

I went and told Keith Lamb, the chief executive, that if I was going to run the butts off the players in pre-season training, they shouldn't have to pay for their own tea and biscuits. The club should provide them. I also told him we needed a water dispenser and I wanted the dressing room painted white, to brighten up the place.

For pre-season training we had the use of pitches at Kirklevington Prison, about a fifteen-minute drive from the ground. So we all piled into cars and as Viv and I drove along I noticed some kids playing in a field. They were wearing Manchester United, Liverpool and Arsenal shirts. I turned to Viv and said, 'The first thing we've got to do is get these kids wearing Middlesbrough shirts.' We had to make people in the area proud of their local team and want to be associated with them.

The warden opened the prison gates for us and we warmed up by jogging around the pitch, watched by prisoners on the other side of the fence. One of the players shouted, 'Gaffer, Gaffer.' I just carried on running.

'You realise that's you, now,' said Viv, who was running bedside me.

Management was totally new to me, but I had to get used to it pretty quickly. Having to train as a player as well meant I had a hectic schedule. I played most of the matches in that first season and Viv played in quite a few important games, too. I gave myself a sitting role, in front of the defence, and felt quite comfortable at that level. In fact, I didn't find it hard combining management with playing, mainly because the players were so good to work with. They seemed to take to me and called me 'gaffer' without my having to tell them. If I gave them a rollicking they accepted it and never argued.

Although Boro had finished the previous season mid-table, I knew they had some good players and the basis of a decent team. I'd played against Robbie Mustoe and Jamie Pollock in Cup-ties. John Hendrie and Paul Wilkinson rightly had good reputations. The area I felt I had to improve straightaway was the defence. I studied videos of their games and analysed the statistics. They had conceded fifty-four goals in the League, so we had to shore up the defensive side of the team to start with. The chairman, Steve Gibson, who had set out his plan to build a new team and a new stadium, gave me the promised £2 million to spend on players and we began recruiting as soon as we could.

My first signing cost nothing. Clayton Blackmore, a defensive-type of midfield player, came from United on a free transfer. I paid £1 million for Neil Cox and £750,000 for Nigel Pearson, two good, strong, dependable defenders. Nigel became my skipper. Alan Miller, a goalkeeper from Arsenal, cost us £250,000. We opened the First Division campaign with a 2–0 win against Burnley in front of a 23,000 crowd, and that set the tone for the season. We won our first four games on the bounce and were unbeaten in seven. The place came alive. I knew the potential was there and that we just had to tap into it. The confidence grew from that first run of results.

I brought in a German striker, Uwe Fuchs, who scored some important goals for us. I'd used up my initial budget, but as we were top of the table, the chairman said I could bring in somebody else for a final push. I said we should go for another goalscorer. So we bought Jan-Aage Fjortoft from Swindon for £1.3 million just before the transfer deadline. He gave us that extra edge to finish the job, scoring some vital goals in the last few matches. Even though we had more draws than we would have liked towards the end, we were three points clear in the final table and deservedly champions.

It was a terrific feeling to take the club up to the Premiership in my first season, but better still to know we were capable of building on that. Our new stadium, the Riverside, would be ready for the following season and the whole of Teesside was excited at the prospect. It made all the effort on and off the pitch worthwhile. United lost their title to Blackburn that season and I watched them play Everton in the FA Cup final on television, while we were on holiday in Barbados. They lost that trophy, as well. I don't know whether I might have been able to make a difference in certain matches, but there was no point in dwelling on what was, for me, the past. Boro was my team now and we had plenty to look forward to.

When I'd changed jobs, I'd been able to stay at home in Hale thanks to the daily ICI executive flight from Manchester to Teesside. ICI had a 20 per cent stake in our club, so I travelled up in the morning and back in the evening, free of charge. When I needed a hotel, I used one owned by ICI, and again it cost the club nothing. The arrangement worked well for four years, until ICI began selling off their plants and cut back on the flights. The following year, Viv and I commuted by car, sharing the driving, but that was hard, especially in winter. So Denise and I bought a place at Aislaby, near Yarm, and stayed there for a couple of years. We kept the house in Hale, though.

Middlesbrough's new home was a 30,000-seater, state-of-the-art stadium and we had no trouble filling it. The fans clamoured for season tickets and, just as we'd hoped, the kids in the area started wearing Boro shirts – and the grown-ups, too. We knew we would have to bring in more quality players for the Premiership and I signed Nick Barmby for £5 million. It was a big fee at the time, but he was a good, young player and I felt we would be able to get our money back if we sold him on. We did eventually sell him, to Everton, for £6.5 million.

Gary Walsh, another ex-United player, became our regular goal-keeper in the 1995–96 season but I was no longer a regular. I would have managed another year in the First Division, but the pace of the Premiership was too much for me, and I made just a couple of League appearances. I had trouble with sciatica, which affected my calf muscles and hamstrings.

We kicked off the season with a 1–1 draw at Arsenal and then played Chelsea in our first match at the Riverside. They had Ruud Gullit and my old mate Sparky in their side. It was a massive day for the club, but things didn't quite go to plan. I wanted to organise our match days as United did, with the players meeting at the stadium to have their pre-match meal together. Then they could relax and watch television or read before the game, but a fire alert in the kitchen set off all the fire extinguishers. The players' meals, along with all the corporate sponsors' food, were ruined. I took the players to one of the ICI hotels, where they managed to rustle up something for us. The club had to give everybody else their money back. It was the worst possible preparation for our big day, yet we won 2–0. There was no temptation to make that our regular routine, though. One drama like that was more than enough.

Our form held up into the autumn and we went to Old Trafford on the back of five consecutive wins. We were fourth in the Premier-ship. The United fans gave me a fantastic reception, but we lost 2–0 and that took some of the momentum out of our play. Fergie brought in a lot of his now famous kids that season and they went on to win the Championship, wrapping up the title at the Riverside. We had our own fresh-faced player to marvel at from the autumn of 1995. In fact, he got the whole of football talking about Middlesbrough. His name, of course, was Juninho.

I got on to him as a result of working with England. Juninho played for Brazil in the Umbro International Trophy, a tournament staged that summer in England as part of our preparations for the European Championship, held the following year. Sweden and Japan were the other countries involved. We played Brazil at Wembley and I was impressed by Roberto Carlos and Juninho, who scored in their 3–1 win. An agent told me there could be a chance of buying Juninho, so I got Keith Lamb to send a fax to his club, São Paulo, asking if they were interested in doing a deal. We got a bit of a stroppy reply, effectively saying there was absolutely no chance.

We persisted and the agent, an Italian guy, got more involved because he could see a cut in it for him. We sent more faxes and got more blanks until they finally said they might be interested. They asked if I would go across to see them, so Keith and I went to Brazil. The negotiations lasted five days because São Paulo were a sporting club, run by a committee. It wasn't like dealing with a chairman or chief executive in this country. We watched Juninho play in a match while we were there and he wasn't the only decent player they had. I wouldn't have minded bringing a few of them back with us. Anyway, Keith finally agreed a fee for Juninho – $7 million, which worked out then at £4.75 million.

I knew we were getting someone special. He could do a bit of everything. He had great pace with the ball, he had skill and vision and scored fabulous goals – Brazilian Player of the Year and still only twenty-two. He was tiny, but that didn't worry me because you could see he was brave and he was never intimidated. The Premiership didn't bother him at all.

The one frustrating thing about the trip was that when I asked the agent about the left-back – Roberto Carlos – he said we'd missed him. He'd just signed for Internazionale. We could have had him for £4 million. Imagine what he might have done for us! We had Juninho, though, and he lit up the Riverside. Our fans loved him and I think the whole country took to him because he was such an exciting and likeable player.

Juninho came from a tightly knit family and he brought his parents and sister across to stay with him. We put them in a club house. His dad was always at his side. Juninho was more than worth the effort and expense it took to sign him and make him happy on Teesside. It was a great coup for us. The charisma he brought to Boro was unbelievable.

We finished that season in twelfth place, which was a solid start for us in the Premiership. There were no relegation issues and I think most teams would have settled for that, but I felt we would do better over the following years. I thought we could, given the ambitions of the chairman, become a top club, although nobody envisaged the level of support we got straightaway. We couldn't fit in everybody who wanted to see us, so the chairman eventually had the corners of the stadium filled in to take the capacity to 35,000. It was great and really satisfying to be involved with the club at that time.

I carried on trying to bring in the best players I could. I think it's fair to say we stunned a few people in the game with the Juninho signing and a number of other exotic names followed him to the Riverside. We attracted genuine world stars. We didn't succeed in signing everybody we wanted. We missed out on Kanchelskis and Spain's Miguel Angel Nadal, known then as 'The Beast of Barcelona' and now as the uncle of the tennis player, Rafael Nadal. I was beaten also to the signature of Gianluca Vialli, by Chelsea, so I asked Juventus about the availability of his fellow Italy striker, Fabrizio Ravanelli. They said every player had his price and we eventually agreed on £7 million.

To sell the club to Ravanelli, I took over photos of the stadium, along with plans for the extension work and the new training ground. I'd visited a lot of training facilities on my scouting trips around Europe and made sure our training ground would lack for nothing. Ravanelli didn't know much about Middlesbrough – I think some of the players we went for had never heard of the place – but when I showed him the plans and the pictures, and told him the place was packed out every week, he was impressed. I suppose it was an advantage that they knew me because of my international career. It didn't just help with the player, it got me in the door in the first place.

Ravanelli was a great player, but also a pain in the butt. He had a terrific attitude to training and was a fantastic goalscorer. He scored all kinds of goals and lots of them. The problem with Ravanelli was that he could be a big moaner. When things were going well he was fine, but if they weren't, nothing would be right for him. If we had a bad result, he would go on about how unprofessional we were for not having proper training facilities. The trouble was that he had come from Juventus, the European champions and Italy's most famous club, to a club where the structure was totally different, where there was no training ground and building work was still going on. We had trained at Ayresome Park in our first season at the Riverside, but then the old place was knocked down, so we were back to training at a college ground, ten minutes away. We put on a bus to take the players there from the stadium but then some players would be ready to leave sooner than others and they'd be sitting on the bus, getting cold and irritated. It wasn't ideal, but it was a situation the other players accepted.

I don't know whether Ravanelli was misquoted sometimes, but his name appeared on a number of articles about that. So I said to him, 'Hang on, you knew it was like this, that we were having a new training ground built.' He'd seen the plans, he knew exactly what the situation was. That's why he used to drive me daft. We were moving to a lovely area, where we would have the best training facilities in the country. Everything was in place, but it couldn't be done overnight.

Then he started getting selfish on the pitch. He was all, 'Me, me, me.' For instance, he wouldn't help Mikkel Beck, a young striker we signed from Fortuna Cologne. He would never encourage Mikkel or do anything to boost his confidence, which was what the lad needed. All he did was knock him, saying he was hopeless and generally putting him down. He was a poor team player in that sense. Ravanelli worked hard and tried his best for the team, no question about that. He had a fantastic left foot and scored thirty-one goals for us in the 1996–97 season, but he just didn't have the personality to make him a popular player. He wasn't well liked within the group and was the only one who didn't really hit it off with the other lads.

Another Italian, Gianluca Festa, a defender, was totally different. He was a brilliant bloke and team man, setting a great example to the other lads. A fitness fanatic, he stayed at the club for something like seven years, which was pretty well unheard of for a foreign player.

Most of the foreign players we signed were no trouble at all and fitted in well at the club. Emerson, a Brazilian we bought from Porto for £4 million, was a good, solid character who always had a smile on his face. He left home and went to Portugal at the age of seventeen and could speak reasonable English, so the move to us didn't faze him. Most of the others learned to speak English quite well. It was only Juninho who struggled with the language.

It probably helped Juninho and Emerson that quite a large Brazilian community had settled on Teesside, which I didn't know until we signed them. We took on a Brazilian lady who lived in the area to help them sort out any domestic matters or problems they might have. Ravanelli and Emerson also moved into club houses. This was a bit of an issue with the club because it meant they had to buy a number of houses, but I explained to Steve and Keith that this was normal practice in Italy and Spain, and players expected it. Besides, any property we bought was a good investment for the club. They realised that and agreed to buy the houses we needed.

A bit of jealousy arose among the British lads, because they were reading in the papers about how much money the foreign players were being paid. I had a few problems with players saying that although they didn't expect to be on the same money as top internationals, they felt they should be brought more into line with them. I put up a few of the players' wages, but only those I thought were worth it. In any case, some of the figures bandied about in the press were way out. We had to pay Ravanelli top money because he had come from a top club in a country where they paid top wages. He came in on around £30,000 a week. Juninho, coming in from Brazil, was on nothing like that.

Some of the articles about our spending were a joke. They were talking as if Steve Gibson hadn't got a business head on him. The club was run efficiently and structured according to what we could afford. We knew that even if we were relegated – which did happen – the club would be in no financial difficulty. Some of the London press were a disgrace in the way they wrote about Middlesbrough as a place. They went on about ICI plants and chimneys and all that sort of thing. The truth is that there are some lovely places in that area. You'll find some of the nicest villages in the country, with great restaurants and a way of life anyone would enjoy.

Some people suggested I was encouraging a foreign invasion and taking jobs from British players by buying from abroad, but it was my job to do the best I could for Middlesbrough. I couldn't get the best British players. They wanted to go to Manchester United, Liverpool or Arsenal, the big clubs with tradition and records of success. To get players with the same ability, I had to go abroad. We brought in quality players and those we sold on generally went for a good profit. These days, of course, every club buys foreign players. Our lads got on well together and realised they were part of something new and special. I've heard stories about club reunions and how Juninho and Emerson love coming back to see their old team-mates again. They say they regretted leaving. I don't think Ravanelli got an invite.

Ravanelli showed what a good player he was in our first League fixture of the 1996–97 season – he scored a hat-trick in a 3–3 draw with Liverpool. Emerson was soon on the score-sheet, too. He started really well for us and had some rave reviews. He was worth watching just for his goal celebrations. The trouble was that, after a while, we heard Barcelona were tapping him, through his agent. That definitely unsettled him and caused us no end of problems.

We had a fantastic run in the Coca-Cola Cup, starting with a 10–0 aggregate win against Hereford. We then beat Huddersfield 5–1, Newcastle 3–1 and Liverpool 2–1 to reach the semi-finals. The downside was that the extra fixtures and injuries started to take their toll. We had a terrific team if we could put them all out together, but didn't have the strength in depth that some of the top clubs had. Things really came to a head just before we were due to play a League match at Blackburn in December.

We had a lot of long-term injuries and then a virus went through the club, leaving us with less than the bare bones of a team. Virtually all our defenders were out. Even Viv and I were injured. I was basically left with forwards and a bunch of untried YTS boys. I went to Keith on the Friday, the day before the match, and told him it was impossible to raise a team. So Keith contacted the Premier League to see if we could call off the match. One or two of the senior people were unavailable, but the most senior official he could speak to advised him to get medical confirmation of our injuries and illnesses. The doctor said he would issue the certificates and Keith rang Blackburn to say we would have to postpone the match. They were against that because they knew we had problems and were desperate for points themselves, but it wouldn't have been fair to us, our fans or the rest of the Premiership to put out the players we had left.

Later in the day, Keith got a call from a more senior official at the Premier League, who'd been playing golf. He said we couldn't postpone the match, but we said it was too late. We had been encouraged to take the course of action we took and there was no talk of punishment, although we felt we might be fined. If there had been any suggestion that we'd have points deducted I would have played the YTS boys and the laundry lady. We would have had nothing to lose. In the end, we were deducted three points and our appeal was thrown out. To my mind they were calling our doctor a liar. It was an absolute joke. Even top lawyers described it as a kangaroo court and a disgrace. It was only after the final match of the season that we realised how serious a miscarriage of justice that was.

We had to patch up the team and try to get through the Christmas holiday fixtures as best we could. We were still so short of bodies for the New Year's Day trip to Arsenal that I turned out for my one and only League match of the season. It also proved to be the last of my playing career. Losing 2–0 was bad enough, but that was only part of the pain for me. Running around after Ian Wright and Dennis Bergkamp finished me off. I couldn't move for three weeks. I was only ten days away from my fortieth birthday, but there was no way I could have played again in the Premiership as a forty-year-old. Enough was enough.

It wasn't really sad having to accept that my playing days were over. In fact, the way I felt at the time, it was a blessing! I'd had a long and fantastic career and there comes a stage when you simply can't do what you used to do. I was lucky to play for as many years as I did and I've turned out in a number testimonial and charity matches since then. Playing the odd match for fun or a good cause will do for me now.

We might have been having a hard time in the League, but we absolutely stormed it in the Cup competitions. We beat Stockport County, 2–1 on aggregate, to reach the Coca-Cola Cup final, and had another great run in the FA Cup. We knocked out Chester, Hednesford Town, Manchester City and Derby to earn another semifinal place. The whole of Teesside was buzzing. Boro had never been to a major final and yet we were one tie away from securing a second trip to Wembley in the same season.

The Coca-Cola Cup final against Leicester City was goalless at the end of normal time. I felt we could win it in extra time and was even more confident when Ravanelli gave us the lead early in the first period. We were dominating the game and should have finished them off. Towards the end they threw everybody forward. Steve Vickers was warming up because I wanted to play another centre-half alongside Nigel Pearson and Gianluca Festa to give us more aerial protection, but before we could bring him on, they took a throw-in and Emile Heskey equalised. There were only two minutes left and the match ended 1–1.

It meant we'd have to start from scratch in a replay, but before that we had to play Chesterfield in the FA Cup semi-final at Old Trafford. It turned out to be one of those Cup classics – full of drama and controversy, with a lower division club giving the Premiership side a real run for their money. The atmosphere was terrific and both sets of fans lapped it up. Not surprisingly, most people go on about the Chesterfield goal that wasn't given. There's no doubt about it, the ball did cross the line and they were unlucky. It was typical of the referee that day, David Elleray, to even it up by sending off Vladimir Kinder for something and nothing. We came back from two goals down to equalise and went behind again in extra time. Festa made it 3–3 and we had another replay on our hands.

Three days later we were at Hillsborough for the Coca-Cola Cup final replay. Again it was tight and again we got to the end of normal time at 0–0. Steve Claridge scored for Leicester in the first half of extra time and, much as we tried, we couldn't get the equaliser. We were in the middle of a hell of a schedule and it was beginning to tell. That was a big disappointment, but we had the chance of another final and did the business when we returned to Hillsborough to play

Chesterfield again. This time we made no mistake and won 3–0, booking our return to Wembley for the FA Cup final against Chelsea. Now we switched our attention to the job of trying to stay in the Premiership.

We'd had a decent League run in March, winning four on the trot to climb out of the bottom three. That came just after I brought in a new goalkeeper, Mark Schwarzer, a £1.2 million signing from Bradford City. He's proved his worth for Boro and Australia since then, but he broke his leg at West Ham, which meant we lost him for the vital last few weeks of the season. I'm sure he could have kept out some of the goals we conceded. The main problem, though, was the heavy load of fixtures and having to play important League matches straight after Cup games. We lost 1–0 against Sunderland and by the same score at Tottenham, on a Thursday night. We dug in to beat Aston Villa 3–2 and drew 3–3 away to Manchester United.

After a 0–0 draw at Blackburn in the rearranged fixture, we went into the last League match of the season, at Leeds, needing a win to avoid relegation. Brian Deane scored for them, which made the task even more difficult, and although Juninho's goal gave us a 1–1 draw, it wasn't enough. The little man was down on the ground in tears at the end. He had worked so hard to try to save us. The whole squad had put everything into it and we were all devastated.

The lads gave it their best shot that day, but we were never really able to get going. There were a lot of tired bodies and minds out there. I have absolutely no doubt that the Cup runs drained them. The fatigue was obvious and we didn't have a big enough squad for me to freshen up the team. I couldn't change things around. The decisive factor, though, when you tot up the sums, was the three points deduction. We finished nineteenth, two points from safety. The points we lost over the Blackburn postponement cost us our place in the Premiership.

We still had an FA Cup final to prepare for and I felt we managed to pick up the players' morale for Wembley. Then we conceded what was, from our point of view, a crap goal in forty-three seconds and found ourselves up against it. It may have looked a spectacular goal to Roberto di Matteo and Chelsea, but it flew straight over the head of our young goalkeeper, Ben Roberts. The lads just couldn't find the spark we needed and Chelsea scored again, near the end, to win 2–0.

It was a cruel way to finish the season, but the fans were fantastic with their support, even when everything went wrong for us. They appreciated what we had achieved in reaching two finals and bringing such exciting times to the club, and had enjoyed the roller-coaster ride with us. I was proud of the players for the way they had performed under difficult circumstances. As a young manager in the game, I believed I had a lot to be optimistic about. We had the players, stadium and support to come straight back up and I was convinced that was what we were going to do.

15
UP TO STAY

THE MIDDLESBROUGH TEAM of 1997 could, I have absolutely no doubt, have gone on to great things. If we had been able to keep all those players and added one or two more, we would have been one hell of a force. We would have been capable of challenging the very top clubs, but relegation changed things for a lot of those players. They had their eyes on the World Cup, at the end of the following season, and the First Division was no good for them. Their national managers wouldn't pick them unless they were playing in the top division.

So we lost some of our best players. Juninho left that summer, moving to Atletico Madrid for £12 million. He'd been great for the club and we made a huge profit on him. Ravanelli said he wanted to go and there were leaked stories that he was looking for £50,000 a week. He was just plain greedy. Everton were linked with him, but he played the first couple of matches for us and then joined Marseille for £5.5 million. I wasn't too sorry to see him go because his attitude did nothing for team spirit. Emerson stayed with us until midway through the season. We were flying at the time and I thought we had a chance of holding on to him, but he said he needed to move on and joined Tenerife for £4.2 million.

We'd brought in nearly £22 million from the sale of those players, which gave me the funds to try to buy top-class replacements. Our aim was to sign players good enough to take us straight back up to the Premiership and keep us there. Paul Merson came into that category. He had loads of natural ability and experience at the highest level. I felt he was worth the £5 million he cost from Arsenal, and we gave him the chance to prove it. We paid Aston Villa £500,000 for Andy Townsend, another excellent player who knew the game inside out. Later in the season we gave ourselves more attacking options by signing Marco Branca from Internazionale and Alun Armstrong from Stockport. They chipped in with some important goals, as did Craig Hignett, from midfield.

We always looked good for promotion, but we also had another great run in the Coca-Cola Cup, beating Barnet, Sunderland, Bolton and Reading to reach the semi-finals, where we played Liverpool. We lost 2–1 at Anfield, but won the home leg 2–0 to go through to our third final. Our opponents were Chelsea, who'd beaten us in the FA Cup final the previous season. This time they didn't get a flying start and neither side took the initiative in normal time. Then they scored twice in extra time and we couldn't come back at them.

It was disappointing to lose another final, but we'd shown our ability by getting to Wembley and our priority was to win promotion to the First Division. I thought we needed a little more flair to make sure of that. We had a solid, hard-working team, all good lads, but sometimes you need a player with that something different, a player who can open a defence with one bit of brilliance. That's why we paid Rangers £3.45 million for Paul Gascoigne before the transfer deadline and he gave us exactly what we wanted. He was terrific in the last few weeks of that season and well into the next. He actually made his debut as a substitute in the Coca-Cola Cup final, but it was in the League that he really did the business for us. He played a major part in securing our promotion.

Some people ask me why I went for Gazza, knowing him as I did. Sure, I knew he'd had bingeing problems. I'd seen it throughout his career. He had a binge mentality, and whether it was eating, drinking, fitness or whatever it was, he would just throw himself into it for a short burst. But I also knew what he could do with a football. I'd always had a good rapport with him in the England camp and he convinced me he was determined to prove he could still do it in the English game. The World Cup was coming up and he was desperate to go to France.

I now know, because he wrote about it in his autobiography, that there was much more to his problems in Scotland than I realised. He got into tablets and if I'd known he was on any kind of drug I wouldn't have signed him. I wasn't aware of that at the time, though, and the way he played when he came down from Glasgow suggested he could still deliver on the pitch. He went through phases when he stopped drinking and that's what he did when he first joined us. His fitness was first class and he helped us to a run of five wins and a draw from our last six matches. We finished second in the table, behind Nottingham Forest, and were back in the Premiership.

Gazza brought a lot more than his skill to the club. He was always hyper, always having a laugh, always up to mischief. I'd seen plenty of his pranks and daft antics over the years, but he was popular with other players and that was good for team morale. Before the start of Italia '90, when we were all relaxing, the girls would go out on pedal boats and he couldn't help himself. He had to go and tip the girls into the sea. He can't sit still. He has to muck about.

I once sold him a sports car, a red Caterham Lotus Super Seven. I was keen on cars and this was a quick, open-topped little thing, but it had been stuck in the garage for a few months and when he heard me talking to the other England players about it, he pestered me to sell it to him. I eventually agreed to let him have it for £10,000, but told him it would need a service before he took it on the road. I arranged for Freddie, the garage guy who looked after the United players' cars, to take it up to the North East for him on a trailer. So they set off, with Gazza sitting in the cab next to Freddie.

They stopped at Scotch Corner for fuel and when Freddie returned to the cab there was no sign of his passenger. Then he looked behind him and saw Gazza sitting in the Caterham. He insisted on staying there for the rest of the journey, making hand signals along the way. When he arrived at his folks' house he got the local kids to push him down the street to bump start it and he got it going. The next day he decided to drive it to London, where he was due at a press conference to promote a Roy of the Rovers comic strip or something. He'd not had the car serviced as I'd told him to, so of course it broke down on the way. When he eventually arrived, late, at the press conference, he blamed me. He told the press lads that I was the Arthur Daley of football!

He often phoned me and so when the phone rang at six o'clock one morning I should have known who it was. He was calling from Italy. He was at Lazio's training camp, up in the mountains. He said the coach, Zdenek Zeman, was mad because he had them out training early in the morning, then in for breakfast, then out again. After lunch, they went off to their beds before another training session later in the afternoon. He said none of the Italians would room with him.

'Gaz, there must be a reason,' I said. 'Come on, what is it?'

Then he told me one player did room with him until one afternoon when they were supposed to be having a siesta and Gazza couldn't get to sleep. He was bored so he set fire to his room-mate's pubes!

'Is there any wonder nobody wants to room with you?' I told him.

Our lads thought he was great fun. He and Andy Townsend, who was a really good bloke as well as a smashing player, used to play bingo over at Seaham, where they were living. It was the main banter around the club. Gazza was so generous he'd pay for the old ladies' cards. If he saw an old man in the bookies on his own, he'd give him a fiver or a tenner for a bet. I've spoken at dinners with Gazza and then seen him divide his money at the end – 'That's for me mam, that's for me sister, that's for Jimmy.' Jimmy 'Five Bellies' Gardner was his best mate and I didn't mind him being around because I thought he would keep an eye on Gazza and they were always a good laugh.

Mind you, I wasn't laughing when we were supposed to be setting off for our first away match of the 1998–99 season, against Aston Villa. We'd moved into our new training ground and also had a brand new team bus. The lads had been moaning about the old bus, saying the seats weren't good for their backs and they ought to have a new one with all mod cons. I'd convinced Keith Lamb we should have a new coach, designed to our specifications. It rolled up for that first trip, gleaming and very impressive. I thought all the lads were in the restaurant but it turned out that Gazza wasn't – he'd jumped into the bus and decided to drive it down to the bookies. He turned at the end of the drive but didn't take a wide enough sweep and hit a big boulder at the corner. Instead of reversing, he tried to carry on going forward and ripped most of the side off the bus. He told the security guys, who'd chased him up the drive, to take it back, and legged it. A bit later he phoned me from the bookies.

'Gaffer, you'll not believe what I've done.'

'I know exactly what you've done. Get your arse back to this training ground.'

We had to sit around for an hour or so while we tried to get hold of another bus. The other lads thought it was hilarious. Well, you know what footballers are like. I didn't drop Gazza, but I did fine him two weeks' wages. He also had to pay £20,000 for the repairs. Only Gazza could have done something like that. But then only Gazza could do some of the things he did on the pitch and he carried on where he left off at the end of the previous season.

The person who gave me more concern at that stage was Paul Merson. He was a terrific player and, when I signed him, I thought he had overcome his demons, but then I had no idea his drink, drugs and gambling problems were as serious as they were. I tried to help him and spoke to him about his troubles. It seemed gambling was the root problem for him. If he was having a bad time gambling, he would turn to the other stuff to obliterate his troubles.

You could see how he was in training. On his good days, he was great but on his down days, his attitude and body language were so negative. He just moped about the place and fell into a depression. When he was like that, I told him to go to the gym to train on his own and hoped he would be OK the following day. Sometimes he said he couldn't play because he had family problems, and I'd give him a couple of days off to sort things out.

He had a fantastic season for us in 1997–98. He was player of the year with everybody – the fans, the sponsors, the players, the local paper – but early in the following season Aston Villa offered £7 million for him. I told Keith that he had given us a good year, but he did have problems and Villa were offering a lot of money. As with Ravanelli, it was, on balance, probably better to get him out of the club.

What upset me was his claim at the time that there was a gambling and drinking culture at Middlesbrough. In fact, it was a relative or mate of his who used to bring in one of the racing papers. The other players weren't that interested in gambling. Merse was the one who secretly went out drinking when I thought he was totally off the booze and he has since admitted that ours wasn't really a drinking club. The press made a big thing of it and, of course, it was a way for them to get at me again. I was annoyed for the other players. Steve Vickers, Robbie Mustoe, Gianluca Festa, Neil Maddison, Mark Schwarzer and all the rest went about their work, day in, day out, without giving their manager a moment's bother. It was a terrible slur on the character of those players and smacked of someone trying to blame other people for his own, self-inflicted problems. We didn't have a gambling or drinking culture at the club. We had a lot of superb, dependable, dedicated professionals. Many of them were teetotal.

We brought in more players with the right sort of character for that first season back in the Premiership. Gary Pallister, my old team-mate at United, and Colin Cooper gave us greater strength in defence. Colin is the solid, committed type any club needs. We signed two new strikers, Brian Deane and a Colombian, Hamilton Ricard. Brian may not have been as pleasing on the eye as some players, but he had a lot to offer and was another model professional. Ricard should have done better for us than he did. He had the ability and was strong physically, but he was slack mentally. He'd be loose in training and would not always concentrate in matches, whereas the strong characters, such as Cooper and Townsend, were always tight and focused. If he'd had that mental strength, Ricard would have been a top player.

We went out of both Cup competitions at the third-round stage, but that probably wasn't a bad thing. We couldn't afford to run into problems in the League and we didn't. In fact, we had a terrific first half of the Premiership season, reaching third place and were still fourth when we beat United 3–2 at Old Trafford. We tailed off in the second half of the season and I think that was partly down to the change in Gazza's fitness and form. There had been talk that he might get back into the England team, but then he was injured, went off the rails again and never recovered his earlier level of performance. Any team would have missed that ability. It wasn't just the drink that hastened his decline. He wasn't eating the right food and you could see the effects in the way he trained. By then, I realised the extent of his problems.

While he was out injured, I thought it might be a good idea to let him stay at our house. I think we've always got on so well because we're both from the North East and he probably respected me as a player. Denise has always been good with him, as well. We went to his wedding. I suppose he looks on us like a big brother and sister. Sometimes he needs to feel he's with people he can trust. He likes to have an arm put around him. Yes, he can seem like a yob and he has admitted to a lot of terrible things, but if you go to Dunston, his home town, you'll see that it's a tough place to be brought up in. He can be such a likeable and loveable guy, warm and generous. Fans and team-mates take to him because of his personality as well as his exciting ability.

He was fine at our place, although I didn't find out until some years later that he'd got up one night, restless as usual, and woken up our two girls, as well. They went down to the snooker room. Knowing Gazza, he probably helped himself to a vodka and Coke. I'm assured the girls weren't drinking, though. They'd known Gaz since they were small so he was like a cousin to them. Luckily for the three of them, I slept through it all.

Things went from bad to worse for Gazza. I got a call from him as I was driving Charlotte to college in Nottingham. He was at Stevenage Station, in tears, threatening to throw himself under a train. I explained I couldn't go for him because I had Charlotte with me. I phoned his dad and Jimmy, but they couldn't go for him, either, so I rang his wife, Sheryl. Although they'd been having problems, she picked him up and took him to a hotel. I got there at about one o'clock in the morning and went to his room. He was in a mess. His marriage had been on and off but he was still infatuated with Sheryl. He was on a downer and smashed. I'd already spoken to our doctor and he'd given me the address of the Priory clinic in Roehampton. I took Gazza down there and stayed with him till about three or four o'clock in the morning. I tried and the club tried as hard as we could to help him, but there was only so much we could do.

We finished the 1998–99 season in ninth place, which was a little disappointing after we'd gone so well before Christmas and looked

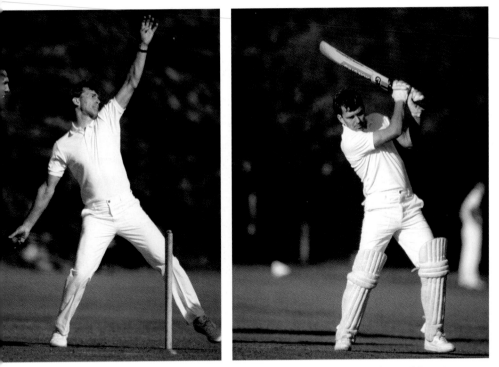

My bowling and batting in this charity cricket match, Chelford v. United, wouldn't give Freddie Flintoff anything to worry about …

… but I shared in a partnership of 130 with Clive Lloyd in another charity match at Old Trafford cricket ground. Clive scored a century.

Getting a few racing tips from Frankie Dettori.

Leading in Taylormade Boy after he won the Northern Handicap at Newcastle. The jockey is Lindsay Charnock.

Robson and Sons – with Dad, Justin, Gary and Dad's wagon near the family home in Chester-le-Street.

Middlesbrough chairman Steve Gibson at our first match at the Riverside, against Chelsea, on 26 August 1995.

Some said it would be a dickens of a job, but I enjoyed my role as player-manager of Boro.

New challenge, new commitment – taking over at Ayresome Park, 23 May 1994.

Fabrizio Ravanelli joined Boro on 22 July 1996. He was a great goalscorer, but drove me daft.

This Italian, Gianluca Festa, was a model professional.

Juninho lit up the Riverside and the whole of the English game.

Paul Gascoigne leaves Dennis Wise trailing on his debut for Middlesbrough in the 1998 Coca-Cola Cup final against Chelsea.

Paul Merson and Gazza were two hugely gifted but troubled players.

Viv Anderson and I try to console Ben Roberts after our 2–0 defeat by Chelsea in the 1997 FA Cup final.

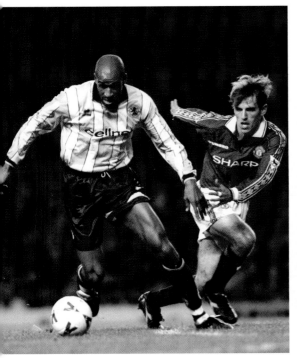

Brian Deane scored our third goal in the 3–2 defeat of Manchester United at Old Trafford in 1998.

Back in partnership, Terry Venables and I saved Boro from relegation but I lost my job.

Alen Boksic is congratulated by Keith O'Neill and Brian Deane after scoring in our 3–1 win at Coventry on the opening day of the 2000–01 season.

Tomasz Kuszczak was a hero in our 1–1 draw against Manchester United at Old Trafford in May 2005.

Geoff Horsfield shares his joy with Zoltan Gera after scoring in our decisive 2–0 win against Portsmouth on the final day of the 2004–05 season.

This is what it's like to pull off the 'The Great Escape'.

My mam and dad.

How they've grown up – Ben, Claire and Charlotte join Denise and me at our twenty-fifth wedding anniversary party, 2 June 2004.

as if we might qualify for Europe, but it was a solid year and that was the kind of base we needed. It was clear, though, that Gazza wouldn't be playing much of a part in our future. He made just eight more League appearances for us and joined Everton in 2000. He tried to get his career going again, but it's harder as the years pass. He was still obsessive in whatever he did and became a fitness fanatic. The trouble was that he didn't eat properly and didn't give his body the fuel it needed. As a result, he lost his old strength and was easily knocked off the ball.

We still keep in touch. He sometimes phones me and I suppose I still worry for him. He's so vulnerable and gullible that I do wonder what will become of him.

For the 1999–2000 season, we signed Christian Ziege, a German full-back, from Milan, Paul Ince, who had returned to England from Internazionale and had a spell with Liverpool, and brought back Juninho on loan. Ziege did brilliantly for us and, like Juninho, Ravanelli and Merson, became our player of the year. I set up the deal directly with Christian and Milan, which annoyed his agent. Christian was happy with everything, but his agent insisted he would scupper the deal unless we put a clause in the contract stating that he could move if we received an offer of £5.5 million and the two clubs agreed to the transfer. We paid £4 million him. He played so well that he inevitably attracted attention from other clubs, including Liverpool, but they slipped up by not approaching us with their offer. They went straight to the player. Witnesses confirmed they had meetings. We took legal action against Liverpool and eventually settled out of court. They had to pay compensation on top of the transfer fee for his services.

One of the frustrations at Boro was seeing players move on after we'd given them the opportunity to launch or resurrect their careers. Paul Merson had been going through a hard time at Arsenal and wanted a fresh start. We gave him that and he got back on to the international scene. Christian was not in the Milan side and had lost his place in the national team. He did so well with us that he was recalled by his country. At least we made money on the deals, but it was difficult for us to field a settled team because it was constantly changing. We'd steady the ship, only to lose more players and have to start looking again. Agents tell their players they can play in Europe and further their careers by moving on. With a club like Boro you are always fighting battles that the big clubs such as Manchester United, Arsenal and Chelsea don't have to contend with because they don't lose their best players. If we could have kept our best players over the period I was at Boro, we would have had a team to take on anybody.

It was great to have Juninho back 'home', but he'd had a bad ankle injury in Spain and was never quite the player he had been first time around. When you don't have great physical strength, you rely on pace to get away from your opponent and Juninho had lost a yard of pace. He could still beat people with his skill, but he couldn't get away from them. So we had a different Juninho, who used his vision and experience to play clever balls.

I brought in Paul Ince to give us leadership. We'd had good leaders at the club in Nigel Pearson and Andy Townsend and I felt Incey was the man to take over as captain. He took a pay cut to join us from Liverpool, which showed everybody at the club the type of character he was. I knew him well already and had no doubts he would give us the drive and commitment we were looking for. I had a lot of nice, quiet lads in the team, and felt we needed that aggression and bite. He would have a go at the lads, which was his way of lifting the team, but he could also play and still had a powerful shot. Off the pitch he got up to his old pranks – cutting trouser legs, hiding socks and stuff like that. He was a great signing for us and carried on playing into his late thirties.

Despite a promising start, we had an average season, mainly because of the many changes that were forced on us, finishing twelfth in the League. We thought we might be on for another final in the Worthington Cup, but lost at Tranmere in the fifth round after Juninho had two blatant penalties turned down and a dodgy offside decision went against us. Wrexham put us out of the FA Cup in the third round and that was the first time I'd been in shock after a match. I played a full side and we should have had no problem, but we were lacklustre and lost 2–1. We got what we deserved – nothing.

We had the usual turnover of players before the 2000–01 season, but I honestly thought we'd cracked it that year. We brought in Alen Boksic, Christian Karembeu, Ugo Ehiogu, Joseph-Desire Job and Paul Okon. Real Madrid were our opponents in a pre-season friendly in Gibraltar. They had just signed Luis Figo for a world record fee of £37 million. We lost 2–1, but we didn't half give them a good game. After that, we went into the Premiership season genuinely confident. Our first match was away to Coventry and we won 3–1. The new players bedded in really well. Boksic scored twice and Job got the other. I remember thinking to myself, 'We've got a real team here.' We had plenty of good options on the bench, as well.

Boksic, Ince and Cooper were all injured during the match, though, and that set the pattern for the season. Before we knew it, Okon was out with a broken leg and Ehiogu for a hernia operation. We had a beast of a time with injuries and found it difficult to pick up, managing one point in nine matches from mid-October to mid-December. We were bottom of the League, in danger of being cast adrift, and the fans started to get on my back. I felt we shouldn't get relegated because we had too many good players, but then I thought, 'Hold on a minute, is my judgement on these players right?'

I felt sure we did have the ability, but with so many injuries, relegation was a possibility. I had to be realistic about the situation. I couldn't allow things to go on like that. We'd worked so hard to build up the club and get it established in the Premiership. I couldn't let it all slip away. I had to do something about it. Another voice, someone with a fresh eye on things, just might give us a few new ideas and perk us up.

Gordon McQueen had become my first-team coach after John Pickering was taken ill with cancer, but he struggled to get about the pitch because of an ankle injury. I phoned Archie Knox and Brian Kidd, the two assistants to Sir Alex Ferguson during my time at United. Both were in jobs and happy. I phoned Sir Alex, Ron Atkinson and a few other old mates to ask them for their thoughts on anyone I could bring in to help. They couldn't come up with anybody. Then one day I was sitting talking to Keith Lamb and I made the point that because Terry Venables was a manager, people tended to forget he was still one of the best coaches in the game and good at working with players on the pitch. I said I thought he could be the man we were looking for. Keith backed me and I asked Terry if he was interested.

My main concern was to get through that season, although I did have it in my mind that if it worked out well for Terry and me, as it had done for us with England, we might take our partnership forward at the club. Terry made it clear from the outset that he would be able to help us only until the end of the season because he had his business interests in Spain and his TV work. He would have to cut back on that work while he was with us, but didn't mind for the half season or so. The agreement suited both sides.

Terry was that different voice I felt we needed, and the players responded. He introduced one or two new ideas, just little tweaks he thought would help us after watching videos of our matches. He thought we needed to get tighter, more compact, and move up and down as a unit. He suggested filling the midfield a bit more. We worked together and I ran things as usual on the days he was away, but he had the final word on team selection and fronted up for the media. Results picked up and, as players returned from injury, we had a decent run towards the end of the season. No one was more important to us in those last few weeks than Alen Boksic. He stayed fit and his goals kept us up – no question about that.

We took some criticism from the media and punters over Alen. He cost us £2.5 million from Lazio and word went around that we were paying him £63,000 a week. That wasn't true. He was on £40,000. That's still a lot of money, but he was one of the best centre-forwards I ever saw and I think he proved his value by the end of that season. Some fans thought he was lazy and it's true to say he didn't have great stamina, but he played in a way almost no one else did. He would either sprint or walk. He didn't have an in-between gear. That's why he injured himself as often as he did. He was such a big, explosive guy, that he could pull a muscle or twist a joint when he ran at speed, but if he thought he could do some damage to the opposition by attacking them or closing them down, he would sprint. If he didn't think it was worth the effort, he would walk. He wasn't lazy, he was intelligent.

He had genuine injuries and was a genuine player. If we weren't playing well, it affected him. He would get frustrated, but he was absolutely nothing like Ravanelli. When we really needed him to turn it on, when we needed his goals to avoid relegation, he produced. Alen and Paul Ince shone above everybody else because they were really up for the fight. Every game was like a cup final for them and their pride wouldn't let them be relegated.

At the end of the season we were in fourteenth place and I'd done what I was determined to do. I'd made sure we stayed in the Premiership. But the crowd had been on my back again towards the end of the season. They saw Terry as the acting manager and felt the improvement in results was down to him. Terry had tried to get me to do some of the press conferences to show it was a joint effort, but I told him I didn't want to push myself forward just when things were going well. I felt we should carry on as we had been doing.

Looking back, I obviously cut my own throat, but when I made the decision to bring in Terry my only concern was the future of the club. I didn't want Boro to go down. I wanted us to keep going forward, to keep building on what we had already achieved. We'd gone through so much together, we'd accomplished so much together. I couldn't stand by and allow it all to be thrown away. Towards the end of that season, though, I could see I had put myself in a difficult situation. I had undermined my position at the club. You can become a victim of your own success. We had raised expectations. The players and fans expected to be challenging for Europe. If we'd had our best players available more often, we could have done that, but when injuries and results go against you it knocks confidence and suddenly you're in the relegation zone. I had to act.

Would we have stayed up if Terry hadn't joined us? It's a hypothetical question and nobody knows the answer. The fact is we did stay up and I can argue I made the right decision because the outcome was all that mattered. As we now know, though, that was the downfall of Bryan Robson as manager of Middlesbrough. What angered me was the way in which I lost my job.

Steve Gibson traditionally entered a staff team for the Singapore Sevens, an end-of-season tournament that was always a lot of fun. Viv and I joined Steve's party for the trip at the end of that season. When I was at the airport for the flight out, I had a phone call from a pal who said he'd heard Steve McClaren, Sir Alex's number two at United, had been lined up to take my job. So I asked Steve Gibson if he was thinking of bringing in a new man. He assured me he wasn't. While we were in Singapore, I rang my parents and my dad said, 'Robbo, what's going on like? I keep reading reports in the papers that Steve McClaren's got your job and Steve Harrison is coming from Villa as his assistant.' I told him it was OK, I'd spoken to Steve Gibson and he said it wasn't true.

It all came to a head when we got back from Singapore and to make matters worse it was the day of John Pickering's funeral. John had lost his fight against cancer. That morning I went through the press cuttings, which we kept at the training ground. There were loads of them and it was obvious to me there was something in the stories. So I asked Keith Lamb if he'd come to see me and I threw the cuttings in front of him.

'Don't tell me there's nothing in those stories,' I said. 'I know how it works, Keith. Surely you could have had the honesty and decency, after seven years, to come to me when we were together in Singapore, and tell me the truth.'

Keith obviously felt uncomfortable and spoke to Steve, who called me over to the stadium for a meeting later that afternoon, after John's funeral. I didn't need to be told what it was going to be about. Steve said he thought my position had become awkward because I'd brought Terry in. He thought the club needed a change.

'Steve,' I said, 'I've got absolutely no problem with that, but when I asked you the question at the airport about bringing in Steve McClaren, you said it wasn't true. We've just been away for a week in Singapore and all this has been going on. You've been having phone calls with Steve McClaren and you couldn't tell me to my face. I just can't believe you. You could have had the decency to tell me before I read it in the papers and had my dad on the phone to Singapore telling me that somebody's got my job. That's the only gripe I have with you.'

'Yes, I should have told you,' he said. 'I shouldn't have let it go so far down the line, but it was difficult for me because we've had seven really good years. I'm sorry it's come to this, but it was awkward for me to find a way to tell you.'

I was angry because I'd had a good relationship with Steve before that point and I've got a good relationship with him now. We worked hard together to build up that club from nothing. Steve is a hard-bitten, cut-throat businessman and I realise what it's like in the game. I know the score. I was annoyed with him for a time, but now it's water under the bridge. I can understand how he felt, and why the situation developed as it did. I think it was difficult for him because we did get on so well together, although we didn't go out for drinks and meals together every other day, as some sections of the press made out. Even if we'd wanted to it wouldn't have been possible because he was away so much on business. We socialised occasionally, along with our wives and Keith and his wife. Maybe it was because we had such a pleasant environment that Steve felt awkward. Overall, my time at Boro was good and that's why I don't bear any grudges. The past is the past and we're friends again. Steve did what he thought was right for the club. These things happen in the game and you have to be big enough to face that.

It was a strange feeling, realising that it was suddenly all over at Boro. At the end of the season I'd carried on as normal, planning for the next one. Gordon was due to have an operation on his ankle, and it was expected he would be fine. Instead, I was out of work and Viv and Gordon went with me. At least Steve was as good as his word over my compensation. He paid me what he said he would.

I left Steve that day feeling gutted and disappointed. Nobody wants to be sacked. It's an awful feeling. That was the first time in my career I'd been in that position, but when I looked back and assessed myself, I realised that getting the sack might not have been such a bad thing after all. Maybe it made me stronger for the next time around. You don't necessarily stop to think and analyse your performance if your contract runs out and you just move on to another job. When you're sacked it concentrates your mind. You ask yourself questions and tell yourself you won't make the same mistakes or you won't do things in a certain way.

I don't think I made any big mistakes at Boro, but perhaps I could have been tighter on one or two matters, mainly to do with discipline. Some of the players and staff I have spoken to since then have admitted they got away with things when I wasn't around. I maybe gave the players a bit too much rope and they hung themselves. Not only that, they hung me in the end. But then people change their tune when things aren't going well. When we were winning promotion and getting to Cup finals, they were saying I was a great manager and Viv was a great coach. When we were having a bad run, suddenly I wasn't doing it right and Viv was useless. I saw that opinion shift in reverse when I went back to West Brom as manager. That's how people are, especially in football.

Whatever lessons had to be learned, I made up my mind that I was going to take a year out of the game. I wanted to spend time with the family. That last season at Middlesbrough was hard not just for me but also for all my family. I got hate mail, as I did in my first few months back at West Brom. I was getting aggravation around the bars and restaurants in the Middlesbrough area when things were going wrong and in the end I just didn't go out. I had to put up with people sneering, telling me, 'The team are shit, you're shit.' People are brave when they've had a couple of pints. I didn't get involved and walked away.

I accept that, as a football manager, I am there to be shot at, an easy target. If you can't take it, you have the choice of getting out, but I can't accept it when members of my family are in the firing line. It's difficult for your wife, kids and parents when they're sitting in the stand and the punters are hammering you. My mam and dad sat through a lot of that at Boro. Our Ben started getting bullied a bit at school. He came home one day with his shirt ripped. He never complained to us but we knew what was going on. Mentally, he's stable and he's quite a tough lad, so I think he stood up for himself, but he was happy when we left Teesside and went back down to Manchester.

It was a low period for me because it was difficult to accept the disappointment of not doing well after a career that had generally been successful. Even at Middlesbrough, it had mainly gone well.

We'd been relegated, but we came straight back up by winning promotion for a second time, we reached the three Cup finals and there were so many other positives from that period. We'd built up a club with great players and fantastic facilities. The club was worth a hell of a lot more to Steve by the time I left. How can that be failure?

What really angered me was the perception that I had been a failure at Middlesbrough. Some people judged me on what happened in the last few months rather than over the whole seven years, but I soon discovered those people were mainly from outside Middlesbrough. I received loads of fan mail from Boro fans, thanking me for what I'd done for them. When I went to Bradford and then West Brom, they wrote to me wishing me well in my new job. When I returned to the Riverside with West Brom, I got a brilliant reception from the fans.

Before getting back into football, though, I needed a break. I was looking forward to going away with the family in school holidays, spending Christmas and New Year with them and doing all the other things you can't do when you're a football player or manager. Then I would be back. I had unfinished business. But things didn't work out quite as smoothly as I'd hoped.

16

NEW LIFE
WITH THE BAGGIES

Denise and I had just one thought in our minds after I left Middlesbrough – to get away and enjoy ourselves. The kids were away on holiday, so we jumped in the car, threw some clothes in the back and set off. We drove around France and Italy, stopping off wherever we fancied, and had a good time for a couple of weeks. I suppose it was our way of releasing all the tension that had built up. We both needed it.

In fact, we had a great year, just as I'd promised myself and the family we would. I didn't close the door totally on football. I kept in touch with the game and would have been interested in any Premiership job that became available, but I was determined to get some time back with the family. Denise and I liked to take breaks in Majorca, Marbella or Dubai, but that year gave us the opportunity really to unwind. Every time Ben was on holiday from school, we went away. That Christmas, we went to Australia. As a footballer and manager, I'd never had the chance to go away at that time of the year. We did have some pretty good Christmas staff parties, but it was great to be able to have a long trip like that with the family.

I kept my hand in with some TV and promotional work and Sir Alex gave me tremendous support. I went to have a cup of tea and a chat with him and he said I could train with Brian McClair, who was then in charge of United's reserves, any time I wanted. He said it would help keep me involved on a training pitch. All I had to do was phone him or Brian and check what the lads were doing. I took him up on that offer and it was great. Brian was a good pal anyway and he knew I was no threat to him. He was different class. He even invited me to take sessions. He felt, as I did with Terry, that a new voice could freshen things up. On the odd occasion I also helped Jimmy Ryan with the first team. Everyone at the club was brilliant. I used to wind up Brian and Mike Phelan, Jimmy's assistant, by sending them a postcard every time I was away on holiday.

I never tried to force the situation as far as a job was concerned because I felt I needed that year out. At the start of the following season the boss – after working with him for eight years it's hard to stop calling him 'boss' or 'gaffer' – said I could carry on with Brian. I told him it was good of him to offer, but I had to concentrate on getting a job. I'd enjoyed training with Brian and the lads at United and the TV work was bringing in some money, but I was in danger of getting into the comfort zone. I did ask him, when he was looking for a new assistant, if he'd thought about me. I'd looked at the quality of the players and facilities and thought it would be a good place for me. He said he had thought of me but saw me as a number one. He was also well on the way to bringing in a foreign coach and eventually Carlos Queiroz joined him.

One of my main aims during that period was to take the coaching courses and get my badges. I got my B licence in that first year, then went for the A. Since then, I've added my Pro-Licence, which gives me the full range of qualifications to work anywhere in the game. It was during that second year out of work that a bit of frustration set in. I was seeing other managers who had achieved nothing like as much as I had getting sacked and then finding new jobs straightaway.

I couldn't help thinking, 'Why hasn't anybody looked at my record and realised what I've done?'

That hurt. It also angered me because some people's perception was still being coloured by those last few months at Boro. Then, of course, there were always the snidey comments about my drinking. Let me just make a point about that. Through the whole of my playing career at West Brom, United and Middlesbrough, I missed only one day's training other than through injury and that was because of food poisoning. I'd had a kebab with a couple of the England lads after an international match, woke up the next morning and couldn't move out of bed. I couldn't go training with United that day. I never missed a day with flu, colds – or a hangover. Even so, the reputation follows me around. Perhaps if I'm seen out it's assumed I'm on a bender, but most managers, like most normal people, go out for a meal and a few drinks now and then. It's called living. The trouble is that I've been knocked so many times down the years that I'm always on my guard when I go out. I think I've been generally more relaxed since I came back into management, although I'm still careful not to give anyone ammunition to shoot me down. I do keep a lot of feelings and emotions bottled up but when I'm with mates and people I know aren't going to stitch me up, I can switch off and be myself. I'll have a right good laugh.

Most people are fine when they see me out with Denise or friends. You get used to the requests for photos and autographs and, as long as people are polite, it's not a problem. In the eighties people had a more aggressive manner, but nowadays you tend not to get that. I find it a bit rude of people to interrupt me when I'm eating in a restaurant. That can be irritating, but I think I'm pretty patient and easygoing in general, just as I think I'm patient and fair with my players.

I suppose we all get calmer as we get older. You're less likely to do daft things. I've certainly done my share of daft things over the years, some funny, some not so funny. Those are the daft things I wish I'd not done. I've let myself down a few times in my private life, such as drink-driving. I'm no saint, but I'd like to think I've learned from my mistakes. That applies to my private life and my career in football. I've no real regrets in football. How can I have? Some people would give their right arm to have had the career I've had, not just as a player but also as a manager. You see lads working in the lower divisions, struggling every day because they have no money to spend. Outside the game, people are stuck in boring jobs or striving just to make ends meet. I've been very lucky in life. Football has opened doors and given me opportunities most people can only dream about. I've had invitations to all sorts of wonderful places and events, and met all sorts of interesting people. Denise and I have eaten in some fantastic restaurants and visited champagne houses in France. I wouldn't claim to be a wine-tasting expert, but I was made an honorary Tastevin at a magnificent French chateau in recognition of that twenty-seven-second goal at the 1982 World Cup. For the record, I prefer white wine to red – that's just my taste buds.

Pop stars have a thing about football, so I've met many over the years. I've done a few charity events with Rolling Stone Bill Wyman and played for a Westlife team in a charity seven-a-side tournament at Stamford Bridge. Mark Owen, from Take That, played as well. We beat Ant and Dec's team – which included Peter Beardsley – in the final and celebrated as if we'd won the FA Cup. We had a bus to take us to a Japanese restaurant on the King's Road and were all hanging out of the windows. Bryan McFadden told me to go and get my medal and put it around my neck. I had a great time getting involved in The Match, which was an old pros v. showbiz charity challenge game played at St James' Park. It was shown on Sky but the ground was still packed. 'Superstars' was fun, meeting top performers from other sports. It was also interesting to talk to them about their different training methods and preparations.

I enjoy watching other sports and really top sportsmen, such as Jack Nicklaus and Seve Ballesteros in golf, Ian Botham and Freddie Flintoff in cricket, and of course Muhammad Ali. I admire them not only as sportsmen but also as people. Ricky Hatton is another boxer I admire and he's a smashing lad. All the great boxing champions are amazing guys because that really is the toughest sport. I followed horse racing when I was a player, but I didn't bet to lose – I bet to win. I gathered all the inside information I could. I got friendly with Walter Swinburn and he didn't give me many bad tips. Denise and I have bumped into Frankie Dettori quite a few times, in Dubai and at other courses.

I've had five horses over the years and it was terrific fun, but it's a case of been there, done that. Don't believe anybody who tells you it's an easy way to make money. Unless you're a really top owner, forget it. You can enjoy the sport by just going to the races. One of my horses was joint owned with Gerry Taylor, who ran a sporting events company called Taylormade Sports and had a box at Haydock. The horse was called Taylormade Boy. We won thirteen races. Sir Alex wasn't too pleased about it at the time, but I was quite happy going racing without having a drink.

We were at the races together one day and Gerry brought with him his girlfriend Janet and her fourteen-year-old son. I could see the lad was getting a bit bored up in the box so I asked him if he'd like to go down to the parade ring and have a look at the horses, close up. As we were walking back, I asked him what he wanted to do in life. He said he was going to be a musician. He didn't say he wanted to be, he said he was going to be. I said, 'That's great. If you're as positive as that and want it that badly, you'll probably do it.' That lad was Robbie Williams. He and Take That did a lot for the Bryan Robson Scanner Appeal. Robbie, of course, went on to become a superstar.

I enjoy an occasional game of golf or tennis and I was once offered the chance to take part in a celebrity motor race at Silverstone. I was up for that, but unfortunately I couldn't make it because of England commitments. I've managed to move on since those early days of dodgy cars. For some years I've been a Mercedes man. When you're on the road as much as I am, you appreciate the quality and reliability of a Merc. I don't own any other fancy toys, but I do like to hire a yacht or a boat for the day when we're on a family holiday in Spain or Portugal. That's a terrific way of spending a day.

The main family concerns over a period of about ten months, spanning 2002 and 2003, were for my dad, who was dying from cancer. He had been such a big part of my life and an inspiration in my career. He had started me playing football and taken me to my first match. Dad and Mam supported me all the way. I think he would have wanted me to do all I could to get back in the game.

I had a number of offers from lower division clubs but felt that would mean having to take too many steps back before I could go forward again. I applied for the Aston Villa job and didn't get a reply until the chairman, Doug Ellis, said they were taking on someone else. That was David O'Leary. I spoke to Trevor Brooking about the West Ham position, but he said the directors were well down the line towards making an appointment. That was Alan Pardew.

I had approaches from abroad. A couple of Arab countries contacted me and then Nigeria came in. That interested me because I knew they had some good players and I thought that if I could win the African Nations Cup with them it would build up my reputation again. I was interviewed by the Sports Minister and we agreed to set up an office in Manchester because most of Nigeria's international players were based in Europe. I gave him an estimate of costings and expenses to run the operation the way I felt was needed. The Sports Minister was all for it and for about six weeks led me to believe the job was mine, but he was overruled by his government and the deal fell through. They said they weren't prepared to come up with the funds. It wouldn't have been an easy job. Their infrastructure was apparently a nightmare. I spoke to a few of the players, who told me of trips when they'd had to pay their own way and then turned up at hotels to find they didn't have enough rooms, so they ended up sleeping on lounge settees.

The organisation of the Republic of Ireland team attracted a lot of attention when Roy Keane had his bust-up with Mick McCarthy, but that certainly didn't put me off when Mick left and that job came up. Again, I did my homework and got in touch with people who knew about the set-up of the Irish camp. I spoke to Roy Keane, Andy Townsend and Denis Irwin, all experienced former Ireland internationals, knowing I'd get three honest and different opinions. Roy is a straight talker and I knew he wouldn't hold anything back. I had a three- or four-hour meeting with him and he was hard-hitting with everything. Denis, in his own, quiet way, gave me a sound, balanced judgement, and Andy told me exactly how it was. They all left me in no doubt that the standards of organisation and facilities had to be raised.

At my interview with the FAI in Warrington, I was able to tell them what I understood to be wrong and what needed to be changed. I felt that issues with training grounds, time-keeping and general preparation had to be addressed. The perception that the Irish have a fairly casual, laid-back attitude to things is, I suppose, part of their charm, but I explained that standards in club and international football were rising all the time and they had to keep pace with the best. I didn't tell them I'd spoken to anyone or that Roy had told me he would come back. I didn't want to put him in an awkward position.

The feedback I got was very positive. Peter Reid and Brian Kerr were also in the running, and Frank Stapleton and one or two other former Ireland internationals had been mentioned, but apparently there was a strong feeling in favour of me and I fancied it. The squad had enough good, experienced players, plus younger talent in Damien Duff, Robbie Keane and John O'Shea, to give them a chance. They had a good track record in the major tournaments and had the backing of fantastic fans. I felt I knew enough about international football to take on the job, and relished the challenge.

Then everything seemed to turn around almost overnight and I got a phone call telling me Brian Kerr was going to get the job. I suppose that, in the end, they felt they should give it to an Irishman and Brian had come through their system, working with the youngsters, so that was fair enough. It was disappointing, but on the other hand I was encouraged that I'd had a couple of interviews and put myself back in the picture. When Bradford City approached me in the 2003–04 season, I liked what I saw and heard, and decided to give it a go.

The club had been a bit of a financial wreck when Julian Rhodes and Gordon Gibb, the chairman, took over, but they were very enthusiastic and eager to breathe new life into it. They had the stadium and general structure in place, and although they made it clear I would have no money to buy players, I figured I could add to what was already a decent squad with a few more on loan. Dave Wetherall, Dean Windass, Nicky Summerbee and Wayne Jacobs were there, and the squad had ability, Premiership experience and good character. The objective was to try to stay in the First Division. I felt we had a good chance of doing that and told Julian I'd come in until the end of the season.

Colin Todd had been interviewed for the job, as well, so after they offered it to me they suggested Colin could be my assistant. Funnily enough, he's another Chester-le-Street lad, yet we'd rarely bumped into each other until then. I phoned him up, arranged a meeting, and we both decided we'd be able to work together. Colin had loads of coaching and managerial experience, from working at Derby and Bolton, and we hit it off.

The whole place got a lift when we came back from two down to beat Millwall 3–2. Danny Cadamarteri, who scored our first goal in that match, was a real talent and should have been playing at a higher level. Unfortunately, he had a lot of injury problems. Injuries are always the worry for a manager with a small squad. With everyone fit, and especially after we brought in some loan players, we had a side good enough to hold its own in that division. I brought in four players on loan – Alun Armstrong from Ipswich, Ronnie Wallwork from West Brom, Nico Vaesen from Birmingham and Gareth Farrelly from Bolton. We had a run of three wins and a draw from five matches going into March and were confident of avoiding the drop, but then came the bombshell.

I got a phone call from the chairman, telling me the club were going back into administration.

'Why?' I asked. 'We're on our best run of the season, the lads on loan have settled really well and things are looking good.'

'I've had enough,' he said. 'I'm not putting any more money into the club.'

He'd made his decision and there was nothing I could do. The problem for me was that the players on loan had to go back to their clubs because the administrator wouldn't pay their wages and we had to consider offers for our contracted players. Sheffield United offered us £50,000 for Andy Gray and Simon Francis, who was probably the best young player coming through at the club. I told them 'No' and the administrator held them off for a while. In the end, we got £200,000 from Sheffield United for the pair.

I could easily have gone, as well. I could have argued this wasn't part of the deal when I took the job on, but I'd got attached to the place and the players. We never saw the chairman again, although he owned the ground. Julian and his family had to take over everything. The players were trying like beasts to keep us up. Wetherall and Windass were terrific, the type you'd want with you in the trenches. Windass scored goals and made his presence felt with his character

and banter. There were lots of good, genuine, dependable professionals at the club, even though their wages were being deferred. I
thought to myself, 'You can't just walk out now and leave them to
it.' So I stayed until the end of the season.

We were relegated, as I feared we would be once the odds were
stacked so heavily against us. Going into administration made our
task impossible. I think Julian was still hopeful I would stay on with
them the following season. I said I would consider doing so if the
club came out of administration. He phoned me while I was on
holiday to say that wasn't the case and, unless I'd changed my mind,
he was going to offer the job to Colin. I said that was fine by me.
Colin phoned me and said he wanted to stay on and I told him I had
absolutely no problem with that.

Bradford's difficulties illustrated the dangers for all clubs who
over-reach themselves financially or are in any way mismanaged. It
has happened even to big clubs, such as Leeds. Clubs now realise they
have to structure themselves so that if they are relegated, they can
cope for at least a couple of years and give themselves a chance of
getting back up. Wages can be the killer, which is why clubs insert
get-out clauses to release them from their contracts. Some people say
we have too many clubs but I disagree. I think it's good that fans all
over the country have a local club to support. It's just that the
financial lessons of the recent past should never be forgotten.

Despite the disappointment of relegation with Bradford, I don't
think it seriously damaged my reputation. The feedback I got
suggested people in the game appreciated what we had done in
the circumstances. We'd put together a decent football team, we'd
played the game in the right way and the players had liked the way
we trained and prepared. I felt it had been a positive spell for me
because I'd got back into the job and I enjoyed working at Bradford.
The players and the fans were brilliant. It was a real pity the financial
burden eventually dragged us down.

During that summer and into the autumn of 2004, I did some promotional work for Manchester United and their major sponsors, Vodafone and Nike. I made appearances at corporate functions at Old Trafford and then I started getting offers to work for them in the Far East. Sky TV also asked me to join their panel. I wanted to get back into management, but it crossed my mind that if nothing came up by that Christmas, I might speak to United about coming to a firm arrangement. I was doing more and more work for them and didn't want the uncertainty of my future to go on forever. I'm pleased to say I didn't have to make that proposition.

My old club, West Brom, parted company with Gary Megson and I sensed this was the opportunity I had been waiting for. They were in danger of being relegated back to the First Division from the Premiership, but I had always felt the structure and potential at The Hawthorns made it a really good job. I knew the club was sensibly run and financially sound. They wouldn't spend big but they wouldn't end up in a fix, as Bradford had. The stadium had been developed and I'd seen how they had built up the training facilities when our Ben played there for Macclesfield against West Brom's academy team. If they had any sort of success they would be assured a great following and, of course, I had a personal attachment to the club.

I put my CV together and sent it down to the chairman, Jeremy Peace. Then I phoned Ron Atkinson, because I knew he still had good contacts at the Albion. Ron spoke to a few people and came back to tell me they were interested in me and I had a good chance of making the short list. As far as I knew, Gordon Strachan, Glenn Hoddle and Gerard Houllier were also on the list. Things were moving on the West Brom front when I got a text message from Paul Ince. He had moved on to Wolves and he was eager to tell me they were also looking for a new manager to replace Dave Jones. Wolves was another of those jobs I felt was an attractive proposition. I certainly would have been interested and I was led to believe they wanted to speak to me, but by then I had arranged to meet Jeremy Peace.

Stories in the national press claimed that Hoddle was a virtual certainty for the West Brom job and that he was going to get a £1 million a year contract. I think that upset the chairman, who wanted to conduct business in a quiet, confidential way until he had reached a decision. I gather Strach didn't convince the chairman he was ready to get back into football at that stage and Houllier was apparently never really a front-runner. Glenn eventually went to Wolves, Gordon to Celtic and Houllier to Lyon.

In my interview we covered the usual footballing matters and then, with just about the last question, the chairman asked me about the drinking culture he'd heard about at Middlesbrough. I explained to him that all stemmed from Paul Merson's comments. I told him I wouldn't allow anything of the sort and that I had a strict code of conduct for my players. It is annoying that this subject keeps cropping up, but I could understand the chairman's concerns. Certain sections of the press are always going to look for a chance to churn out the same old rubbish and knock me. At least the chairman was straight enough to bring it up and give me the opportunity to deal with it. He was obviously satisfied with my response and I know that Steve Gibson gave me a very positive reference, which I greatly appreciated. The job was mine and I felt it was right for me. I was given a twelve-month rolling contract, which I think is a fair and sensible arrangement these days.

I wasted no time contacting the man I wanted as my number two – Nigel Pearson. He had played for me at Middlesbrough, where he showed his leadership qualities as captain. He always had the right attitude to work and discipline and was positive and enthusiastic by nature. I had also seen him at coaching courses and was impressed with his communication skills. He was working with the FA at the time, coaching the Under-20s, but he was keen to join a club and the FA agreed to release him. We were both up for what we knew was going to be a tough job, but we looked at the squad and thought we had a chance.

I took some hammer from the Albion fans when I left the club in 1981 and for two or three years afterwards, but I didn't sense any deep resentment when I returned as manager. It was a long time ago. I had furthered my career at United and West Brom had put my transfer fee to good use. It more or less paid for the £2 million Halfords Lane Stand, which a lot of supporters called the 'Robson Stand'. What all fans want is a team playing well and winning matches. It's fair to say that, initially, we didn't give them what they wanted.

As fate would have it, my first match as manager of West Brom – at The Hawthorns on 14 November – was against Middlesbrough. We would have come out of it with a respectable 2–2 draw if Kanu hadn't somehow spooned the ball over the bar from a yard in stoppage time. That miss had to be seen to be believed. A 1–1 draw at Arsenal was a good result, but five defeats in a row left us eight points adrift at the bottom. Going down 4–0 away to our neighbours Birmingham and 5–0 at home to Liverpool were particularly painful, and the fans gave me flak. I had no complaints because we were playing badly and deserved those hammerings.

If anyone thought I was beginning to regret taking the job, they were wrong. That was never the case. It was bound to take time to get to know the players and make our presence felt. In the bad times, when you are being thumped by four and five goals, you learn more about your players and discover who are the strong characters. We had a squad of thirty-four professional players and it was clear that too many of them weren't good enough for the Premiership. We trimmed the squad by nine in the first three months and then concentrated on those we felt could improve as individuals and team players.

We were hearing and reading in the media that no club had survived in the Premiership after being bottom at Christmas, and turned that into a motivational tool, urging the players to make their own piece of history and silence the critics. Records are there to be broken, we said. We realised, though, that we had to do something about the way we played. Nigel and I had felt we shouldn't try to change things too quickly because that could make things worse, but in the Premiership you can't afford to keep giving the ball to the opposition and the lads at the back were doing that all the time. They explained they had always been told to get the ball forward. We got them to play the ball across the back and keep possession. The lads took the instructions on board and the more we passed the ball the more our confidence grew and the more we improved.

The ProZone service, which provides clubs with statistics and detailed analyses of matches, isn't everybody's cup of tea, but I believe it is a valuable aid. The statistics showed that our passes per match increased during the course of the season from 250–270 to 350–380. That was the major difference and the reason for the better results. People questioned why I tended to use Rob Earnshaw as a substitute rather than start with him. The statistics showed that defenders made far fewer runs and covered far less ground as they tired in the later stages of a match and therefore were less likely to be able to cope with Robbie's pace and energy.

We had a lucky draw at Manchester City, but less than a month later we beat them convincingly 2–0 at home and that was probably the turning point. By then we had taken advantage of the January transfer window and brought in new players. Kevin Campbell came on a free from Everton, Kieran Richardson on loan from United and I paid Burnley £1.5 million for Richard Chaplow, a young player with a lot of promise. Most of that we recouped by selling Rob Hulse to Leeds.

Campbell had a good track record of scoring goals and had vast experience of playing at this level. With his strength of character, he was a massive influence in the dressing room. Kevin, Kanu, Robbie and Geoff Horsfield gave us good options up front and I felt that Earnshaw was bound to benefit from playing alongside those seasoned professionals. I'd liked the look of Kieran since I'd had that spell at United, working with Brian McClair and the reserves. I'd watched him progress through the ranks. He had skill, a good shot, pace, stamina, a willingness to learn and that bit of devilment you want in a player. When I look back through match programmes, his is one of the names I ringed as a player likely to do well. I tried to take him to Bradford on loan, but Sir Alex turned me down. This time he let me have him.

Kevin gave us leadership and Kieran an extra dimension to get at the opposition. He didn't come in with a Big Time Charlie attitude because he was from Manchester United. He trained hard and mixed well with the lads, and his desire rubbed off on them. We gave him the chance of playing first-team football and he more than repaid us. I was delighted for him when he made his England debut that summer and scored twice in the United States.

There was a fresh belief and optimism in the camp, even after a 3–2 defeat at Norwich. We battered them, played them off the park and yet lost to a last-minute goal. I said to Nige after the match, 'I enjoyed watching us today and if we carry on playing like that we'll win more games than we lose.' We'd been unlucky to concede late goals to Fulham and Crystal Palace, as well. We were playing the right way and the fans appreciated that. The talk in the area was about our football and the chances we were creating. That gives you encouragement. The backing of the fans was vital in the final push.

Another important factor was a bonding trip to Orlando. We'd gone out of the FA Cup in the fourth round, so I took advantage of a gap in our fixture list to get the players away together. I hadn't realised how many of the players were new to the club that season and I felt they still didn't know one another as well as they might. Those few days in a different environment, going on the rides at Disney World, playing golf and just having a laugh together definitely brought them closer. It also helped me to get to know them all better. They had plenty to do without feeling the need to tour the bars, as they might in Spain or Portugal.

Maybe my kids helped, as well. For the first time, our Claire, Charlotte and Ben went on holiday together without Denise and me that winter. They went to Tenerife. When they got back they started laughing and said they'd brought me a lucky charm, a little plastic Buddha. Ben said I had to keep it in my pocket. I've never had any superstitions or rituals as a player or manager and I don't have any strong religious beliefs, although I'm Church of England and respect the church. Anyway, I took my little Buddha with me to the home match against Birmingham and we won 2–0. Then we went to Chelsea and lost 1–0. Ben asked me if I'd had the Buddha with me and I realised I'd left it in my briefcase. He said, 'I told you to keep it in your pocket!' I didn't dare go to a match without it after that and we lost just two of our last nine matches.

As well as giving the 'boing, boing' cry a good airing, the Baggies fans adopted 'The Great Escape' as our theme tune. The club traditionally put on free buses for one away match each season and chose the trip to Charlton that March. We took 2,000 fans to The Valley and our sponsors, T-Mobile, got into the mood by providing 'survival kits' of goodies and refreshments to help them through the day. The atmosphere our fans created was unbelievable and the players responded. We won 4–1, with Robbie coming on to score a hat-trick.

A 1–1 draw at Aston Villa lifted us out of the bottom three for the first time since I joined the club, but we had probably the hardest run-in of all the relegation-threatened teams. Our rivals for the one survival spot were Southampton, Crystal Palace and Norwich. The club decided to lay on free travel again for the trip to Middlesbrough. Boro's fans gave me a great reception and my players did me proud in the first twenty-five minutes. We were all over them and should have been three up, but we blew our chances and by half-time we were three down. I was left wondering what we had done to deserve that. In the end, we lost 4–0. It was my mam's seventieth birthday party that night but not quite the double celebration I'd been hoping for.

We were back down to nineteenth in the table. After a 1–1 draw with Blackburn, we were still nineteenth. Our three remaining fixtures were Arsenal at home, Manchester United away and Portsmouth at home.

Against Arsenal we played well and created the better chances. Up to the sixty-fifth minute we produced eleven or twelve crosses to Arsenal's one, but they beat us with two late goals and we faced United needing to get something from the match. We knew we could be relegated when we left Old Trafford if the various results went against us. It was an early evening kick-off and we were given a boost by Southampton's late equaliser against Palace. You never know how developments at other matches are going to affect your team and we just didn't get going in the first half. For the first time in months, I had a real go at them at half-time. Fortunately for us, United missed chances, as they had done throughout the season, and they were only 1–0 up instead of being out of sight. Tomasz Kuszczak, who came on in goal for the injured Russell Hoult, performed heroics for us. In the second half we started passing and got a break with a penalty, which Robbie put away.

The way our players ran over to our fans and celebrated with them at the end showed how important that draw was. We were bottom of the table, yet we'd given ourselves a fighting chance for the last day of the season. That was all I could have asked for. People said Sir Alex wasn't too warm towards me at the end, but he was livid with his team and I understood why. He sets high standards and his team under-performed. I could imagine them getting the hairdryer treatment. He was fine with me later and we had a drink together. I told my players they had responded really well in the second half and played their way back into it.

Although we were the bottom club going into the final round of matches, I felt we had the easiest fixture. We were at home to Portsmouth and confident we would win, but that wouldn't be enough to save us if one of the other three teams won. Norwich were at Fulham, Palace at Charlton and Southampton at home to United. Norwich and Palace had one away win between them all season so why, I thought, were they all of a sudden going to win their last away match? Southampton had home advantage, but I knew United would be determined to win after losing at home to Chelsea in midweek. They hate to lose two in a row – that's the mentality at the club.

We had to win, so in that sense the day was simple and uncomplicated for us. The players weren't nervous. They had prepared well and listened to everything we told them. We had Horsfield and Kanu on the bench, so we could change things if we needed to chase a goal. It was still 0–0 at half-time but no one showed any sign of panic. I told my staff I didn't want to be given the scores at the other matches because I needed to concentrate on making sure we won, but in the second half you couldn't avoid knowing what was happening. Fans were listening on their radios and word was going around the ground. By then, Norwich were pretty well gone. They were on their way to a 6–0 thrashing. Southampton took the lead, but United came back and beat them 2–1. Palace were a goal down at half-time, yet became our main concern.

During the half-time break, Horsfield had said to me, 'I always score important goals.' He is the kind of character you need in a situation like that, someone who will stand up to be counted. So I sent him on in the second half and within about thirty seconds he scored with a great strike. At about the same time, Palace equalised.

Kieran put us 2–0 in the lead, but the elation of the crowd was stifled. They'd gone flat and I could guess why. Palace had scored again and gone in front. Then some fans with a radio, just behind the dug-out, jumped up in the air. Palace had conceded a goal. It was 2–2. If it stayed like that, we were safe. Suddenly, the whole stadium erupted. Everybody was going daft.

We saw off the last five minutes of our match and won 2–0, but everybody wanted to know what was happening at Charlton. We heard they were playing six minutes of stoppage time and our whole crowd went quiet and nervous. Fans, players and staff just stood there, waiting. I was standing by the dug-out. The final four minutes seemed like an eternity. Then it was all over at The Valley – Charlton 2, Palace 2, Palace relegated, Albion staying up! Another eruption.

We're screaming with joy and relief. We're hugging each other and jumping up and down. Within seconds the fans are swarming on to the pitch and the place is a mass of bodies. It's a fantastic sight, just the best ever.

Much of what happened after that is a blur. I remember getting drenched in champagne by Kieran and Kevin, then going round all the players, not only those in the team that day, to thank them and let them know how important they were to the club. My emotions were all over the place. Everything was just a crazy whirr. I felt over-whelmed because although I believed in myself and Nige and the players, we were still deep in trouble until the final few minutes of the season and you wonder if it can possibly all go in your favour at the end. You think back to all the bad days and the knocks before it started coming good. Then you just try to soak up all the elation around you.

I said at the time that it was my greatest achievement and now, in the cold light of day, many months on, I still say the same. I won so many trophies at United and caps for England, but we were expected to have success at Old Trafford. That was normal. This was an achievement against the odds. At Albion, the expectation was to be relegated. The players were being written off as failures. I was glad for them because they had risen to the challenge of proving to themselves as much as to everyone else that they were good enough for the Premiership. We had to help them clear that mental barrier, but then everything we achieved was done together. We'd all been in it together and we all came out of it together.

Everybody was saying, 'I bet you'll celebrate tonight,' but I didn't really. I was too drained. The season, especially the last day, had taken so much out of us all. A few members of my family had come down for the match, so a group of us went out for a quiet Indian meal. We made up for it the following day. I had the players in to give them a run-down on what we were planning for pre-season and what they should be doing through the summer. Then Kevin and Geoff Horsfield asked me what I was going to do for the rest of the day. I told them I was going to see if Nigel and the staff wanted to go over to the pub and then on to the club's player of the year function. They asked me whether we'd like to go with the players to a Thai restaurant in Birmingham, instead. So we joined them and then went on to the player of the year award at the stadium.

Ronnie Wallwork won the award, which I thought was deserved and fitting. A lot of talented players had contributed, Zoltan Gera and Jonathan Greening as well as the others I've already talked about. But lads such as Ronnie, Neil Clement and Paul Robinson typified the honest, hard-working effort that had kept us in the Premiership. They were all magnificent for us. I knew Ronnie and felt I could get the best out of him. He showed what he could do and everybody acknowledged that. Ronnie had a good night, and he wasn't the only one.

17
TALKING A GOOD GAME

Maureen Robson

One of the best nights we had following Bryan was the European Cup-Winners' Cup final against Barcelona in Rotterdam. Manchester United made us so welcome. We went to the party afterwards and it was great. In fact, we never got to our beds that night. We just picked up our things and went straight for the ferry. Our Justin couldn't remember a thing about it. He wasn't used to champagne and had a terrible hangover.

We used to go to France on holiday a lot because Brian liked driving. We'd drive up to Holland to watch Bryan playing in a pre-season friendly match for United and then on to another place in Holland to see Gary playing for West Brom. I've been to matches where they've called our Bryan all sorts. I just turned a blind eye to it. I've never turned round and said anything to anyone if they've had a go.

I like to watch Bryan's team at West Brom if I can. I used to go down to Boro when he was manager and watch them. It all got a bit nasty for him at the end. When he went there they had that old ground and no team or anything. He got them into the Premiership and to three Cup finals and all that. Then Steve Gibson took them to Singapore when he had already got Steve McClaren. I thought that was a dirty trick. Bryan was hurt, after all he had done for them, but then not a lot seems to affect him. He gets over things. He was a bit down after two years out of the game. He's got a good wife in Denise. She helps him to cope with the highs and the lows.

It really hurt him when his dad died. It was the way his dad died, but the family were with him at the end. Middlesbrough sent a wreath, which was good of them. Bryan offered to buy us this house, but Brian said no, he'd buy it when he could and that's what he did. I'm happy here. Our Susan is next door, the other lads are near and our Bryan rings me nearly every day. I don't drive any more but our Susan and the lads take me all over.

I went down to look after our Ben when Bryan and Denise were going away and he said, 'I'll come and collect you, Mam.' Well, it costs so much in petrol and he would have had to take me back again, so I said, 'Look, Bryan, there's no need. I'll go to the station and check the trains.' It was only £50.70 return to Manchester Airport, which is not far from where they live.

We've collected piles of photos and cuttings of Bryan over the years. He spent time while he was out of work sticking the photos in albums. When our Bryan comes home he always says, 'Mam, make us some mince and Yorkshire puddings.' I've no time for this nouvelle cuisine stuff. The rest of the family tell me to cook for him because he's so fussy.

Denise Robson

It was hard when Bryan did the two jobs, with Middlesbrough and England, because he was never here, really. I was quite lonely. Ben was little and the girls were teenagers and wanting to go out, so I had to be a bit of mum and dad. He doesn't bring his work home with him, though. He can switch off. He'll still have phone calls and he deals with those, but normally he can leave his work behind. I don't know a lot about football, so it's no good talking to me about it anyway, but

Bryan says he's happy with that. The only thing is that when he's watching sport on television you might as well talk to the wall.

I never wish he'd had a different job and wasn't so well known. We've had a good life and I always say we've been lucky. You accept the hard parts. The worst was when things weren't going well at Middlesbrough. We were living at Aislaby, near Yarm, and Ben was having quite a hard time at school with some other lads, but he handled it quite well. He cheered when we told him we were going back to Manchester.

It was worse for Claire when she was attacked one night as she was waiting for a taxi in Durham. Our girls never say who their dad is when they're out, but one of the girls Claire was with mentioned to this guy that she was Bryan Robson's daughter. When she walked out to the taxi, he butted her. She had to have ten stitches in her head. I've not had any hassle personally and generally we've not had any trouble.

I was in Barbados with Claire and Ben when stories appeared that Bryan was going to be sacked by Middlesbrough. I said to him, 'What's the point in going to Singapore if they're going to give you the sack? You might as well ask the question.' I told Bryan it couldn't just be paper talk. He asked the question and they denied it. Then they tell him on the day of John Pickering's funeral. But you move on. Bryan had seven good years there and they were great times. They were sociable, down to earth, normal people.

Bryan's become more serious and responsible. I tell him he's becoming a miserable old bugger, a grumpy old man. He says he's not as bad as his dad – yet! I suppose that's just growing older – and management. He does hide his emotions. He's quite deep. He doesn't show his temper at home – he does that at football. It takes a lot for him to snap. I can really wind him up before he goes. He's not bad at remembering birthdays and anniversaries. He's got better as the years have gone by. He might bring me flowers on special occasions – or when he's in the bad books!

He's quite particular about his food. He likes good food, pastas, things like that. He doesn't eat a lot of junk. Occasionally, he'll get stuck into the Quavers, or really spoil himself with chips and curry sauce. He's not fussy with clothes. He's a pain in the butt there because I have to buy his clothes. He'll go shopping no more than twice a year. I have to bring him his clothes and if they don't fit I take them back again.

I wouldn't say I'm looking forward to his retirement because I hope a lot of good things are to come before then. I'm sure I'll look forward to it in a few more years, but Bryan's too young to retire. He enjoys his work and he's still ambitious. He had those years out of the game and we enjoyed ourselves. We had some lovely holidays and were lucky to be able to do that. When we're older, we'll do a lot more of that.

I HAVE BEEN FORTUNATE in my career because the good times have outweighed the bad and there can have been no better feeling at the end of that 2004–05 season than being the manager of West Bromwich Albion. It's at times like that, especially, that you realise there's no better job than being in football. Nothing beats playing, which is why I tell players to look after themselves and play as long as they can, even if it means dropping down a division, but management is a good second best. Just being involved in the game always gives you a buzz.

At the highest level, I believe the standard is very good. The quality and fitness of the players are exceptional, but I don't think we have the quality in depth that we had ten and twenty years ago. The standard of players in the lower divisions used to be good and many of them were able to make the step up to top clubs. Now you find fewer players doing that because there just aren't as many who are good enough. The quality gap has widened significantly.

The Premiership has produced some fantastic and entertaining football and I think twenty clubs is about the right number. There are, in effect, three or four mini leagues within the Premiership and it would be very difficult for a Derby or Nottingham Forest to win the Championship again. Provincial and smaller city clubs can't compete financially with Chelsea, Manchester United or Arsenal, so their only hope would be to strike it lucky and bring through five or six outstanding players from their academy. That has happened on very few occasions in my memory. Arsenal, United and Leeds have produced batches of top kids, but they are the exceptions rather than the rule.

In a sense, Chelsea broke away into their own league when Roman Abramovich arrived with his limitless funds. There were concerns that clubs would overstretch themselves again in an attempt to compete with Chelsea in the transfer market. That is unlikely to happen because the other clubs, even Manchester United and Arsenal, know they can't compete with them. It amazes me when people assume all those involved in running football clubs are idiots. The vast majority are sensible businessmen who understand the dangers of gambling. They are not prepared to gamble and lose big-style, as Leeds and a few other clubs did. Chelsea have to pay their own prices because everybody knows how much money they've got.

Clubs across the board look at their own budgets, assess what they can and cannot afford, and stick to that. Within those bounds, you may have different strategies, depending on your results. If you are promoted or know you are going to be comfortable in a higher division, you may be prepared to spend more. If relegation is on the cards, you don't want to overspend and find you can't cope financially. So you have a plan A and a plan B.

Finances, TV revenues especially, determine so much of the modern game and the glaring example of this is the Champions League. To my mind, though, it has been devalued because it is no longer the league of champions. It should be the competition for champions only, as it used to be. I realise that in that case United wouldn't have been there to win the Cup in 1999 and Liverpool wouldn't have won it in 2005, but the Champions League doesn't have the stature or aura of the old European Cup.

Now the leading European football countries have four clubs entered and the competition has become bloated, with too many meaningless matches. It doesn't capture the imagination as it did – not until the later stages, anyway. For the players, it's great. You get far more opportunities to play in the top club competition. I wish it had been so easy to qualify in my playing days. I would have played in it a hell of a lot more than I did. Now the usual clubs are virtually guaranteed their places and that's the whole point of the present structure. It's a money-making machine for those who already have plenty.

The quality and appeal of the UEFA Cup has suffered as a result. You only have to look at some of the poor attendances at English grounds in the early rounds. Supporters can't be expected to keep forking out their hard-earned money. Heavy fixture demands will affect supporters and clubs alike. The more successful a club, the bigger the squad required. They are also the clubs more likely to be supplying players for internationals. I think there is a case for restricting the League Cup to the clubs below the Premiership. It would give those clubs a bit more revenue, prestige and the chance of winning a trophy – but then the League Cup gives clubs such as West Brom a better chance of success and playing in Europe.

No matter what level you play at these days, the chances are that you will play in a fine facility and on a near perfect surface. The improvement in the standard of stadiums and pitches is one of the positive features of the modern game. Right down the divisions, there are some terrific grounds. I remember going to Crewe with Middlesbrough and we couldn't get all our players and staff in the dressing room at the same time. Some had to stand and wait outside while the others changed. We had to change in shifts. Now Crewe have built up their stadium and the facilities are really good. As a player, my favourite stadium was probably Barcelona's Camp Nou. It may well be for today's players, too. It's brilliant, but now there are so many fantastic grounds, in this country as well as abroad.

I used to enjoy playing at Maine Road and Villa Park because they had big pitches. It might also be because we had some important wins on those grounds, but most players will tell you they prefer a pitch with wide open spaces. Players also like a good surface, which we didn't always have. Most pitches now are unbelievably good all the way through a season. We had terrible problems with our pitch at Old Trafford in the eighties. It was like a sandpit one season. Now there are no excuses for mis-controlling the ball because you don't get the bad bounces we used to have. You can get the ball down and play, which suits the better, passing sides such as United and Arsenal.

Some might say the standard of football ought to be better, considering the wages paid to today's footballers. I don't want to sound like a miserable, cynical old pro and go on about my playing days, because every player is entitled to do the best he can for himself. I got myself the best deal I could. No player in his right mind is going to say 'No' if he gets the offer of a fabulous new deal. Again, I go back to the point – clubs aren't as stupid as many people seem to believe.

What concerns me far more than the money being paid to players is the money going out of the game to agents. The problem nowadays is that a club very rarely deals directly with a player. I sometimes look at a player and think, 'Why don't you stand on your own two feet?' Only a handful of them do. Agents unsettle players to force moves and then demand massive fees to do the deals. I sit there in amazement at some of the things they ask for. You can have a situation where an agent does a deal for a player in a £2 million transfer and then wants 10 or 20 per cent on top. They must think we've got rocks for brains.

It's up to clubs to be firmer with agents. The trouble is that you will sometimes miss a player. When I was at Middlesbrough I missed out on Robbie Keane, who was then at Wolves. We dug in our heels and refused to pay the agent what we thought was ridiculous money. Keane went to Coventry, instead. Players are on good contracts and you'd think they should be paying their advisers, but unfortunately that's not where we are any more. Nearly all the clubs accept they will have to pay the agent a separate fee once the player's contract has been agreed.

I discussed the subject of agents with David Dein, the Arsenal vice-chairman, some years ago and suggested that clubs caught paying agents above a certain rate should be heavily fined. David said the players would then go abroad because agents would still be able to command huge fees from foreign clubs. Trying to regulate agents world-wide would be a nightmare. In fairness, I must say some agents are helpful and reasonable, genuinely have the interests of their players at heart and care about the game. The problem I have is with the rest of them.

Identifying and signing good players is a vital part of management. In fact, when I'm asked what makes a good manager, I say, 'The short answer is good players.' If you watch coaches at work, nobody does anything really different. New methods of training have evolved with advanced scientific knowledge. For instance, we do far more power work, with weights, than when I was a young player. A number of the United players, including Roy Keane and Ryan Giggs, incorporated yoga in their training and preparation. We are opening up to a far wider range of methods. Diet is more controlled with a greater use of vitamins and nutrients, and general discipline is much tighter.

Then you need the right tactics, organisation, dedication and motivation. You have to get the blend of players right and bring the best out of them, but without the right players in the first place, there is only so much you can do. I've always said that if you've got the eleven best players in a 4–4–2 formation, you'll win a hell of a lot more often than the team who haven't got the best eleven players – and it doesn't matter how good a coach you are.

I believe I have become a better manager through experience, the coaching courses and self-assessment. I'm stricter with the lads at West Brom. I won't allow players to do what they want, as Andy Townsend, Gazza and others told me people were doing behind my back at Boro. I handle situations head-on. I think I'm patient and fair with players. I give them a chance. It takes a lot to get me annoyed, but if they let me down, I'll come down on them. I'm still fair game for a laugh and a joke. The lads will stick photos of me with Sir Alex on the dressing room wall and, of course, if I fall over in training it's hilarious. I don't get away with anything. The fun and banter help keep me young.

Working with players, especially when you see the improvement in their football, is the best and most satisfying part of the job. Dealing with directors, agents and the media is a part of the job that has to be done. I've said my piece about agents. With directors you accept that there will be slaps on the back when things are going well and snidey comments when they're not going so well. At Albion the board are OK, although I work mainly with the chairman. I have always had a reasonable relationship with the press and players are better prepared to give interviews than when I started playing. We also tell young players to be careful where they go and what they do because there's always someone ready to tip off the tabloids if they get involved in any bother. There are plenty of nice places to take their wives or girlfriends without going to nightclubs and risking a confrontation with some smart aleck.

The media picked up on the fact that I've become more hands-on at matches than I used to be, another lesson I learned from my days at Boro. I used to stand back and communicate with the players through my number two. Now I talk to them directly from the touchline and get my message across more quickly. I also feel more involved this way. You get caught up in the game almost as if you are a player. I think the fans like to see that from their manager.

There is a theory that great players don't make great managers. When I went into management, it was pointed out that Bobby Charlton and Bobby Moore, two of England's greatest ever players, didn't have the best of careers in management. First of all, I took it as an amazing compliment to be mentioned in the same breath as those two and, to use an example from the same era, I would suggest Franz Beckenbauer didn't do so badly as a manager. Today, you see a lot of top Dutch players, for instance, making good managers – Marco van Basten with the national team and Frank Rijkaard at Barcelona, to name two. I think this is an example of where the coaching courses can be so valuable, because you are taught how to communicate and put across your points to players. Perhaps some of those great players of the past found it difficult to explain what they wanted of their players.

Four of us from the same United team found ourselves in Premier League management at the same time. I was pitting my wits against Steve Bruce's Birmingham and Mark Hughes' Blackburn, while Gordon Strachan was in charge at Celtic. Steve, Gordon and I always had our opinions and were perhaps more obvious managerial material. Sparky was quiet, but always a deep thinker. He didn't say too much when we were arguing with the gaffer or Archie about something, but, typical of Sparky, he was taking it all in.

We're all British and another common belief I don't accept is that foreign coaches are better. I think it's more the case that they are lucky enough to get the best clubs. Sir Alex had a chance with United and look what he did with it. The other top clubs are going for foreign managers and coaches and British managers aren't getting a fair chance. Are we saying we can't find another Busby, Shankly,

Paisley, Clough or Ferguson? I can't help wondering what Sam Allardyce would do if he was at Liverpool, Chelsea, United or Arsenal. He couldn't possibly do more than he has done at Bolton. It would be interesting to see what Arsene Wenger or Jose Mourinho could do at Bolton or West Brom on the budgets of those clubs, or how they would get on in the Championship if they were asked to build up a club such as Middlesbrough. I'm in no way putting down Wenger and Mourinho, but we can't prove the argument one way or the other until British managers are given a crack at the big clubs.

Wenger has undoubtedly done a fantastic job at Arsenal. The main reason for that was his insight into French football. He was able to nick all the good young players who came through the French system, paying modest fees for them and selling on Nicolas Anelka and Patrick Vieira for huge profit. He also saw something in Thierry Henry that others didn't, and did a terrific job in prolonging the careers of Tony Adams and those other British stalwarts of the Arsenal defence. Tony is full of admiration for him. When I was at Middlesbrough I never had a proper conversation with Arsene, but he came into my office at West Brom and we chatted for about twenty-five minutes over a glass of wine. He speaks sense, as, in fact, do most top managers.

Even Sir Alex and Wenger don't have the budget Mourinho has, but no matter how much money you have to spend, you've still got to structure the team well and deliver results. In his first season in England, Mourinho won two trophies, including Chelsea's first Championship in fifty years and only their second ever. He's got some fantastic players, he operates a system that suits them, and so far he's produced the results.

Mourinho has broken the United-Arsenal domination of the Premiership, just as Sir Alex overcame the Old Firm and then the Merseyside clubs. Chelsea raised the bar and challenged United and Arsenal to match them. It was a big ask, but you would be a fool to write off Sir Alex. He still has a lot of experienced players who've seen it all and he's added terrific young talent in players such as Wayne Rooney and Cristiano Ronaldo. I suppose the biggest problem, though, is finding the player to replace Roy Keane.

United were faced with that situation after parting company with Roy in November 2005. It surprised me because I thought that at the age of thirty-four he had another two good years in him, but criticising team-mates is not good for dressing-room spirit. It's up to the manager to criticise players and I got the impression Sir Alex felt matters had become too awkward, so he moved Roy on. I was definitely interested in signing Keaney and so were many other clubs, including Real Madrid. He eventually joined Celtic, fulfilling a long-held ambition. The move also meant that he would not have to play against United.

I admire Roy not only because he is a great player but also for the way he has changed his lifestyle around. He was keen on boxing when he was young and you could see that aggression in him off the pitch as well as on it. He did have something of a mentality problem, and when he had a drink he could turn really nasty. He and Gary Pallister were big mates, but then had a bust-up and Roy just turned on him. As he got older, and wiser, Keaney realised he would have to change if he wanted a long career in the game. He had a couple of serious injuries so he knew he had to get into the gym and rebuild his body. He cut out drinking totally and became a fitness fanatic. I know it sounds unlikely, but he really did take to yoga. You've got to hand it to him. It's not easy to do what he's done when you have that aggressive streak running through your character.

People speculated about who might replace me at United, but first Paul Ince and then Roy came along. That said, it's difficult to see an adequate replacement for Keaney at the moment. Steven Gerrard is the obvious player who fits the bill, but Chelsea couldn't get him to leave Liverpool and United admit they've no chance of buying him from their great rivals. Vieira would have been a candidate, but he left Arsenal for Juventus and his best years may be behind him. Players with their ability and flair, who can command the midfield, produce a defence-splitting pass or score a goal are few and far between.

Comparing players is difficult because everyone has his own strengths and characteristics, but I think it's fair to say that Gerrard hasn't got the aggression that Roy has and I had. Then again, I didn't have the pace that Gerrard's got. He's tremendously quick across the ground. Roy's pace is similar to mine, if not better, but I don't think either of them has my stamina and the records suggest Keaney doesn't score as many goals as I did. He scored more regularly when he was younger, but the goals have dried up in recent seasons.

I think also that Gerrard and I have better temperaments. Again, the records provide the proof. I was sent off once. Gerrard has been sent off, I think, three or four times, Keane thirteen times. If you are the captain of the team, you have got to be able to control your temper better than that. As I have said, he has worked at that and he definitely controls himself better now. Gerrard and I have probably found it more natural to control our aggression.

In fairness, the laws are more strictly applied now than in my playing days, so I no doubt got away with a lot more than those two can. The referees started clamping down when I went to Middlesbrough. Then again, you know the rules whenever you are playing and have to be disciplined. I played regularly in that first season at Boro and was booked, I think, only once. What you should do as a player is push the rules right to the limit – and no further. There is a case for calling it cheating, but you'll find most top sportsmen do that, not just footballers.

It's harder for referees now because the laws of the game allow nowhere near as much physical contact as when I played and every decision comes under such intense scrutiny. TV cameras cover every angle and capture every incident. Referees are also put under immense pressure by the watching assessors. They know that if they don't perform well they could be demoted. I see no good reason why match officials should not be assisted by the technology we have available, but only for goal-line and penalty decisions. They could have the verdict from the fourth official within seconds and it would save time on all the arguing. I wouldn't use video evidence for offside decisions because I think that over a season those do balance out. I'm not sure that penalty decisions do.

Character and mental strength are so important in football, for a player or a manager. I have already talked about Alan Shearer and it is not only his ability that marks him out. His attitude and the way he conducts himself make him an example to any young player. Another player I admired enormously was Kevin Keegan. He was the first player after George Best to exploit commercial possibilities, helped of course by Harry Swales, who was nothing like some of the agents who have popped up in recent years. Kevin would be the first to acknowledge he wasn't the most naturally gifted and that, to a certain degree, he manufactured himself. To win the European Footballer of the Year award twice and all his other honours through sheer hard work and dedication speaks volumes for his character.

Just as there are more foreign managers coming into the English game, so there are more foreign players and I have certainly been willing to go down that route for the good of my club. I don't believe it is as hard, though, for British players to make their mark and we have probably more home players at Albion than most clubs have. I think that if you are a good enough player, you will get a chance. It just may take longer to break through at a top club. You'll never lose the very good or good players, but the average players might drop down the divisions or even out of the game altogether. They could become disenchanted and pack in.

The thorny subject of nationality was most controversially raised when England put Sven Goran Eriksson, a Swede, in charge of the national team. Predictably, that issue was in the spotlight again when England suffered an embarrassing defeat against Northern Ireland in a World Cup qualifying match. I would have no great objection to the appointment of a foreign manager if we had no Englishman good enough to do the job, but I believe we have coaches who are more than capable. You don't get too many leading football nations who employ a foreign manager and the FA's decision was a bit of a slap in the face for our lads.

We have some genuinely top-class players in this country and it would be a great opportunity for an English manager to make his mark with them. As well as Sam Allardyce, we have Alan Curbishley, Steve Bruce, Steve McClaren and Stuart Pearce. Hopefully one of them will get a chance eventually. The FA want English managers and coaches to take their courses, and they go on about how important it is for us to get our badges, yet they gave the England job – with a massive contract – to a foreign manager. After the World Cup, though, Sven goes.

Any manager would have to think long and hard about what he would be taking on with England. We all know public scrutiny and criticism comes with the territory, but some of the abuse our managers have had to take from the media has been outrageous. The treatment Bobby Robson received was a disgrace, and no one should have to be subjected to the 'turnip' insults that Graham Taylor came in for. Attacks like that are too personal. The pressure and attention can also impact on your family. All these factors would have to be considered very carefully by anyone offered the job.

Would I be interested? I take the view that you have to see how your life and career progress. I may never get near the job again. I was interviewed when Terry Venables left, but at the time I wasn't ready. I didn't have the coaching badges or the experience. If the opportunity does come around, I would certainly consider it. Just to be mentioned in connection with the job is an honour. I am more experienced and hardened to management now, so I would have an open mind about it. You have to take that attitude because you never know what's around the corner in this business.

I'm always being asked about the prospect of managing United and I'd like to think that my record at Middlesbrough and West Brom would be good enough possibly to get a chance at some stage in the future. I think the real challenge would be to work in Italy, a country that has produced some of the very best coaches. I nearly went there as a player and I wouldn't have any worries about going there as a manager, but right now my only concern is West Brom and trying to build us into a solid Premiership club.

As for England, I think Sven has, overall, done a good job in the matches that matter. We have qualified for the major tournaments since he got the job. We haven't missed out, as we did during the seventies and nineties. There's nothing worse than watching the World Cup on TV when England aren't involved. The danger is, when we approach a major tournament, that the country will get carried away and raise expectations too high. But I do believe we have a chance in 2006 – probably our best chance since 1990.

As a manager you can never be sure of your side because of injuries, suspensions or loss of form. Even in the final preparations for a World Cup, a player could come from nowhere and stake his claim for a place. It is more difficult still to pick an ideal England line-up several months ahead of the event, but I'll attempt to do so anyway to give you an idea of my personal thoughts on the players and the system that might deliver for England in Germany.

My first consideration would be to give us a solid base. You don't want to be conceding too many goals, otherwise your World Cup could be over before it's begun. Paul Robinson has become a good, reliable, number one goalkeeper and I can see Chris Kirkland challenging him at some stage, so we are looking strong again there.

Then I look at our abundance of riches in central defence and ask whether any country has three as good as ours. John Terry, Rio Ferdinand and Sol Campbell would get into any international team so, if they are all fit and flying, I'd have the three of them in my team. They would take some getting past. I have spoken to Sven about his defence and asked him whether he would change from a back four. He said, 'No.' I would.

With a back three, the full-backs would effectively become wing-backs, and Ashley Cole is the perfect player for that role on the left. He is naturally left-sided and likes to get forward. On the right I would play Gary Neville or Shaun Wright-Phillips, depending on the opposition and whether the emphasis is on defending or attacking. David Beckham has played in a midfield holding role, and done a decent job. He has a great range of passing and works hard, but he is not a tackler and if you are in that position, sitting in front of the back three, you have to be able to win the ball. I think that job is made for Steven Gerrard. He can tackle, he can pass and when the opportunity is there, he can get forward. I would have Becks to his right and Frank Lampard to his left. You need to crowd the midfield at international level and we would be doing that with three of the best midfield players in the world. We would have ability, strength and experience. They are also intelligent enough to fill in for each other when one of them goes on a run. That set-up would suit those players.

Up front it has to be Michael Owen, with Wayne Rooney playing just behind him. Michael is a natural, instinctive goalscorer and has a great record with England. Rooney is without doubt one of the outstanding young players in the world. We saw how important he was to England in the 2004 European Championship. If it hadn't been for his injury, we might have won the tournament. He has to learn to control his temper and I believe he will. Mark Hughes became an even better player when he realised you can't afford to push referees too far. I think Wayne could be one of the real stars of the 2006 World Cup.

That team, with the back-up we have as well, has the potential to go all the way. It reminds me of our Italia '90 side. We had that strength and authority at the back, quality in midfield and an out-and-out goalscorer in Gary Lineker, supported by a brilliant player in Peter Beardsley. I think that system would bring the best out of those players. You have to be flexible with systems. At West Brom I have generally played 4–4–2, but if it's not working I may throw on another striker and play 4–3–3. A lot of clubs are now going with one central striker and two wide, or a midfield five. As a coach, you are constantly looking at ways to outwit the opposition.

As for the England captaincy, I have to say that Becks wouldn't have been my choice. He hasn't done a bad job and he has matured, but he's not a leader on the pitch. Gerrard and Terry are more natural leaders and have the aggression that most managers like in a captain. To my mind, Terry has probably edged ahead of Gerrard as the best choice. He leads by example, is an excellent organiser and has the presence that everyone in the team will respect. He also scores goals, a great bonus for a defender.

England could hardly have had a better draw for the opening group stage of the World Cup. Sweden may give them a tough game, but you would expect them to beat Paraguay and Trinidad and Tobago to progress to the last sixteen comfortably enough.

When you are trying to assess the contenders for any World Cup, Brazil inevitably have to come into the reckoning and from what I have seen of them they again look the team to beat. Their attacking options are frightening. At the last Confederations Cup they played with Adriano, Robinho, Ronaldinho and Kaka. Imagine that talent plus Ronaldo, Roberto Carlos, Cafu and Emerson. They even have a decent goalkeeper now, in Dida. If Brazil put it all together, they could be awesome and, as they have proved time and again, they are a tournament team.

I have a feeling the Dutch might do well. They have some good young players coming through and they've got goals in them. Germany also appear to be bringing through some young talent again and they will have home advantage. Like Brazil, they always seem to come good when it matters. Another country you can never write off is Italy. They are traditionally difficult to beat and always have players capable of producing something special to turn a game. Argentina have had their World Cup successes in the past, but I wasn't impressed with them in the Confederations Cup. Unless they have some more players coming through, I don't think they will be a serious threat. I don't really fancy France this time, either, not even with Zinedine Zidane back.

The Brazilians apart, there shouldn't be too much out there to worry England. Any team that wins a World Cup will need to have some luck and avoid too many injuries and suspensions, but we do have the players capable of winning. The dream final would be England v. Brazil, although they could meet in the semi-finals.

The main thing for our lads is to make the most of this opportunity and enjoy it. You never know whether you'll get the chance again. I tell my players at West Brom the same thing. I want them to enjoy their football and their training because if they are enjoying what they do, I am going to get a better performance from them. It's no different for the top players with England. You have to go out there with no fear and just play. Whatever happens, I'll be following every kick and header. Nothing compares with the Olympic Games and World Cup for sporting spectacle and I'll be hooked, as I always am.

I know I am sticking my neck out giving my thoughts on how it may go in Germany, and I could be getting it badly wrong, but that is all part of the fun of our great game.

At West Brom, the first objective for the 2005–06 season again had to be staying in the Premiership. At Middlesbrough I put down the stepping stones and we progressed a long way. I want to do the same with Albion, but it has to be one step at a time. The important thing is to keep going forward. We're working hard to build the whole club. We've invested in an academy and improved training facilities. I was happy for £3 million to be taken out of my transfer fund and put into that development project.

We had the smallest budget in the Premiership, but I still had money to spend and strengthen our squad. We bought Wigan striker Nathan Ellington and Luton's young central defender Curtis Davies for £3 million each. We also signed midfield player Darren Carter from Birmingham, Diomansy Kamara from Portsmouth and Steve Watson from Everton. Ellington is powerful and quick, and has a good scoring record. People had been comparing Davies with Rio Ferdinand, but he reminds me of Paul McGrath. If he becomes half as good as Paul, we have got a player. We weren't able to get Kieran Richardson on loan for another season, which was a disappointment, but we took Chris Kirkland on loan from Liverpool. He has all the assets you need in a keeper and he is prepared to work at his game. I gave him his chance at the start of the season and he took it with both hands. Later, Tomasz Kuszczak did the same.

Geoff Horsfield showed why he deserved a new, two-year contract with four goals in his first two games. Four points from our first two League matches was solid enough, but then three consecutive defeats reminded us that we had no margin for error. Defensive lapses cost us dear. We had to face up to the fact that it would take another season of hard graft and application if we weren't going to undo all the good work of the previous year. That meant total commitment from everyone at the club. That's why I've never liked to get too involved in speculation about the future. I had more than enough to think about at Albion.

We managed to start a good run in November 2005, playing to the standard I'd expected of us, but the whole of football was over-shadowed late that month by the death of George Best. We were the first team to play against United at Old Trafford after he died and it was a very emotional night. The outpouring of grief and affection for George was amazing. The following Saturday, back home in Belfast, he was given what seemed virtually a state funeral. The tributes, including one from Denis Law, portrayed George as the nice, loyal bloke he was. It is just so sad he hadn't been able to cope with his drink problems.

I'm certainly not planning anything beyond football. I've dabbled in business with the Birthdays card shops but, as with the horses, I've ticked that off. I am building up a portfolio of properties for the family's future and we bought a little place close to the Albion training ground. I stay there for most of the week, although we still have our house in Hale. Our Char has been working with a yacht crew in Florida, but Claire and Ben are still at home. Ben is doing his A levels and playing part-time with Altrincham. He wants to be a player and seems to be doing OK, so maybe there will be a Robbo around in the game even after I call it a day.

Football has been good to me and I'd like to think it's been a two-way street. It's really nice when people say they appreciate my approach to football because I always gave everything. If that's how I'm remembered, I'll be more than happy.

BRYAN ROBSON
– CAREER RECORD

Born Chester-le-Street, 11 January 1957

INTERNATIONAL PLAYING RECORD

England Under-21: 7 caps
England B: 3 caps
England full: 90 caps

England appearances

1980

1	6 February	Rep of Ireland (Wembley) ECQ	W	2–0
2	31 May	Australia (Sydney) F	W	2–1
3	10 September	Norway (Wembley) WCQ	W	4–0
4	15 October	Romania (Bucharest) WCQ	L	1–2
5	19 November	Switzerland (Wembley) WCQ	W	2–1

1981

6	25 March	Spain (Wembley) F	L	1–2
7	29 April	Romania (Wembley) WCQ	D	0–0
8	12 May	Brazil (Wembley) F	L	0–1
9	20 May	Wales (Wembley) HIC	D	0–0
10	23 May	Scotland (Wembley) HIC	L	0–1
11	30 May	Switzerland (Basle) WCQ	L	1–2
12	6 June	Hungary (Budapest) WCQ	W	3–1
13	9 September	Norway (Oslo) WCQ	L	1–2 (1 goal)
14	18 November	Hungary (Wembley) WCQ	W	1–0

1982

15	23 February	N Ireland (Wembley) HIC	W	4–0 (1 goal)
16	27 April	Wales (Cardiff) HIC	W	1–0
17	25 May	Holland (Wembley) F	W	2–0
18	29 May	Scotland (Hampden Park) HIC	W	1–0
19	3 June	Finland (Helsinki) F	W	4–1 (2 goals)
20	16 June	France (Bilbao) WCF	W	3–1 (2 goals)
21	20 June	Czechoslovakia (Bilbao) WCF	W	2–0
22	29 June	West Germany (Madrid) WCF	D	0–0
23	5 July	Spain (Madrid) WCF	D	0–0
24	22 September	Denmark (Copenhagen) ECQ	D	2–2
25	17 November	Greece* (Salonika) ECQ	W	3–0
26	15 December	Luxembourg* (Wembley) ECQ	W	9–0

1983

27	1 June	Scotland* (Wembley) HIC	W	2–0 (1 goal)
28	12 October	Hungary* (Budapest) ECQ	W	3–0
29	16 November	Luxembourg* (Luxembourg) ECQ	W	4–0 (2 goals)

1984

30	29 February	France* (Paris) F	L	0–2
31	4 April	N Ireland* (Wembley) HIC	W	1–0
32	26 May	Scotland* (Hampden Park) HIC	D	1–1
33	2 June	USSR* (Wembley) F	L	0–2
34	10 June	Brazil* (Rio de Janeiro) F	W	2–0
35	13 June	Uruguay* (Montevideo) F	L	0–2
36	17 June	Chile* (Santiago) F	D	0–0
37	12 September	East Germany* (Wembley) F	W	1–0 (1 goal)
38	17 October	Finland* (Wembley) WCQ	W	5–0 (1 goal)
39	14 November	Turkey* (Istanbul) WCQ	W	8–0 (3 goals)

1985

40	26 March	Rep of Ireland* (Wembley) F	W	2–1
41	1 May	Romania* (Bucharest) WCQ	D	0–0
42	22 May	Finland* (Helsinki) WCQ	D	1–1
43	25 May	Scotland* (Hampden Park) RC	L	0–1
44	6 June	Italy* (Mexico City) MCT	L	1–2
45	9 June	Mexico* (Mexico City) MCT	L	0–1
46	12 June	West Germany* (Mexico City) MCT	W	3–0 (1 goal)
47	16 June	USA* (Los Angeles) F	W	5–0
48	11 September	Romania* (Wembley) WCQ	D	1–1
49	16 October	Turkey* (Wembley) WCQ	W	5–0 (1 goal)

1986

50	26 February	Israel* (Tel Aviv) F	W	2–1 (2 goals)
51	17 May	Mexico* (Los Angeles) F	W	3–0
52	3 June	Portugal* (Monterrey) WCF	L	0–1
53	6 June	Morocco* (Monterrey) WCF	D	0–0
54	15 October	N Ireland* (Wembley) ECQ	W	3–0

1987

55	18 February	Spain* (Madrid) F	W	4–2
56	1 April	N Ireland* (Windsor Park) ECQ	W	2–0 (1 goal)
57	29 April	Turkey* (Izmir) ECQ	D	0–0
58	19 May	Brazil* (Wembley) RC	D	1–1
59	23 May	Scotland* (Hampden Park) RC	D	0–0
60	14 October	Turkey* (Wembley) ECQ	W	8–0 (1 goal)
61	11 November	Yugoslavia* (Belgrade) ECQ	W	4–1 (1 goal)

1988

62	23 March	Holland* (Wembley) F	D	2–2
63	27 April	Hungary* (Budapest) F	D	0–0
64	21 May	Scotland* (Wembley) RC	W	1–0
65	24 May	Colombia* (Wembley) RC	D	1–1
66	28 May	Switzerland* (Lausanne) F	W	1–0
67	12 June	Rep of Ireland* (Stuttgart) ECF	L	0–1

68	15 June	Holland* (Dusseldorf) ECF	L	1–3 (1 goal)
69	18 June	USSR* (Frankfurt) ECF	L	1–3
70	14 September	Denmark* (Wembley) F	W	1–0
71	19 October	Sweden* (Wembley) WCQ	D	0–0
72	16 November	Saudi Arabia* (Riyadh) F	D	1–1

1989

73	8 February	Greece* (Athens) F	W	2–1 (1 goal)
74	8 March	Albania* (Tirana) WCQ	W	2–0 (1 goal)
75	26 April	Albania* (Wembley) WCQ	W	5–0
76	23 May	Chile* (Wembley) RC	D	0–0
77	27 May	Scotland* (Hampden Park) RC	W	2–0
78	3 June	Poland* (Wembley) WCQ	W	3–0
79	7 June	Denmark* (Copenhagen) F	D	1–1
80	11 October	Poland* (Katowice) WCQ	D	0–0
81	15 November	Italy* (Wembley) F	D	0–0
82	13 December	Yugoslavia* (Wembley) F	W	2–1 (2 goals)

1990

83	25 April	Czechoslovakia* (Wembley) F	W	4–2
84	22 May	Uruguay* (Wembley) F	L	1–2
85	2 June	Tunisia* (Tunis) F	D	1–1
86	11 June	Rep of Ireland* (Cagliari) WCF	D	1–1
87	16 June	Holland* (Cagliari) WCF	D	0–0

1991

88	6 February	Cameroon* (Wembley) F	W	2–0
89	27 March	Rep of Ireland* (Wembley) ECQ	D	1–1
90	16 October	Turkey (Wembley) ECQ	W	1–0

Overall

P	W	D	L
90	46	26	18

*Denotes captain – 65 of Robson's caps were as captain
ECQ = European Championship Qualifier
F = Friendly
WCQ = World Cup Qualifier
HIC = Home International Championship
WCF = World Cup Finals
RS = Rous Cup
MCT = Mexico City Tournament
ECF = European Championship Finals

– Robson scored 26 goals for England.
– In 1989 Robson scored the fastest goal in a professional match at Wembley. He took just 38 seconds from the kick-off to find the back of the net against Yugoslavia. England won 2-1 for their 100th victory at the famous stadium.
– In 1982 Robson put England ahead against France after 27 seconds in Bilbao – the fastest goal in the World Cup finals until Hakan Sukur's strike for Turkey against South Korea in 2002.

CLUB PLAYING CAREER

Club honours

FA Cup: 1983, 1985, 1990 (Manchester United)
European Cup-Winners' Cup: 1991 (Manchester United)
Premier League: 1993, 1994 (Manchester United)
Division One: 1995 (Middlesbrough)
Charity Shield: 1983, 1993 (Manchester United)

Club playing record

			P	W	D	L	Goals
1974–75	WBA	Division Two	3	2	0	1	2
1975–76	WBA	Division Two	14+2	8	5	3	1
1976–77	WBA	Division One	21+2	9	6	8	8
1977–78	WBA	Division One	35	15	12	8	3
1978–79	WBA	Division One	41	23	11	7	7
1979–80	WBA	Division One	35	10	16	9	9
1980–81	WBA	Division One	40	18	12	10	10
1981–82	WBA	Division One	5	1	1	3	0
		League Total	194+4	86	63	49	40
		FA Cup	10+2	5	4	3	2
		League Cup	17+1	7	6	5	2
		Others	12	7	2	3	3
		Totals	233+7	105	75	60	47
1981–82	Man Utd	Division One	32	18	8	6	5
1982–83	Man Utd	Division One	33	16	10	7	10
1983–84	Man Utd	Division One	33	18	9	6	12
1984–85	Man Utd	Division One	32+1	17	8	8	9
1985–86	Man Utd	Division One	21	13	4	4	7
1986–87	Man Utd	Division One	29+1	10	11	9	7
1987–88	Man Utd	Division One	36	22	9	5	11
1988–89	Man Utd	Division One	34	12	12	10	4
1989–90	Man Utd	Division One	20	9	4	7	2
1990–91	Man Utd	Division One	15+2	7	7	3	1
1991–92	Man Utd	Division One	26+1	16	9	2	4
1992–93	Man Utd	Premiership	5+9	10	2	2	1
1993–94	Man Utd	Premiership	10+5	8	4	3	1
		League Total	326+19	176	97	72	74
		FA Cup	33+2	21	10	4	10
		League Cup	50+1	32	10	9	5
		Others	32+2	14	13	7	10
		Totals	441+24	243	130	92	99
1994–95	Middlesbrough	Division One	21+1	13	5	4	1
1995–96	Middlesbrough	Premiership	1+1	1	0	1	0
1996–97	Middlesbrough	Premiership	1	0	0	1	0
		League Total	23+2	14	5	6	1

	P	W	D	L	Goals
FA Cup	1	1	0	0	0
League Cup	1	1	0	0	0
Others	0	0	0	0	0
Totals	25+2	16	5	6	1
Overall Totals					
League	543+25	276	165	127	115
FA Cup	44+4	27	14	7	12
League Cup	68+2	40	16	14	7
Others	44+2	21	15	10	13
Totals	699+33	364	210	158	147

– Robson joined Manchester United for £1.5 million, then a British record fee

MANAGERIAL RECORD

(Note: all records up to and including 2 January 2006)

Middlesbrough: 18 May 1994 – 5 June 2001
Bradford City: 24 November 2003 – 16 June 2004
WBA: 9 November 2004 – present

			P	W	D	L	F	A	Pts
1994–95	Middlesbrough	D1	46	23	13	10	67	40	82
1995–96	Middlesbrough	P	38	11	10	17	35	50	43
1996–97	Middlesbrough	P	38	10	12	16	51	60	39†
1997–98	Middlesbrough	D1	46	27	10	9	77	41	91
1998–99	Middlesbrough	P	38	12	15	11	48	54	51
1999–00	Middlesbrough	P	38	14	10	14	46	52	52
2000–01	Middlesbrough	P	38	9	15	14	44	44	42
	League Total		282	106	85	91	368	341	400
	League Cup		34	20	5	9	60	28	
	FA Cup		23	10	6	7	36	27	
	Others		4	0	3	1	2	4	
2003–04	Bradford City	D1	27	7	1	19	22	40	22
	League Cup		0	0	0	0	0	0	
	FA Cup		1	0	0	1	1	2	
	Others		0	0	0	0	0	0	
2004–05	WBA	P	26	5	10	11	25	39	25
2005–06	WBA	P	21	5	4	12	20	31	19
	League Total		47	10	14	23	45	70	44
	League Cup		3	2	0	1	8	6	
	FA Cup		3	1	1	1	4	3	
	Others		0	0	0	0	0	0	
TOTALS	League		356	123	100	133	435	451	
	League Cup		37	22	5	10	68	34	
	FA Cup		27	11	7	9	41	32	
	Others		4	0	3	1	2	4	
	Totals		424	156	115	153	546	521	

†Three points deducted

Index

Aberdeen 80, 102
Abramovich, Roman 281
Adams, Tony 164, 190, 199, 287
Addison, Colin 34, 36
adidas 59
Adriano 294
agents 74, 283–4
Albiston, Arthur 52
Allardyce, Sam 287, 291
Allen, Ronnie 33, 44–7
Anderson, Viv 37, 116, 123
  Middlesbrough 224, 254–5
Anelka, Nicolas 287
Argentina 295
Armstrong, Alun 240, 265
Arsenal 163–4, 287
  v Man U (1982) 64; (1984)
    80; (1990) 138
  v Middlesbrough 235
Ashman, Alan 15
Asprey, Bill 25
Astle, Jeff 22
Aston Villa, v Man U (1985) 90;
  (1993) 155; (1994) 168
Atkinson, Ron 140, 183, 250,
  267
  Aston Villa 168
  Manchester United 44, 45,
    48–9, 51–2, 61, 69, 83,
    94, 96, 104, 196, 198
    character 105
    FA Cup 66–8
    new players 54, 61, 66,
      70–2, 80, 92, 100
    sacked 99–101
  West Brom 33–4, 36, 41, 44,
    45
Atletico Madrid 149–50

Bailey, Gary 52, 67, 73, 77, 87,
  91, 114
Ballesteros, Seve 261
Barcelona 75, 141, 277

Barlow, Andy 150, 167
Barmby, Nick 227
Barnes, John 186, 192, 200
Barnes Peter 27, 90, 98, 176
Batson, Brendan 36–7
Battiston, Patrick 181
BBC TV broadcasting 207
Beardsley, Peter 84, 192, 201,
  260, 294
Beck, Mikkel 231
Beckenbauer, Franz 286
Beckham, David 112, 223–4, 293
Benfica 58
Bergkamp, Dennis 235
Best, George 10, 23, 57, 116,
  197, 290, 297
Biggins, Wayne 71
Birmingham Evening Mail 40,
  42, 48
Birthdays shops 60, 108, 297
Birtles, Garry 52, 62
Birtley Lord Lawson
  Comprehensive School
  4–5, 9, 12
Birtley South Secondary
  Modern School 9
Blackburn, v Middlesbrough
  234–5, 237
Blackmore, Clayton 98, 125,
  136–7, 142, 226
  goals 137, 140
Boksic, Alen 249, 251
Bolton, Joe 12
Boniek, Zbigniew 77, 78
Bosnich, Mark 143
Botham, Ian 261
Bournemouth, v Man U (1984) 85
Bowyer, Lee 99
Bradford City 264–6
  BR as manager 264–6
  new players 265
  relegation 266
Brady, Liam 78

Branca, Marco 240
Brazil 294
Brazil, Alan 62, 80, 83, 91–2,
  100
Bright, Mark 133
Brindley, Doreen (mother-in-
  law of BR) 38
Brindley, George (father-in-law
  of BR) 38, 50
Brooking, Trevor 178, 181–2,
  262
Brown, Ally 29
Brown, Mick 44, 51, 65
Brown, Tony 29, 36, 37, 47
Bruce, Steve
  Birmingham manager 286
  goals 118, 140, 158
  Manchester United 45, 107,
    117–18, 121–2, 128,
    134, 137, 141, 143, 147,
    150, 159–60, 162, 291
Bryan Robson Scanner Appeal
  189, 261
Buchan, Martin 52–4, 61
Burnley Football Club 13
Burton, Ken 27
Busby Babes 131
Busby, Sir Matt 57–9, 68, 148,
  160, 167–8
Butcher, Terry 176, 179, 192,
  200, 201
Butt, Nicky 112, 173
Byrne, Roger 57

Cadamarteri, Danny 265
Cafu 294
Campbell, Kevin 270–1
Campbell, Sol 293
Cantello, Len 29, 36, 45
Cantona, Eric 107, 120, 151,
  156–7, 161, 166–9
  goals 157, 167, 172
  Istanbul incident 167

Cardiff City, v West Brom (1975) 26
Carlos, Roberto 229, 294
Carter, Darren 296
Case, Jimmy 130
Chamberlain, Mark 200
Champions League 281–2
Chaplow, Richard 270
Chapman, Bill 5, 9, 14–15
Chapman, Lee 143, 151
Charity Shield 70, 90
Charles, Gary 207
Charles, John 105
Charlton
  v Man U (1990) 133
  v West Brom (2004) 272
Charlton, Bobby 10, 57–8, 193, 196, 286
Chelsea 287
  v Man U (1994) 171–2
  v Middlesbrough 237, 240
Cherry, Trevor 41
Chester-le-Street 4, 7, 19
Chester-le-Street Grammar School 12
Chesterfield, v Middlesbrough 236
Claridge, Steve 236
Clemence, Ray 41, 42, 143, 185
Clement, Neil 276
Clough, Brian 130
Cole, Ashley 74, 293
Colman, Eddie 57
Confederations Cup 294, 295
Cooper, Colin 245, 249
Coppell, Steve 41, 52, 55, 62, 70, 133, 179
Cork, Alan 123
Coventry City, v Man U (1984) 85; (1989) 129
Cox, Neil 226
Crerand, Paddy 57–8
Croker, Ted 181, 184, 186
Crooks, Garth 71
Cruyff, Johan 141, 197
Crystal Palace, v Man U (1990) 133–4, 206
Cumbes, Jim 21
Cunningham, Laurie 36–7, 41–2, 45, 66–7, 69
Curbishley, Alan 27, 291
Curtis, Mrs 17

Dalglish, Kenny 46, 118, 126, 162
Darlington 12
Davenport, Peter 62, 92, 100, 124

Davies, Alan 66–7, 77
Davies, Curtis 296
Davies, Wyn 10, 11
Deane, Brian 237, 245
Dein, David 284
Dettori, Frankie 261
di Matteo, Roberto 238
Dida 294
directors 285
Dublin, Dion 155
Duff, Damien 264
Dukla Prague 72–3
Dundee, v Man U (1984) 85
Duxbury, Mike 85, 98
Dyer, Kieron 99

Earnshaw, Rob 270–3
Easy Jeans 189
Edwards, Dr Vernon 193
Edwards, Duncan 57
Edwards, Louis 127
Edwards, Martin 48, 69, 74, 77, 127–8, 196
Edwards, Roger 74
Ehiogu, Ugo 249
Elleray, David 236
Ellington, Nathan 296
Ellis, Doug 262
Emerson 232–4, 239, 294
England 292
  B team 37
  South America tour 186
  Under-21 31, 37, 40
  v Argentina (1986) 196
  v Australia 176
  v Brazil (1980) 176
  v Denmark (1983) 185
  v France (1981) 179
  v Greece (1982) 183
  v Holland (1988) 199–200; (1990) 206
  v Israel (1986) 188
  v Luxembourg (1982) 184
  v Mexico (1986) 188, 193
  v Morocco (1986) 195–6
  v Norway (1980) 176, 177
  v Paraguay (1986) 196
  v Poland (1986) 196; (1990) 201
  v Portugal (1986) 194–5
  v Republic of Ireland (1980) 41, 175; (1988) 199, 205
  v Romania (1980) 176
  v Spain 182
  v Turkey 149; (1986) 188; (1988) 199
  v West Germany 181; (1986) 188

  v Yugoslavia (1988) 199
  World Cup (2006) 294
  youth team 27
Eriksson, Sven Goran 188, 291, 292
European Championship 41, 175, 183, 198–9
European Cup 57–8, 90, 112, 149, 165, 208
European Cup-Winners' Cup 72–3, 80, 90, 102, 113, 119, 127, 141, 148, 277
European Super Cup 149
Everton 65, 85, 88–9, 97, 115
  v Man U (1983) 65; (1984) 85; (1985) 88–9; (1985) 227
  v West Brom (1968) 22
Express and Star 40

FA Cup 57, 77, 235–6
FA Cup final (1977) 57; (1983) 66–8; (1985) 88–9; (1988) 124; (1990) 133–4, 206; (1994) 171–2; (1995) 227; (1997) 237–8
Farrelly, Gareth 265
Fashanu, John 123–4
Fenwick, Terry 192, 197
Ferdinand, Rio 293
Ferguson, Duncan 143
Ferguson, Sir Alex 59, 223, 250, 257, 261
  Manchester United manager 102–73, 112, 273, 286
  new signings 116, 121, 125, 144–5, 15
Festa, Gianluca 232, 236, 244
Figo, Luis 249
Finland 27
Fjortoft, Jan-Aage 226
Flintoff, Freddie 261
foreign players 290
Foulkes, Bill 58
Francis, Simon 265
Francis, Trevor 78, 181
Francombe, John 96
Frost, Freddie 121
Fuchs, Uwe 226

Galatasaray, v Man U (1994) 165
Gardner, Jimmy 243
Gascoigne, Paul 104, 122, 202–4, 207–8, 285
  Middlesbrough 240–3, 245–7
Gascoigne, Sheryl 246
Gera, Zoltan 276

Germany 295
Gerrard, Steven 288–9, 293, 294
Gibb, Gordon 264–5, 268
Gibson, Colin 118
Gibson, Steve 170, 174, 226, 233, 252–4, 277
Gibson, Terry 62, 92, 98, 123
Gidman, John 52, 91
Giggs, Ryan 59, 112, 119–21, 144, 284
  goals 150, 159
Giles, Johnny 27–30, 32, 33, 55
Glazer, Malcolm 74
Godden, Tony 36
Graham, Arthur 69, 73, 90
Gray, Andy 36, 265
Greening, Jonathan 276
Greenwood, Ron 40–2, 104, 176, 178, 181–3
  England manager 176, 178, 181–3, 185
Grimes, Ashley 70
Grobbelaar, Bruce 65, 88
Guardian Royal Insurance 189
Gullit, Ruud 200, 228

Hansen, Alan 46
Hardy, Jack 4
Hardy, Judy 4
Harrison, Steve 252
Hartford, Asa 29, 38
Hartlepool Hospital Cup 12
Hateley, Mark 186, 192
Hatton, Ricky 261
Hayward, Jonathan 169
Hayward, Sir Jack 170
Hendrie, John 225–6
Henry, Thierry 287
Heskey, Emile 236
Heysel Stadium disaster 90, 142
Hignett, Craig 240
Hill, Jimmy 96, 207
Hill, Pete 30, 40
Hinton, Irene 18
Hinton, Pete 18
Hinton, Ron 18
Hirst, David 156
Hoddle, Glenn 27, 37, 40, 176, 192, 267–8
Hodge, Steve 192
Hogg, Graeme 121
Holland 295
Horsfield, Geoff 271, 274, 276, 296
Houghton, Ray 199
Houllier, Gerard 267–8

Hoult, Russell 273
Howe, Don 15, 20, 24–6, 104
  England coach 178, 179, 202
Hughes, Mark 54, 92, 106, 121, 128, 145, 223, 293
  Barcelona 97
  Blackburn manager 286
  Chelsea 228
  goals 84–5, 88, 133, 139, 141, 155, 167, 169, 172
Hulse, Rob 270–1
Hunter, Norman 6
Hurst, Geoff 28

Ince, Paul 59, 125, 134, 145–7, 151, 157, 162, 164, 223
  goals 159
  Middlesbrough 247–8, 251
  Wolves 267
Ipswich, v West Brom (1977) 31; (1978) 34
Irwin, Denis 133, 137, 156, 263
Italia '90 241, 294
Italy 295

Jacobs, Wayne 264
Job, Joseph-Desire 249
Johnson, David 41
Johnston, Willie 28, 39
Jones, Chris 30
Jones, Dave 267
Jones, Vinnie 123
Juninho 228–30, 232–3, 237, 239, 247–9
Juventus, v Man U (1984) 76–7

Kaka 294
Kaltz, Manny 52
Kamara, Diomansy 296
Kanchelskis, Andrei 107, 144, 150
  goals 151, 168–9, 223, 230
Kanu, Nwankwo 269, 271, 274
Karembeu, Christian 249
Kaye, John 21
Keane, Robbie 264, 284
Keane, Roy 59, 107, 137, 145, 157, 162, 164, 288
  and McCarthy 263
  suspension 169, 208
Keegan, Kevin 41–2, 49, 59, 63, 290
  England 175, 178, 181–3
  injuries 179
Kempes, Mario 37
Kerr, Brian 263–4
Kidd, Brian 57, 112, 144–5, 158, 250

Kinder, Vladimir 236
Kirkland, Chris 292, 296
Kirton, Glen 180, 187
Knighton, Michael 127–8
Knox, Archie 103, 108, 112, 139, 144, 147, 250
Kuszczak, Tomasz 273, 296

Lamb, Keith 225, 229, 234, 243, 250, 253
Lampard, Frank 187, 293
Law, Denis 10, 57–8, 297
Lawrence, Lennie 170
League Cup final 70, 140, 150, 155, 168, 240
Leeds 151
  v Man U (1991) 139; (1992) 150–2
Leicester City, v Middlesbrough 236
Leighton, Jim 121–2, 133–5, 137
Limpar, Anders 141
Lineker, Gary 192–3, 196, 201, 204
  goals 193, 199, 294
Liverpool 46, 60, 81, 97, 130, 133, 223, 247
  v Man U (1981) 55; (1982) 64–5; (1983) 70; (1985) 88, (1990) 137–8
  v Middlesbrough 234

Mabbutt, Gary 142
McAllister, Gary 151
Macari, Lou 52–4
McCarthy, Mick 263
McClair, Brian 107, 116–18, 258, 271
  goals 118, 138
McClaren, Steve 252–3, 291
McDermott, Terry 41, 49
Macdonald, Malcolm 11
McFadden, Bryan 260
McFaul, Willie 94
McGrath, Paul 54, 98, 105, 106, 122, 125–6
McGregor, Jim 86, 96
McIlroy, Sammy 49, 52
Mackay, Dave 84
McMahon, Steve 130
McNeill, Billy 116
McPherson, Albert 20, 25
McQueen, Gordon 52–4, 64, 71, 106
  Middlesbrough 224, 250
Maddison, Neil 244
Maddix, Danny 124

management 284–5
managers 290–1
Manchester City
  v Man U (1981) 55; (1989)
    129, 144
  v West Brom (1976) 31
Manchester United 44, 267
  Charity Shield 70
  drinking culture 106–8
  European Cup 57, 112, 165
  European Cup-Winners' Cup
    72–5, 80, 113, 127, 137,
    141–2, 148, 277
  European Super Cup 149
  FA Cup 57, 66–8, 71, 89,
    133–5, 140, 171–2
  fitness training 94
  League Champions 57, 158–
    60, 168
  Milk Cup 54, 63, 64, 71, 85,
    92
  Premier Division 155, 158–
    60
  Robson signs for 48
  South Africa tour 16
  UEFA Cup 63, 81, 85, 87
  v Arsenal (1982) 64; (1984)
    80; (1990) 138
  v Aston Villa (1985) 90;
    (1993) 155; (1994) 168
  v Atletico Madrid (1992)
    149–50
  v Barcelona (1984) 75, 127,
    142; (1991) 141, 277
  v Benfica (1968) 58
  v Bournemouth (1984) 85
  v Charlton (1990) 133
  v Chelsea (1994) 171–2
  v Coventry City (1984) 85,
    87; (1989) 129
  v Crystal Palace (1990) 133–
    4, 206
  v Dukla Prague 72–3
  v Dundee (1984) 85
  v Everton (1983) 65; (1984)
    85; (1985) 88–9; (1985)
    227
  v Galatasaray (1994) 165
  v Juventus (1984) 76–7
  v Leeds (1991) 139, 149;
    (1992) 150–2
  v Liverpool (1981) 55; (1982)
    64–5; (1983) 70; (1985)
    88, 92; (1986) 114;
    (1987) 118; (1990) 137–8
  v Man City (1981) 55;
    (1989) 129, 144
  v Montpellier 113, 139

  v Newcastle (1964) 10;
    (1984) 84; (1987) 104
  v Nottingham Forest (1989)
    132; (1992) 150
  v Oldham Athletic (1990)
    132–3; (1991) 149–50;
    (1994) 169
  v Oxford United 71, 118
  v PSV Eindhoven 85
  v QPR (1988) 124; (1992)
    150
  v Raba Gyor 85
  v Red Star Belgrade (1992)
    149
  v Sheffield Wednesday
    (1985) 91, 97; (1991)
    140; (1992) 148; (1994)
    158
  v Southampton (1986) 98, 99
  v Spartak Varna 73
  v Spurs (1981) 54; (1991) 142
  v Stoke City (1984) 85
  v Sunderland (1981) 55;
    (1985) 95–6
  v Videoton (1984) 87
  v Warsaw 140
  v West Brom (1976) 31;
    (19767) 37; (2004) 273
  v West Ham (1984)
    87;(1985) 96, 97
  v Wimbledon (1986) 103–4;
    (1987) 123
  v Wolves 49
  youth 112
Mandela, Nelson 164
Maradona, Diego Armando
  73–5, 156, 196–7
Mariner, Paul 176, 179, 181,
  192
Martin, Alvin 192
Martin, Lee 129, 134, 140
Martin, Mick 28
Martyn, Nigel 133
Matts, Ray 40–1, 42, 48
Maxwell, Robert 74
Megson, Gary 267
Menotti, Luis Cesar 73
Merrett, Ken 110
Merson, Paul 164, 240, 243–4,
  247, 268
Middlesbrough 224–56, 296
  drinking culture 106, 110,
    244
  FA Cup final (1997) 237
  League Cup final (1998) 240
  new players 227–33, 239–40,
    245, 247, 249
  Premier Division 227, 241

relegation 238–9
  v Arsenal (1996) 235
  v Blackburn (1997) 234–5,
    237
  v Chelsea (1997) 237; (1998)
    240
  v Chesterfield (1996) 236
  v Leicester City (1996) 236
  v Liverpool (1996) 234
  v Real Madrid (2000) 249
  v West Brom (2004) 273
Milan 79
Milburn, Jackie 11
Milk Cup 54, 63
Miller, Alan 226
Millichip, Bert 35
Mills, Mick 63, 182
Mitchell, Bobby 11
Molloy, Lyn 58
Molloy, Pete 58
Moncur, Bobby 11
Montpellier 113, 139
  v Man U 113, 139
Moore, Bobby 11, 286
Moran, Kevin 5, 65–6, 89–90,
  98, 106, 108, 122
Moses, Remi 46, 52, 66, 79,
  84, 91, 98–9
Mourinho, Jose 287
Muhammad Ali 261
Muhren, Arnold 61–3, 72–3,
  76, 84–5, 90
Mulligan, Paddy 28
Munkas, Pecsi 138
Murphy, Jimmy 57, 131
Mustoe, Robbie 226, 244

Nadal, Miguel Angel 230
Neville, Gary 112, 124, 171,
  173, 293
Neville, Phil 112
New Balance 60, 189
Newcastle
  BR trial 14
  Inter-Cities Fairs Cup 10
  v Man U (1964) 10; (1984)
    84; (1987) 104
  v Northampton Town 10
Nicholas, Charlie 66, 69
Nicklaus, Jack 261
Nicolas, Peter 66
Nigeria 262
Nike 267
Nottingham Forest
  v Man U (1989) 132; (1992)
    150
  v West Brom 27

Okon, Paul 249
Oldham Athletic, v Man U
    (1990) 132–3; (1991)
    149–50; (1994) 169
O'Leary, David 262
Olsen, Jesper 71, 80, 83–4, 87,
    95, 98–9, 123, 183
Osborne, John 22
O'Shea, John 264
Owen, Mark 260
Owen, Michael 293
Oxford United, v Man U 71, 118

Pallister, Gary 107, 125, 128–9,
    133, 134, 137, 141, 143,
    145, 147, 288
    goals 159
    Middlesbrough 245
Palmer, Roger 132
Pardew, Alan 262
Parker, Paul 137, 144, 202
Parlour, Ray 164
Peace, Jeremy 267–8
Peake, Trevor 129
Pearce, Stuart 202, 291
Pearson, Nigel 145, 199, 248
    Middlesbrough 226, 236
    West Brom 268, 275–6
Pele 156, 197
Phelan, Mike 125, 258
Phipps, Kath 190
Pickering, John 224, 250, 252
Platini, Michel 78, 197
Platt, David 202
Pollock, Jamie 226
Portsmouth, v West Brom
    (2004) 274–6
Premier League 153
PSV Eindhoven, v Man U 85
Puskas, Ferenc 165

Queen's Park Rangers, v Man U
    (1988) 124; (1992) 150
Queiroz, Carlos 258

Ravanelli, Fabrizio 230–3, 236,
    239, 247
Real Madrid 224
    v Middlesbrough 249
Red Star Belgrade 149
Regis, Cyrille 36–7
Reid, Peter 89, 192, 263
Rhodes, Julian 264–6
Ricard, Hamilton 245
Richardson, Kieran 270–1, 275,
    296
    England 271
Rijkaard, Frank 200, 286

Ritchie, Andy 133
Rix, Graham 181
Roberts, Ben 238
Robertson, Alistair 29, 35, 36
Robinho 294
Robins, Mark 132–3
Robinson, Paul 276, 292
Robson, Ben (son of BR) 131,
    138, 147, 255, 257, 278–
    9, 297
    Macclesfield 267
Robson, Bobby 63, 104, 183
    England manager 183–6,
    193–4, 196, 202–3, 291
Robson, Brian (father of BR)
    1, 3, 7, 175, 262, 278
Robson, Bryan
    LIFE
        awarded OBE 131
        birth 4
        drinking reputation 106–
            10, 259–60
        endorsements 59–60, 189
        horse racing 261
        marriage 38–40
        new life 257
        school 4–5
    FOOTBALL
        Bradford City, manager
            264–6
        business deals 58–9
        coaching licences 258
        England 41–2, 175–91
            assistant to manager 174
            B 37
            captain 63, 183
            goals 177, 179, 214, 260
            Under-21 31, 37, 40
            World Cup 61, 260
            youth team 27
        injuries 30–2, 76, 86, 91–3,
            96–7, 114, 124, 131–2,
            136, 190, 193, 195, 206–7
        Manchester United 10, 48,
            50–64, 222
            captain 63–4, 81–2, 129
            contracts 48, 83, 140
            drinking habits 106–10
            goals 55, 67, 73, 81,
                133, 140, 164
            promotional work 267
            relations with Ferguson
                108–11
            testimonial match 138
        Middlesbrough 170, 174,
            222–56
            FA Cup final 237
            League Cup final 240

sacked 252–5
West Brom 5, 14–47, 56,
    295–6
    apprentice 14–22
    first team 26
    goals 26, 27, 31, 44, 88
    manager 110, 255, 267–8,
        295–6
    signs contract 24–5
    transfer to Man U 47
    youth team 22–3
Robson, Charlotte (daughter
    of BR) 61, 131, 138,
    179–80, 297
Robson, Claire (daughter of BR)
    43, 131, 138, 279, 297
Robson, Denise (wife of BR)
    31, 45, 48, 50, 59, 78,
    131, 162, 246, 278–80
    children 43, 61, 179–80
    marriage 38
Robson, Gary (brother of BR)
    4, 5, 6
    West Brom 5, 93, 277
Robson, Justin (brother of BR)
    4, 5, 6, 7, 94, 277
Robson, Maureen (mother of
    BR) 3, 4–6, 277
Robson, Maurice (cousin of
    BR) 13, 18
Robson, Susan (sister of BR)
    3, 4, 7, 278
Robson's Choice 189
Rojo, Francisco 75
Ronaldinho 294
Ronaldo, Cristiano 288, 294
Rooney, Wayne 126, 288, 293–4
Rosenthal, Jim 180
Rossi, Paolo 76–7
Rostron, Wilf 12
Rowell, Gary 12
Royle, Joe 24, 38
Rummenigge, Karl-Heinz 181
Rush, Ian 46
Ryan, Jimmy 258
Ryan, Reg 'Paddy' 14, 16, 20

Sadler, David 58
Salako, John 134
Sansom, Kenny 41, 179, 192
Schmeichel, Peter 143, 144,
    168, 185
Scholes, Paul 112, 173, 208
Schumacher, Toni 181
Schwarzer, Mark 244
Scudamore, Peter 96
Sealey, Les 134, 137, 139, 141
Sexton, Dave 44, 175

Sharpe, Lee 107, 119–20, 129, 144, 164
goals 138–9
Shearer, Alan 11, 153–4, 162, 169, 290
Sheffield Wednesday (1985) 91, 97; (1991) 140; (1992) 148; (1994) 158
Sheridan, John 140, 158
Shilton, Peter 42, 143, 200–1, 204
England 185, 192, 197
Silk, Tom 45
Siveback, John 92
Smith, Denis 30
Smith, Gordon 67
Smith, Jim 71
Smith, Richard 95
Souness, Graeme 49
South Africa 163
Southall, Neville 89
Southampton, v Man U (1986) 98, 99
Spartak Varna 73, 73
Speed, Gary 151
Speedie, David 129–30
Stam, Jaap 223
Stapleton, Frank 52, 54, 62, 72–3, 92, 263
goals 67, 73, 75, 87–8
Statham, Derek 36
Steven, Trevor 192, 201
Stevens, Gary (Everton and Rangers) 192, 193, 201
Stevens, Gary (Tottenham) 67, 192
Stiles, Nobby 57
Stoke City, v Man U (1984) 85
Strachan, Gordon 80, 83–5, 91, 118, 125, 151, 267–8
Celtic manager 286
and Ferguson 102–3, 111
Street, Fred 195, 204
Sturrock, Paul 85
Summerbee, Nicky 264
Sunderland, v Man U (1981) 55; (1985) 95–6
Swales, Harry 59–61, 189, 290
Swinburn, Walter 261
Switzerland 27

Taylor, Gerry 261
Taylor, Graham 170, 291
Taylor, Tommy 57
Taylormade Sports 261
Terry, John 187, 293, 294
Thomas, Geoff 134
Thomas, Michael 125
Thompson, Bobby 50

Thompson, Phil 41
Todd, Colin 6, 264, 266
Tottenham Hotspur
v Man U (1981) 54; (1991) 142
v West Brom (1976) 30
Townsend, Andy 240, 242, 248, 263, 285
Trewick, John 28, 35
Tueart, Dennis 31, 35
Turner, Chris 91, 98, 114

UEFA Cup 282

Vaesen, Nico 265
van Basten, Marco 199–200, 286
van den Hauwe, Pat 89
Venables, Terry 25, 104, 174–5, 291
BBC panelist 207
Middlesbrough 250, 252
Venison, Barry 95
Vialli, Gianluca 230
Vickers, Steve 236, 244
Videoton 87
Vieira, Patrick 124, 287, 289
Vodaphone 267

Waddle, Chris 158, 192, 202
Walker, Des 202
Walker, Jack 153–4
Wallace, Danny 125
Wallness Charity 189
Wallwork, Ronnie 265, 276
Walsh, Gary 98, 114
Middlesbrough 228
Walsh, Paul 88–9
Warsaw 140
Watson, Dave 41
Watson, Steve 296
Webb, Neil 125, 132, 134, 136, 204
goals 137
Wenger, Arsene 287
West Bromwich Albion 5, 14–47, 267–72, 296
BR joins as apprentice 14–21
BR as manager 110, 255, 267, 295–6
v Charlton (2004) 272
v Man U (2004) 273
v Middlesbrough (2004) 273
v Portsmouth (2004) 274–6
China tour 34–6
First Division 30
v Ipswich (1977) 31; (1978) 34

v Man City (1976) 31
v Man U (1976) 31; (1977) 37
v Tottenham (1976) 30
Second Division 21–2
v Cardiff City (1975) 26
v Everton (1968) 22
v Nottingham Forest 27
v York City (1975) 26
youth team 22–3
West Ham, v Man U (1984) 87; (1985) 96, 97
Wetherall, Dave 264–5
Whelan, Billy 57
Whitehills 6
Whitehouse, Brian 25, 26, 44, 51, 84
Whiteside, Norman 54, 61, 65, 73, 92, 98, 106, 125–7, 147, 182
goals 64, 67, 77, 89
Wicks, Steve 27
Wile, John 33, 36
Wilkins, Ray 27, 28, 52, 61–4, 67, 70–2, 76, 79
England 179, 183, 192, 195, 200
Wilkinson, Howard 156
Wilkinson, Paul 226
Williams, Graham 22–3
Williams, Robbie 261
Willis, Peter 89
Wimbledon, v Man U (1986) 103–4; (1987) 123
Windass, Dean 264–5
Wise, Dennis 123
Witton Gilbert 3, 4, 6
Wolverhampton Wanderers 49, 169–70
Wood, Ronnie 60, 108
Woodcock, Tony 41, 65
World Cup
goals 179
songs 190
World Cup (1982) 61, 176–82; (1986) 188; (2006) 293–5
Wright, Ian 133, 235
Wright, Mark 202
Wright-Phillips, Shaun 293
Wyman, Bill 260
Wypler, Jane 49

York City (1975) 26

Zeman, Zdenek 242
Zico 197
Zidane, Zinedine 295
Ziege, Christian 247–8